Collector's Library of Essential Thinkers

MONTAIGNE

Montaigne

Essays

(SELECTIONS)

The Collector's Library of
ESSENTIAL THINKERS

This edition published in 2005 by
The Collector's Library of Essential Thinkers
an imprint of CRW Publishing Limited
69 Gloucester Crescent, London NW1 7EG

ISBN 1 904919 59 6

1 3 5 7 9 10 8 6 4 2

Typeset in Great Britain by Antony Gray
Printed and bound in China by Imago

Contents

BOOK TWO

BOOK THREE

Introduction

A French country gentleman retires to live on his estate. He develops the habit of taking a quiet ramble through his thoughts, reflecting on his own likes and dislikes, the great and small deeds of the past, the world with all its follies and delights. He begins to write down his musings, mixing in a little gossip and some reminiscences of youth. He sprinkles the text with quotations from his favourite authors. Gradually it turns into a book, something to help his family and friends remember him after he is dead. Then the book is published during the author's lifetime and quickly makes him famous. He carries on writing, adding material, bringing out a much enlarged fifth edition. Four years later he dies, but his book is already a national treasure.

What had he done, this Michel Yquem de Montaigne, that the French nation should take him to its heart? The title of his book was hardly awe-inspiring: the reader was offered only *essais*, which meant nothing more than trials, or attempts – the literary overtones of the word had not yet begun to resonate. But the simple, unassuming tone was itself revolutionary, and so too was the subject matter. No one before Montaigne had ever taken such a personal standpoint in discussing life. He writes about everything under the sun, but always he comes back to himself and his own opinions, not from any particular love of them but because he wants to find out what he really thinks and so illuminate the hidden corners of the mind. This was a new enterprise in European literature, and for the purpose he invented a new style: intimate, conversational, meandering. Latin was too artificial and polished, too full of rhetorical weight to convey what he wanted to say; so he wrote in French (with bits of Gascon dialect thrown in here and there) and felt it no shame to include any word that was in common use on the streets of Paris.

What, then, of us, more than four hundred years later? Why should we still trouble to read these Essays, whose philosophy is a patchwork of ideas taken from Stoics, Epicureans, Sceptics, Platonists, Aristotelians and anyone else with anything to offer, all strung together without any system save for a stout belief that the old ways are best and all change is for the worse (except his own quite frequent changes of opinion)? The answer lies in the character of their author, who turns out on closer acquaintance to be a very interesting fellow indeed, much wilier and sharper-witted than he would first have you believe. Montaigne makes a lively and exuberant companion, with his keen eyes and ears, his sensitive nose, and his great capacity for observing human affairs. Where praise is due he is generous. Where he disapproves, he says so plainly and with no false airs. His judgements are plain, refreshing and above all transparently honest in intent.

'I am fond of change and variety, unwisely and impetuously fond, and my style and mind have the same vagabond nature.' Montaigne confesses his faults, but only gradually do we realise that he is also warning us of ours. We are vain, wayward creatures, blown here and there by our whims, and always at the mercy of the inscrutable goddess Fortune. To recognise this may be the beginning of wisdom.

Life

The country estate of Montaigne, in the district of Périgord (near Bordeaux), had been bought by Michel's great-grandfather in 1477 from the profits of a business that included selling fish. So the family was comfortably off without being at all grand. The author's father was important enough to be elected mayor of Bordeaux but continued running his business. He conceived the extraordinary idea, when his son Michel was born in 1533, of bringing him up to speak Latin as his mother tongue. A German tutor was hired who knew no French, and servants as well as the two parents had to obey a rigid rule that only Latin words were to be used when communicating with the boy. He first started to learn French at the age of six.

This scheme may just have been a piece of upwardly mobile eccentricity, or there may have been darker causes. These were times when the Catholic religion was meeting open opposition from reformers, and new sects were attracting support – Lutherans in Germany, Calvinists in France. Michel's mother was Jewish by descent, but her family had converted to Protestantism. In the course of time, two of her eight or nine surviving children followed their mother's faith, abandoning the Catholicism of their father. It is not unlikely that he may have devised Michel's education as a means of removing him as far as possible from the early influence of his mother.

When he grew up he began studying for the law, probably in Toulouse, and in 1557 he took up work at the *parlement*, or law court, of Bordeaux. Montaigne tells us that he was a lazy young man. Nevertheless he had high ambitions and seems always to have inspired the trust and confidence of powerful men; without any achievement to his name he was being invited to join in royal celebrations well before the age of thirty. We know practically nothing of his activities over the next decade or so; only that he did some campaigning (but no actual fighting) in the bitter wars of religion that raged in those years and was employed on various occasions as a mediator between the Catholic and Protestant leaders. For a few years he enjoyed a deep friendship, 'so perfect and entire that surely we seldom read the like of it', with Étienne de la Boëtie, a fellow lawyer who died in 1563. He married and had a number of children, though only a single daughter survived into adulthood.

In 1568, on the death of his father, Michel inherited the chateau and estate of Montaigne. A Latin inscription on the wall of his study tells us that in 1571, 'wearied of the slavery of the courts and public functions', he retired there to take up a life of leisure. In his library he was surrounded by a thousand volumes, many of them passed on to him by La Boëtie. There he sat and, for the first time, began to write down his thoughts. But leisure is never without its interruptions. In Montaigne's case, these included periodic agonies from kidney stones, an unexpected invasion of his house by armed horsemen, four years acting as mayor of Bordeaux, and a plague epidemic that forced him to abandon his estate for six months. Life in those days was hard and full of surprises.

Montaigne, who writes of himself as being an old man, never reached the age of sixty.

The wars of religion

'I do not meddle with telling people what they are to do in the world (there are plenty of others who do that); I only say what I do myself.' Without ever claiming any grand purpose for his writing, Montaigne well knew that France had a desperate need for sane counsel. The country had divided along tribal lines between Catholics and Protestants, whose leaders were for the most part filled with fanatical hatred for the opposing side. Collective madness took hold, finding its outlet in acts of treachery and cruelty on a scale unknown anywhere else in Europe.

By 1562 the Protestants (called Huguenots, the name given to Calvin's followers in Geneva) were strongly ensconced, especially in the south and west. With the assassination of their most implacable opponent, the duc de Guise, ultimate victory seemed possible. But the killing roused the Catholics to fury. Civil war broke out and remained endemic for the next fifteen years. A royal marriage arranged in 1572 with the express aim of reconciling the two sides culminated in the ugliest episode of all, the Massacre of St Bartholomew's Day – six days of licensed butchery in Paris after the king had given orders for the Huguenot leaders to be wiped out. In other provincial towns, Bordeaux among them, the violence was repeated while the authorities looked the other way.

Of the two sides, Montaigne regarded the Protestants as more to blame because they were the ones who originally disturbed the peace. Nothing could excuse the fact that they had been disloyal to the king. But his own Christian faith, he was well aware, owed much to tradition and circumstances. He was mystified by the idea that any human beings could be so certain of their religious beliefs that they felt justified in destroying anyone who disagreed. His ideal leader (and a personal friend) was the Protestant Henri of Navarre, who after Montaigne's death was offered the throne of France on condition that he became a Catholic – which he duly did, declaring that 'Paris is worth a Mass.'

Speaking of witches, Montaigne invoked the opinion of St Augustine that where matters are obscure it is safer to doubt; he remarked drily that 'it is to put a very high value on your surmises to roast a man alive for them.' As we read the *Essays* we cannot fail to be aware that the world is full of human follies, and supreme amongst them is the folly of dogmatism and certainty.

The Essays

Montaigne tells us that when he withdrew to his home in the country he hoped that, in reflecting on the world, his mind would become more settled and mature. But his experience was completely opposite. His mind started behaving like a runaway horse; it produced 'chimeras and fantastic monsters, one after another'. To contemplate the strangeness and absurdity of these creatures, he began to write them down, with the hope (he says) that in time he could make his mind ashamed of them.

There was, therefore, no plan at the outset to produce anything as substantial as the *Essays* in their final form, adding up to well over 1,000 pages. Even without Montaigne's own testimony we would still know this from the way his book grew and changed in the course of composition. From the modest first edition of 1580 in two volumes, to the much revised and enlarged Paris edition of 1588 (with a completely new third volume added), to the author's own copy of that edition containing extra material crammed into the margins, the *Essays* were always work in progress. By the end of his life Montaigne was allowing his ideas more room to expand. The chapters of the third book are much longer, some containing not just a single essay but several strung together. Meanwhile, he himself was becoming more indiscreet: one of his handwritten additions, next to a passage dealing with the perils of love, reveals that he had suffered two doses of the clap in his life, information which he had previously withheld. He is struck by the absurdity of self-revelation. 'An amusing idea! Many things that I would not say to a single person I say to the public; and for my most secret knowledge and thoughts I send my most faithful friends to a bookseller's shop!'

Having chosen his theme Montaigne is never reluctant to let himself be distracted by something else. He digresses, tells stories, creates diversions for himself. But his manner has a logic of its own. 'I go out of my way, but rather through licence than inadvertence. My ideas follow one another, but sometimes at a distance; and they look at one another, but askance.' The mind, he suggests, often works best if no one is asking it to arrange its thoughts into a neat pattern. And anyway, our nature is too variable to be capable of entirely consistent views:

> All the contradictions are to be found in me, according as the wind turns and changes. Bashful, insolent; chaste, lascivious; talkative, taciturn;

> clumsy, gentle; witty, dull; peevish, sweet-tempered; mendacious, truthful; knowing, ignorant; and liberal and avaricious and prodigal: all this I see in myself in some degree, according as I veer about.

All is well as long as we are prepared to recognise what kind of beings we are. Our worst enemy is not so much temptation as the mistaken belief that we are uniquely elevated creatures. We have souls, it is true, but we are also 'wonderfully corporeal', and to pretend otherwise is dangerous. 'In trying to make themselves angels men transform themselves into beasts.' The same thought reappears in other forms, each more quotable than the last. 'Man is quite insane. He wouldn't know how to create a maggot, and he creates gods by the dozen.' 'When I play with my cat, who knows if she isn't amusing herself with me more than I am with her?' 'Though we sit on the highest throne in the world, still we sit only on our own bottom.'

Montaigne and the ancients

Carved into the joists and beams of Montaigne's library are over fifty Latin mottoes, each one a nugget of wisdom. His sources were the Bible, Homer, Plato, Horace, Terence and other classical writers. The same pleasure in quoting can be seen throughout the *Essays*, where Montaigne's ideas are frequently interrupted in mid-flow by the appearance of some extract from a favourite author making the same point.

Some writers quote to impress us with their reading or their seriousness. Montaigne does it because he enjoys it. He had read widely and remembered much. It is, quite simply, a pleasure for him to recall a choice phrase from the past and allow the voice of an old friend to interrupt his monologue. Most often it is one of the Roman poets – Horace, Virgil, Ovid and Catullus foremost among them. Stoic philosophy is strongly represented, especially in the words of Seneca and Cicero. For Greek authors Montaigne relies on translations. It should be understood that the *Essays* in their original form never gave the sources of these quotations. Later scholars were interested enough to undertake the laborious process of tracking them all down, with the result that most modern editions include the author's name after each one. This is certainly a great help, but it does obscure the game that Montaigne was playing with his readers. It amused him to know that those who disagreed with him might be arguing with Plato without realising it.

'He who follows another follows nothing,' says Montaigne when writing on education. He knows perfectly well that quoting the authority of someone else proves nothing. Just as important, no one deserves exclusive credit for an idea merely from having expressed it first. 'It is no more according to Plato than according to me, since he and I understand it and see it alike. The bee rifles the flower here and there, but she afterwards makes honey of what she has gathered, which is all her own: it is no longer thyme or marjoram.' As generations of readers have discovered, Montaigne's honey is some of the best there is.

HUGH GRIFFITH

To the Reader

This is a sincere book, Reader. It forewarns you at the outset that in writing it I had no other but a private and family end in view. I thought neither of being serviceable to you, nor of my own fame. My powers are not equal to such a design. I intended it solely for the solace of my kinsfolk and friends: that, when they have lost me (as they must do before long), they may recover in it some lines of my character and humours, and by this means more fully and vividly cherish me in their memory.

Had my intention been to court the world's favour, I should have trimmed myself more bravely, and stood before it in a studied attitude. I desire to be seen in my simple, natural, and everyday dress, without artifice or constraint; for it is myself I portray. My faults may therein be read to the life, and my native form, as far as my respect to the public has permitted.

For, if my lot had been cast among those nations who are said to be still living in the sweet freedom of Nature's first laws, I assure you that I should have been quite prepared to give a full-length, and quite naked, portrait of myself.

So, Reader, I am myself the subject of my book; it is not reasonable to expect you to waste your leisure on a matter so frivolous and empty.

Farewell then, from MONTAIGNE, this first day of March, 1580.

To the Reader

It is an honest book, Reader. It forewarns you at the outset that in contriving it I had no other but a private and family end in view. I thought neither of being useful to you nor of my own glory. My powers are not equal to such a design. I intended it solely for the solace of my kinsfolk and friends: that, when they have lost me (as they must do before long), they may recover some traits of my character and humours, and by this means more fully and vividly cherish their memory.

Had my intention been to court the world's favour, I should have trimmed myself more bravely, and stood before it in a studied attitude. I desire to be seen in my simple, natural and every-day dress, without artifice or constraint; for it is myself I portray. My imperfections are here to be read to the life, and my native form, as far as my respect to the public has permitted.

Even if my lot had been cast among those nations who are said to be still living in the sweet freedom of Nature's first laws, I assure you that I should have been quite prepared to give a full-length and quite naked portrait of myself.

So, reader, I am myself the foundation of my book: it is not reasonable to expect you to waste your leisure on a matter so frivolous and empty.

Farewell then, from Montaigne, this first day of March, 1580.

BOOK ONE

By various means we arrive at the same end

The most common way to soften the hearts of those we have offended, when they have us at their mercy and are able to take revenge, is to move them to pity and commiseration by submission. Nevertheless, bravery and fortitude, quite contrary means, have sometimes wrought the same effect.

Edward, Prince of Wales, the same who was so long regent in our Guienne, a personage who, by nature and fortune, had many and noteworthy attributes of greatness, having been grievously offended by the Limousins, and having taken their city by force, could not be stayed by the cries of the inhabitants, including women and children, given over to slaughter, throwing themselves at his feet and imploring his mercy, until, penetrating further into the town, he perceived three French gentlemen who, with incredible valour, were alone resisting the onslaught of his victorious army. Admiration and respect for this remarkable bravery at once blunted the edge of his anger, and, beginning with these three, he showed mercy to all the other inhabitants of the city.[1]

1 This incident, which took place in 1370, is told by Froissart, who remarks however that the generosity of the

Scanderbeg, Prince of Epirus,[2] was pursuing one of his soldiers with intent to kill him, and the latter, having tried in vain to appease him by humble prayers and supplications, determined in his extremity to await him with sword in hand. This bold attitude put a sudden end to his master's fury, who received him into grace for his noble bearing. This example might be differently interpreted by such as have not read of the prodigious strength and bravery of that prince.

The Emperor Conrad the Third having besieged Guelph,[3] Duke of Bavaria, though offered the most abject submission, would condescend to no milder conditions than that the gentlewomen who were besieged with the Duke should alone be allowed to leave the city on foot, with their honour unsullied, and with only so much as they were able to carry on their persons. The ladies showed their greatness of heart by loading on their backs their husbands, their children, and the Duke himself. The Emperor was so pleased with their pretty courage that he wept for joy, and put away all the bitterness and mortal enmity which he had borne against the Duke, and from that moment he treated him and his people with all humanity.

For my part, I could easily be moved by either of these means, for I am weakly and strangely inclined to mercy and indulgence; to such a degree that I imagine

---

Black Prince towards the three noblemen did not arrest the sacking of the city.

2 George Castriot, an Albanian prince surnamed Scanderbeg (1414–67), an inveterate adversary of the Turks.

3 At Weinsberg in 1140. The incident forms the subject of a poem by Schiller, *Die Weiber von Weinsberg.*

I should more naturally yield to compassion than to admiration. Yet the Stoics look upon pity as a fault: we should succour the afflicted, they hold, without being moved so far as to suffer with them.

Now these examples seem the more appropriate as we observe these souls, assailed and tried in these two several ways, resisting the one without weakening, and bowing to the other. It may be said that to break one's heart in commiseration is the mark of an easy, soft, and gentle nature, whence it comes that the weaker natures, as those of women, children, and the common people, are most subject to it; but that, after disdaining tears and prayers, to give way solely to respect for the sacred image of valour, is the mark of a strong and unyielding soul, that loves and honours a manly and obstinate courage.

Nevertheless, admiration and astonishment may similarly affect less generous natures: witness the people of Thebes who, having put their captains, Pelopidas and Epaminondas, on trial for a capital offence, which was that they had continued their charge beyond the time prescribed to them, were with great difficulty persuaded to absolve Pelopidas who, bowing under the weight of his accusations, relied on appeals and supplications to save himself; whereas Epaminondas magniloquently recounted the deeds he had performed in their service, flinging them, as it were, in the face of the people with a haughty and arrogant mien, with the result that they had not the heart even to take the ballot-balls in hand, and the assembly broke up with loud praises for the lofty courage of that general.

Dionysius the Elder having, after a long and extremely difficult siege, taken the city of Rhegium and with it the captain Phyto, a great and worthy man, who had offered so stubborn a defence, was resolved to take a tragic and exemplary revenge on him. He first told him how he had the day before drowned his son and all his kindred, to which Phyto merely replied, 'that they were a day nearer happiness than he'. He then had him seized, stripped, and dragged through the town by his executioners, whilst he himself mercilessly and ignominiously whipped him, loading him at the same time with cruel insults. Phyto did not lose heart; but, on the contrary, with raised voice and unmoved countenance, recalled the glorious and honourable cause of his death, namely that he would not deliver his country into the hands of a tyrant, and threatened him with the speedy punishment of the gods. Dionysius, reading in the eyes of most of his soldiers that, far from being incensed by the bravado of this vanquished enemy and his contempt for their chief and his triumph, they were not only moved to astonishment by this show of valour, but even half inclined to rise in mutiny and on the point of snatching Phyto out of the hands of his minions, made an end of his martyrdom and sent him secretly to be drowned in the sea.

Truly man is a marvellously vain, fickle, and unstable creature, on whom it is difficult to found a certain and uniform judgement. Here we see Pompey pardoning the whole city of the Mamertines, with whom he was greatly angered, in consideration of the valour and magnanimity of the citizen Sthenon, who took upon himself the whole guilt of the people, and demanded no other favour but to bear alone the punishment; yet Sulla's host, who showed a like valour in the city of

Perusia,[4] gained nothing either for himself or his fellow-citizens.

And, in direct contradiction to my first examples, Alexander, the boldest of men and so gracious to the vanquished, having, after many and great difficulties, forced the city of Gaza, came upon Beltis, who was in command there, and of whose valour he had during the siege experienced some wonderful proofs, now alone, abandoned by his troops, his arms broken in pieces, covered with blood and wounds, still fighting in the midst of a number of Macedons, who were belabouring him on all sides. Provoked by so dearly bought a victory (for among other injuries, he had received two fresh wounds on his person), Alexander said to him, 'You shall not die as you have wished, Beltis; be sure that you shall suffer all the torments that may be invented for a captive'; to which menace the other returned no other answer but a proud and haughty look. Alexander then, observing his fierce and stubborn silence, 'Has he bent a knee? Has any suppliant voice escaped him? Truly I will conquer this silence, and if I cannot wrest a word from him, I will at least wrest a groan', and, his rage turning to fury, he ordered his heels to be pierced and had him dragged alive, torn and dismembered, at a cart's tail.

Can it have been that fearlessness was so familiar to him that he respected it the less for not being able to admire it? Or that he esteemed it so peculiar to himself that he could not suffer to see it in so high a degree in another without vexation and envy? Or was

4 Should be Praeneste, a city of Latium, and not Perusia. This error appeared in the first edition of Amyot's Plutarch, but was afterwards rectified.

it that the natural impetuosity of his anger could brook no opposition? In truth, if he had been capable of curbing it, we may believe that he would have done so at the capture and desolation of the city of Thebes, when he saw so many valiant men, lost and totally destitute of common defence, put to the sword. For no less than six thousand were killed, not one of whom was seen to fly or cry for quarter; on the contrary, they sought, some here, some there, throughout the streets of the city, to confront the victorious enemy, provoking them to put them to an honourable death. Not one was seen so disheartened by wounds but he still tried with his last breath to avenge himself, and, with the weapons of despair, to find consolation for his own death in the death of an enemy. The distress shown in their valour, however, found no pity, and the length of a day was not sufficient to quench Alexander's thirst for revenge; the carnage continued until there was not a drop of blood left to shed, and was not stayed till all were killed except the unarmed, old men, women and children, who were enslaved to the number of thirty thousand.

How the soul relieves its feelings on the wrong objects, when the real are wanting

A gentleman of these parts, who was uncommonly subject to the gout, being urged by his physicians to abstain from all kinds of salt meats, was wont to reply very humorously, that in the throes of his affliction he must needs have somebody or something to lay the blame upon, and that if he could shout and curse the Bologna sausage, or the ham, or the ox-tongues, he felt very much better.

But, in good sooth, when the hand is raised to strike we feel hurt if it misses its aim and falls on the empty air; so also, if the sight is to have a pleasant prospect, it must not be lost and scattered on vacant space, but have an object to sustain it at a reasonable distance,

As the tempests lose
Their strength by sturdy forests unopposed,
Diffused on empty space.

LUCAN

So it would seem as if the soul, when moved and shaken, were lost in itself if it is given no hold; it must always be provided with an object to aim at and work upon. Plutarch says, speaking of those who lavish their affection on apes and little dogs, that the amorous part that is in us, for want of a legitimate object, rather than remain unsatisfied, will forge a false and frivolous one. And we see that the soul in its passions is wont to cheat itself by setting up a false and fanciful object, even against its own belief, rather than not have something to act upon. So it is that animals in their rage attack the stone or weapon that has hurt them, and with vicious teeth wreak their vengeance on themselves for the pain they feel:

Not otherwise a bear
Pannonian, fiercer for the wound received,
Maddened by dart from Libyan thong propelled,
Turns circling on her wound, and still pursues
The weapon fleeing as she whirls around.

LUCAN

What causes do we not invent for the misfortunes that befall us? What will we not blame, rightly or wrongly, that we may have something to fight with? It was not those fair tresses that you tear, nor the whiteness of that bosom that in your anger you so cruelly beat, that with an unlucky bullet killed your beloved brother: wreak your vengeance elsewhere.

Of the Roman army in Spain, after the loss of their two great captains, who were brothers,[1] Livy says, *they all at once began to weep and beat their heads*. It is a common practice. And did not the philosopher Bion say humorously of the king who tore his hair in his grief, 'Does this man think that a bald head will assuage his sorrow?' Who has not seen a man chew and swallow the cards, or gorge himself with a box of dice, to avenge himself on anything for the loss of his money? Xerxes scourged the waters of the Hellespont, placed it in chains and heaped insults

1 Publius and Cnaius Scipio.

upon it, and wrote a challenge to Mount Athos; and Cyrus delayed a whole army for many days to avenge himself on the river Gyndus, for the fright he had had in crossing it; and Caligula demolished a very fine mansion on account of the pleasure[2] which his mother had taken in it.

When I was young the people used to say that one of our neighbouring kings, for a cudgelling received from God, swore to be revenged, and commanded that for ten years no man should pray to him, nor speak of him, nor, as far as lay in his power, believe in him. This story was intended to describe not so much the folly as the vainglory natural to the nation to which it referred.

These two faults always go together, but such actions truly partake more of the nature of overweeningness than of stupidity. Augustus Caesar, having been tossed about in a storm at sea, set about defying the god Neptune, and in celebrating the Circensian games commanded his statue to be removed from among the other deities, as a token of revenge. Wherein he has less excuse than the preceding, and less than he had later, when, after losing a battle under Quintilius Varus in Germany, he ran about in anger and despair, knocking his head against the walls and exclaiming, 'O Varus, give me back my legions!' For they are more than foolish, since they add impiety to their folly, who direct their anger against God himself, or against Fortune, as if she had ears to be assailed by

2 *Plaisir* was evidently a misprint for *déplaisir*, for Seneca says that Caligula demolished a mansion in the Hercules quarter, because his mother had been detained there as a sort of prisoner.

our batteries; such as the Thracians, for instance, who, when it thunders or lightens, start shooting at heaven with Titanian vengeance, as if they could bring God to reason by a flight of arrows. Now, as the ancient poet says in Plutarch,

> 'Tis vain to be angered with things,
> They care not a rap for our wrath.

But when our minds are disordered we can never utter insults enough.

Of liars

There is no man whom it would so little become to boast of his memory as myself, for I can hardly show a trace of it, and I do not think that there is another in the world so marvellously defective as mine. All my other faculties are mean and ordinary, but in this I think I am singular and quite a rarity, deserving of a name and reputation.

Besides the natural inconvenience I suffer by it (for truly, seeing its necessity, Plato is right in calling it a 'great and powerful goddess'), in my part of the country, when they mean that a man has no sense, they say that he has no memory; and when I complain of the defect of mine, they take me up and will not believe me, as though I were accusing myself of being a fool. They can see no alternative between memory and intelligence.

This is spoiling my market. But they do me wrong, for experience rather shows, on the contrary, that an excellent memory is, more often than not, coupled with an infirm judgement. They do me wrong also in this, since I am nothing if not a good friend, that the very words that accuse my infirmity stand for ingratitude. They doubt my affection on account of my memory, and turn a natural defect into a lack of conscience. 'He has forgotten, they say, this request or that promise; He does not remember his friends; He has forgotten to say this, to do that, or to conceal something else, for my sake.' Certainly I am apt to forget, but as for neglecting, through indifference, a thing that a friend has charged me with, that is not in my nature. Let them be satisfied with my misfortune without making it a kind of ill-will, and an ill-will that is so foreign to my temper!

I find some comfort. Firstly, in the reflection that it is an evil which has provided me with the principal reason for correcting a worse evil, which might easily have grown on me, to wit, ambition; for the want of memory is an intolerable defect in one who would encumber himself with the world's affairs;

That, as several like examples of the progress of Nature show, she has generally strengthened my other faculties in proportion as this has weakened, and my mind and judgement could be easily led to follow indolently in the footprints of others, without exercising its own power, as is the way of the world, had the discoveries and opinions of others been present with me, by the gift of memory;

That my speech is the briefer, for the store-house of the memory is apt to be better furnished with matter than that of invention.

Had mine been faithful to me, I should have deafened all my friends with my chatter, the subjects arousing in me the little faculty I possess for handling and employing them, drawing out and warming my eloquence. That would be a pity, as I have experienced in the case of some of my intimate friends: according as their memory supplies them with a full and present view of their subject-matter, they carry their narrative so far back, and stuff it with so many needless details that, if the story be good, they stifle its goodness; if it is not good, you begin to curse either their good fortune in having such a memory, or their misfortune in having such a poor judgement. And when once you are on the high road of a narrative, it is difficult to stop and cut it short. There is nothing in which a horse's power is better seen than in a neat and dead stop.

Even among those who keep to the point I know some who are unable, though willing, to stop short in their career. While searching about in their mind for a point of conclusion, they go maundering on, dragging their feet like a man faint from weakness. Especially dangerous are old men, who retain the memory of things past and have lost the memory of their repetitions. I have known very amusing stories, told by a lord, become very wearisome, each of the company having been drenched with them a hundred times.

Secondly, I find a comfort in the reflection that I am the less mindful of offences received; as that ancient writer said of somebody.[1] I should need a reminder, like Darius who, in order not to forget the injury he had received at the hands of the Athenians, instructed a page, whenever he sat down to table, to sing into his ear three times, 'Sire, remember the Athenians!' On the other hand, places and books that I see again always smile upon me with a fresh novelty.

Not without reason do they say that he who is not very strong in memory should not meddle with lying. I know that the grammarians make a distinction between telling an untruth and lying, and say that to tell an untruth is to tell a thing that is false, but which one thinks to be true, and that by its derivation the word *lie* in Latin (*mentiri*), whence comes our French

1 Thou forgettest nothing, except injuries. – CICERO

word (*mentir*), means as much as to go against one's conscience,[2] and that it consequently applies only to those who say what is contrary to what they know, and of whom I am now speaking.

Now these either invent the whole, pith and all, or they alter and disguise something that has a true foundation. When they disguise and alter, and are often made to repeat the same story, they can hardly avoid tripping themselves up, because the real facts, as first lodged in the memory and imprinted upon it by the medium of conception and knowledge, cannot but present themselves to the imagination, dislodging the false, which cannot have so firm and settled a foothold; and the circumstances as originally learned, ever and again stealing into the mind, will make them lose the memory of those added details that are false and adulterated.

In what they wholly invent, inasmuch as there is no contrary impression to clash with their falsehood, there seems to be less fear of tripping. Yet even this, because it is an empty body without any substance, is apt to escape the memory, if it be not very sure. Of this I have often had amusing experience at the expense of such as profess only to adapt their speech to the matter in hand, and to humour the great persons with whom they are speaking. For, those circumstances to which they are ready to enslave their faith and conscience being subject to many changes, their speech must needs vary accordingly. Whence it happens that they will speak of one thing as now grey, now yellow; to this

2 *Contra mentem ire* was perhaps at the back of Montaigne's mind; or he recalled an expression of Cornelius Nepos: *contra id quod in mente est loqui*.

man in one way, to that in another; and if by any chance these men bring back their booty and compare their contradictory information, what becomes of that fine art? Moreover, they so often trip themselves up when off their guard; for what memory could suffice them to recall the many different shapes in which they have forged one and the same subject? I have known several in my day who craved a reputation for this fine sort of caution; they do not see that if the reputation be there, the results cannot be there.

Lying is indeed an accursed vice. We are human beings, and hold together, only by speech. If we knew the horror of it, and the gravity, we should pursue it with fire, and more justly so than other crimes.

I find that people usually waste their energies in chastising children, very improperly, for innocent faults, and torment them for thoughtless acts which make no impression and are of no consequence. Lying alone, and stubbornness, which stands on a little lower level, are, in my opinion, those faults whose birth and progress should be most earnestly combated. As the child grows, they grow with it; and when once the tongue has been started in this wrong direction, it is marvellous how impossible it is to pull it back. Whence it comes that we find men subject and enslaved to this vice who are honest in every other respect. I have a good fellow of a tailor whom I have never known to speak the truth, not even when it could serve him a good turn. If falsehood, like truth, had but one face, we should know better where we are, for we should then take for certain the opposite of what the liar tells us. But the reverse of the truth has a hundred thousand shapes and a boundless field.

The good, according to the Pythagoreans, is certain

and finite; evil is infinite and uncertain. A thousand ways deviate from, only one leads to, the bull's eye. I am by no means sure that I could tell a solemn and barefaced lie to save myself from an evident and extreme danger. An ancient father[3] says that a dog we know is better company than a man whose language we do not understand, *as a foreigner cannot be a man to a foreigner* (Pliny the Elder). And how much less sociable is false speaking than silence!

King Francis the First boasted of having, by this means, put on the rack one Francesco Taverna, ambassador of Francesco Sforza, Duke of Milan, a man of great fame in the art of talking. This man had been dispatched to excuse his master to his Majesty on account of a thing of great importance, which was this: The King, in order to keep up some communication with Italy, whence he had been recently driven, and especially with the duchy of Milan, had thought it expedient to have a gentleman to represent him at the Duke's court, an ambassador in effect, but ostensibly a private gentleman who resided there under the pretence of being engaged in his own affairs; for, being much more dependent on the Emperor, it was greatly against the interest of the Duke (especially at that time when he was negotiating a marriage with his niece, daughter of the King of Denmark, now Dowager of Lorraine) to be discovered having any intercourse and dealings with us. A fit and proper person for this charge was found in one Merveille, a Milanese gentleman and an equerry of the King's stables. Dispatched with secret credentials and ambassadorial instructions, and, for a cloak and appearance, with other letters of

3 Saint Augustine.

recommendation to the Duke to further him in his private concerns, this man was so long at the Duke's court that the Emperor had some inkling of it, which, as we think, was the occasion of what followed after, which was that, under colour of some murder, behold him one dark night decapitated by the Duke's orders, and his hash settled in a couple of days!

Messer Francesco being come, ready with a lengthy and made-up account of this affair (for the King had written, to demand satisfaction, to all the princes in Christendom, and to the Duke himself), had audience at the morning's sitting of the Council, and there, to bolster up his case, very ingeniously put forward several plausible explanations of the deed: that his master had never regarded our man as any other than a private gentleman and a subject of his, who had come to Milan on his own business, and had never resided there in any other capacity; that he denied any knowledge of his being of the King's household or even known to the King, much less that he was his ambassador. The King, in his turn, after pressing him with divers questions and objections, and attacking him on every quarter, at last cornered him on the matter of the execution carried out by night, and as it were by stealth. To which the poor man, in his embarrassment, assuming the part of the courtier, replied that out of respect to his Majesty the Duke would have been loath that the execution should have taken place in the daytime. We may all imagine how he was caught up, having tripped so clumsily in the presence of such a nose as that of King Francis.[4]

4 A glance at the portrait of King Francis will sufficiently explain the humour of this remark.

Pope Julius the Second sent an ambassador to the King of England to stir him up against King Francis.[5] After he had delivered himself of his charge, the King in his reply dwelt on the difficulties he would find in making the necessary preparations for fighting so powerful a king, and urged several other reasons, whereupon the ambassador very inopportunely answered that he also had considered these difficulties, and had represented them to the Pope. From these words, so foreign to his purpose, which was to incite him to immediate war, the King at once inferred, what he afterwards found to be the case, that this ambassador privately inclined to the side of France. Of which his master having been informed, his property was confiscated, and he himself barely escaped with his life.

5 Actually King Louis XII.

Of steadfastness

The law of resolution and steadfastness does not imply that we should not, as far as lies in our power, take cover against the ills and discomforts which threaten us, nor does it, by inference, forbid the fear of being taken by them unawares. On the contrary, all honourable means of securing ourselves from harm are not only allowed, but commendable, and the game of steadfastness is chiefly played by resolutely supporting those ills which cannot be remedied. So that no bodily activity or wielding of hand-weapons is to be condemned, if it serve to protect us from the blow that is aimed at us.

Some very warlike nations, when fighting, found their chief advantage in flight, and showed their backs to the enemy more dangerously than their faces. The Turks still to some extent practise this ruse.

Socrates in Plato ridicules Laches for defining courage as 'standing firm in the ranks against the enemy'. 'What! he said, can it be cowardice to beat them by yielding ground?' and he cites Homer, who commends the art of flight in Aeneas. And when Laches, on better consideration, admits this practice in the Scythians and more generally in all who fight mounted on horseback, he again cites the example of the Lacedemonian foot-soldiers, a nation trained above others to maintain their ground in fighting, who, at the battle of Plataea, being unable to force an opening into the Persian phalanx, decided to disperse and fall back, in order that the compact mass of the enemy, thinking they were in flight, might be broken and dissolved in pursuit. By this means they gained the victory.

Speaking of the Scythians, it is recorded that Darius, when he went out to subdue them, sent a message to their king, bitterly taunting him for always recoiling and shunning a hand-to-hand battle. To which Idanthyrses, for that was his name, replied, 'That it was not for fear of him or any man living, but that it was the method of proceeding of his nation, who had neither cultivated lands, nor cities nor houses to defend, and so had no fear of the enemy's gaining any profit. But if Darius was so hungry for a bite, let him approach and see their ancient places of sepulture, and there he would meet with somebody to talk with.'

In a cannonade, however, when a man is exposed to the fire, as often happens in war, it is an unbecoming thing to wince before the menacing shot, the more so as by reason of its impetus and velocity we account it unavoidable. And many a man, by raising his hand or ducking his head, has at least provided his comrades with a good laugh. And yet, in the expedition which the Emperor Charles the Fifth conducted against us in Provence, the Marquis de Guast, going to reconnoitre the city of Arles, and coming from behind a windmill under cover of which he had been approaching, was perceived by the Seigneur de Bonneval and the Seneschal d'Agenois, who were promenading on the Amphitheatre. These gentlemen pointing him out to the Sieur de Villier, commissary of the artillery, he aimed a culverin so accurately that, had not the said Marquis, seeing him apply the match, leapt to one side, he would have got it full in the body.

And in like manner, some years before, Lorenzo dei Medici, Duke of Urbino, father of the Queen-mother of the King, laying siege to Mondolfo, a place in Italy, in the territory called the Vicariat, seeing the match being applied to a piece of artillery that was pointed at him, did well to 'play the duck', else he would doubtless have had the ball, which only grazed the top of his head, right in the stomach.

To tell the truth, I do not think that these movements are the result of calculation, for how can you judge a high or low aim in so sudden a matter? It is much easier to believe that Fortune favoured their fright, and that on some other occasion the same movement might bring them into the line of fire, instead of avoiding it.

I cannot deny that if the loud report of an arquebus suddenly strikes on my ear in a place where I have no reason to expect it, I am startled; which I have seen happen to others more valorous than I.

And the Stoics do not claim that the soul of their sage can be proof against the first ideas and fancies that surprise him; but, as we are all by nature subject to them, they acquiesce rather in his yielding, even so far as to be convulsed and to turn pale, to a loud crash in the sky, for example, or the collapse of a building. And so with the other feelings, provided that his judgement remain sound and entire, that his reason be not thrown off its balance, and that it yield no consent to his fright or suffering. With regard to the man who is not a philosopher, it is the same in the first stage, but quite otherwise in the second. For in his case feelings make not a merely superficial impression, but penetrate to the seat of his reason, infecting and corrupting it. He judges according to his feelings, and is guided by them. The state of the Stoic sage is fully and elegantly expressed in this line:

> Though tears may flow, the mind
> remains unmoved.
>
> VIRGIL

The Peripatetic sage is not exempt from perturbations of mind, but he moderates them.

Of fear

Aghast I stood, tongue-tied, with stiffening hair.

VIRGIL

I am not a good naturalist (as they call it), and know not by what springs fear works in us, but so much is true that it is a strange feeling, and the physicians say that there is none that more easily throws our judgement off its proper balance. Indeed I have known of many people going mad through fear, and it is certain that it will produce even in the most sober-minded, as long as the fit is on them, a fearful bewilderment. I leave aside the uneducated, in whom it takes the form, now of their great-grandfathers rising out of their graves wrapped in their shrouds, now of were-wolves, hobgoblins, and monsters; but even in soldiers, who should be less liable to it, how often has it not transformed a flock of sheep into a squadron of mail-coats, reeds and bulrushes into lancers and men-at-arms, friends into enemies, the white cross into the red?[1]

When Monsieur de Bourbon took Rome, an ensign who was on guard at the Borgo San Pietro was seized with such terror at the first alarm that, with his colours in his hand, he rushed through a hole in a ruin out of the town and straight into the enemy, thinking that he

1 i.e. the Frenchman into a Spaniard.

was making for the centre of the city; at last, seeing Monsieur de Bourbon's company rallying to oppose him, who for their part thought that those of the town were making a sortie, he had no sooner come to himself than, facing about, he re-entered by the same hole through which he had advanced three hundred paces into the country. It by no means fell out so happily with the ensign of Captain Juille when St-Pol was taken from us by the Comte de Bures and Monsieur du Reu, for, distracted with fright, he rushed, flag and all, through a loop-hole out of the town, and was cut to pieces by the attacking party. The same siege was remembered for the fear that so seized, contracted, and froze the heart of a nobleman, that he fell without any wound stone dead in the breach.

At times a whole multitude will be seized with a like fear. In one of the encounters between Germanicus and the Germans, two large bodies of troops in their fright ran in opposite directions, the one from the place whence the other had fled.

Sometimes it lends wings to the heels, as in the two first cases; sometimes it nails and shackles our feet, as we read of the Emperor Theophilus who, in a battle which he lost against the Agarenes, was so benumbed and stupefied that he could not make up his mind to flee, *so much does fear dread even the means of safety!* (Quintus Curtius), until Manuel, one of the chief commanders of his army, had tugged and shaken him, as if to rouse him from a deep sleep, saying, 'If you do not follow me, I will kill you, for it is better that you should lose your life than, by being taken prisoner, the empire.'

Fear manifests its utmost power when, under its

influence, we are driven to a deed of valour which our duty and honour had refused. In the first regular battle which the Romans lost to Hannibal under the Consul Sempronius, a body of fully ten thousand foot-soldiers, being seized with terror and seeing no other outlet for their cowardice, threw themselves into the thick of the enemy, whom they charged through with wonderful energy and with a great slaughter of Carthaginians, thus purchasing an ignominious flight at the same price that a glorious victory would have cost them.

It is fear that I stand most in fear of; in sharpness it exceeds every other feeling. What distress could be sharper and more reasonable than that of Pompey's friends who, in his ship, were spectators of that horrible massacre? Yet the fear of the Egyptian sails which were then approaching stifled that feeling to such an extent, that it was observed that they thought only of urging the sailors to make what speed they could and escape by strength of oars until, being arrived at Tyre and delivered from fear, they had leisure to turn their thoughts to their late loss and give a loose rein to the tears and lamentations which the other stronger feeling had suspended:

> Then dread discharged all wisdom from my mind.
>
> ENNIUS

They who have had a good drubbing in a fight may be led back to the charge on the morrow, though still wounded and bleeding; but if they have been given a good fright by the enemy, you will not induce them even to look at them. Such as are oppressed by the fear of losing their property or of being banished or enslaved, live in continual anguish, to the point of losing appetite and sleep, whereas the poor, the exiled, the slaves, often live as merrily as other folk. And the many people who, in their impatience of the prickings of fear, have hanged or drowned themselves, or hurled themselves from a precipice, have plainly taught us that it is even more importunate and more insupportable than death.

The Greeks distinguish another kind of fear, which is not due to an error of judgement, arising, as they say, without any apparent cause and from a celestial impulse. Whole nations are often seized with it, and entire armies. Of that kind was the terror which brought a miraculous desolation upon Carthage, when the air was filled with cries and terrified voices, and the inhabitants were seen to rush out of their houses as to an alarm-bell, and to charge, wound, and kill one another as if they had been enemies come to occupy their city. All was disorder and tumult until with prayers and sacrifices they had appeased the ire of the gods. They call that a *panic terror*.

That to philosophize is to learn to die

Cicero says that philosophizing is nothing more than preparing for death. That is as much as to say that study and contemplation in some sort withdraw our soul outside of us, and keep it occupied apart from the body, and this is a kind of apprenticeship and resemblance to death; or perhaps, that all the wisdom and reason in the world converge in one point, to teach us not to fear death. In truth either reason is a mockery, or it must aim only at our contentment, and all its labour must tend in brief to make us live well and joyfully, as Holy Scripture says.[1] All opinions in the world agree in this, that pleasure is our end, although they differ as to the means of attaining it; otherwise they would be rejected at the outset, for who would give ear to him that should set up pain and misery as our goal? The dissensions of the philosophic sects in this case are verbal. *Let us skip over those subtle trifles* (Seneca). There is more obstinacy and wrangling than is consistent with so time-honoured a profession; but whatever part a man may undertake to play, he always brings in his own personality.

Whatever they may say, the last object we aim at, even in virtue, is voluptuousness. It amuses me to beat this word about their ears, which goes so much against their stomach. And if it signifies some supreme pleasure and excessive satisfaction, it is more

1 Ecclesiastes, 3:12–13.

due to the aid of virtue than to any other. This pleasure, for being more lusty, more sinewy, more robust and virile, is the more seriously voluptuous. And to virtue we ought to give the name of pleasure, as being more suitable, sweeter, and more natural, and not that of vigour, from which it takes its name.[2] That other and baser kind of voluptuousness, if it could deserve the fair name of pleasure, should bear it by way of competition and not of privilege. I find it less free from crosses and troubles than virtue. Besides that the taste of it is more fleeting, thinner, and more feeble, it has its vigils, its fasts, and its pains, both sweat and blood, and moreover particularly its keen-edged suffering of so many kinds and so dull a repletion attending it, that it is equivalent to penance.

We are greatly mistaken if we think that these incommodities serve as a sting and a condiment to its sweetness (as in nature a contrary is quickened by its contrary), or if we say, when we come to Virtue, that she is overwhelmed by the like consequences and difficulties and is rendered austere and inaccessible; whereas, much more really than in voluptuousness, they ennoble, sharpen, and enhance the divine and perfect pleasure that she procures us. He is certainly very unworthy to know her who weighs the cost against the fruit, and knows neither her charms nor her use. They who go about to instruct us that her quest is rugged and laborious, her fruition agreeable, what do they mean by that but that she is always disagreeable? For what human means ever arrived at its enjoyment? The most perfect have been well

2 Montaigne derives *virtus* (virtue) from *vis* (strength, vigour).

contented to aspire to and approach her, without possessing her. But they deceive themselves, seeing that of all the pleasures that we know, the very pursuit of her is pleasing. The attempt savours of the quality of the thing it aims at, for it is a good part of the effect, and consubstantial with it. The felicity and beatitude which glitters in virtue fills all its appurtenances and avenues, even to the first entry and utmost limit.

Now, one of the principal blessings of virtue is the contempt of death, by means of which our life is furnished with a soft tranquillity, and we are given a pure and loving taste for it, without which every other voluptuousness is extinct. For which reason all the rules meet and concur in this point.[3] And although they all in like manner lead us with one accord to despise pain, poverty, and the other calamities to which the life of man is subject, they do not do so with the same solicitude, as well because these calamities are not so inevitable (the greater part of mankind passing their lives without tasting of poverty, and some also without experience of pain and sickness, like Xenophilus the musician[4] who lived a hundred and six years in perfect health), as also because, at the worst, death can, when we please, cut short and put an end to all other discomforts. But as to death, it is inevitable:

> One road, and to one bourne
> We all are goaded. Late
> Or soon will issue from the urn
> Of unrelenting Fate

3 The earlier editions have: 'all the philosophical sects meet and concur in this point of teaching us to despise death.'

4 A slight confusion. Xenophilus was a philosopher; it was the musician Aristoxenes who recorded the fact.

The lot that in yon bark exiles us all
To undiscovered shores, from which is no recall.

HORACE

And consequently, if it frights us, we are subject to continual torment which can be in no way eased. There is no quarter from which it does not blow; we may turn our heads this way or that way without ceasing, as in a suspected country: *ever like Tantalus' rock it hangs over us* (CICERO). Our high courts often send criminals to be executed on the spot where the crime was committed. Take them on their way past fine houses, entertain them with as good cheer as you please;

Not feasts Sicilian shall
With all their cates recall
That zest the simplest fare could once inspire,
Nor song of birds, nor music of the lyre
Shall his lost sleep restore:

HORACE

do you think that they can rejoice in them, and that the final purpose of their journey, being continually before their eyes, will not have dried up their palate and sickened them with all such delights?

He hearkens as he goes and counts the days,
The length of route is measure of his life;
His soul is racked by thoughts of coming doom.

CLAUDIAN

The end of our race is death; it is the necessary object of our aim: if it frightens us, how is it possible to go a step forward without a fit of ague? The remedy of the vulgar is not to think of it, but from what brutish stupidity can proceed so gross a blindness? We must bridle their ass by the tail;

> With forward head he wends his backward way.
>
> LUCRETIUS

It is no wonder if they are so often caught in the snare. You will frighten those people by the mere mention of death, and most of them cross themselves as if we had spoken of the devil. And because a will is not made without a reference to death, you must not expect them to set their hand to it until the physician has given his last verdict; and God knows then, what with pain and terror, how much judgement they will bring to the concocting of it!

Because this syllable struck upon their ears too rudely, and the sound of it seemed unlucky, the Romans had learned to tone it down or extend it into a periphrasis. Instead of saying 'he is dead', they say 'he has ceased to live, he has lived'. So it be life, be it past or no, they are comforted. We have borrowed the same idea in our *feu Maistre Jehan*.[5]

Perhaps it is because, as the saying is, 'the delay is worth my money'. I was born between eleven o'clock and noon on the last day of February, one thousand five hundred and thirty-three, according to our present computation, beginning the year in January.[6] It is just a fortnight since I cleared thirty-nine years; I should

5 The late Master John; probably Montaigne derived *feu* from *fut* = was.

6 Under the first race of kings in France the year began on 1st March; under the second, on Christmas Day; under the third, on Easter Day until, in 1563, Charles IX fixed 1st January as the beginning.

live at least as many more. Meantime it were folly to encumber myself with thoughts of a thing so far off. But what! young and old leave their lives on the same terms. None departs this life otherwise than if he were presently entering into it. Added to which, there is no man so decrepit but thinks, as long as he has the example of Methuselah before his eyes, that he still has twenty years in his body. Moreover, poor fool that thou art, who has set a term to thy life? Thou reliest on physicians' tales; look rather at experience and facts. According to the ordinary course of things, thou hast long been living by extraordinary favour. Thou hast passed the ordinary term of life. And that that is so, reckon up among thy acquaintance how many more have died before thy age than have reached it; make a record of those even who have ennobled their lives by renown, and I will lay a wager that thou wilt find more who have died before than after thirty-five. It is consistent with reason and piety to take example by the humanity of Jesus Christ: he ended his life at thirty-three. The greatest man who was merely man, Alexander, died at the same age.

How many several ways has death to surprise us!

No mortal due provision makes
'Gainst ills which any hour may fall.

HORACE

I leave aside fevers and pleurisies. Who would ever have imagined that a Duke of Brittany could be crushed to death in a crowd as that Duke was, at the entry of Pope Clement, my neighbour,[7] into Lyons?

7 Bertrand de Got, Pope Clement V and Archbishop of Bordeaux, hence 'my neighbour'. King Henri II was

Hast thou not seen one of our kings killed at play? And did not one of his ancestors die through being charged by a hog? In vain did Aeschylus, threatened[8] by the fall of a house, keep out of doors: behold him felled by the roof of a tortoise that had escaped from the talons of an eagle flying in the air! The other met his death through a grape-stone; an emperor from the scratch of a comb whilst combing his hair; Emilius Lepidus through knocking his foot against the threshold of his door; and Aufidius through colliding with the door on entering the council-chamber; and between the thighs of women, Cornelius Gallus the praetor, Tigellinus, captain of the watch at Rome, Lodovico, son of Guido di Gonzaga, Marquis of Mantua, and, of still worse example, Speusippus the Platonic philosopher, and one of our popes.

Poor Bebius, a judge, whilst he is granting a term of eight days to a litigant, behold him taken with a seizure, and his own term of life expired! And Caius Julius, a physician, anointing the eyes of a patient, when behold death closes his own! And if I may bring in myself, a brother of mine, Captain Saint-Martin, twenty-three years old, who had already given sufficient proof of his valour, whilst playing at tennis was struck by a ball a little above the right ear. There being no sign of a wound or contusion, he did not sit down to rest, but five or six hours later he died of an apoplexy caused by this blow. When such frequent and ordinary examples pass before our eyes, how can

---

mortally wounded in a tournament; his ancestor was Philip, eldest son of Louis le Gros.

8 That is to say, threatened by a prophecy, which came true, metaphorically. 'The other' was Anacreon.

we possibly help thinking of death and fancying every moment that he is gripping us by the throat?

What matter, you will say, how it comes about, as long as one does not torment oneself? I am of this mind, and whatever means one may adopt to shelter from the blows, though it were under a calf's skin, I am not the man to despise them. For it is enough if I pass my life in comfort; and I steer the safest course that I can, though it be as little glorious and exemplary as you will.

For my own part, I rather would be thought
Dull as a writer, possibly distraught,
Nor could I but take pleasure in my faults,
Nor see where meaning or where music halts,
Than be of mine own failings quite aware
And gnash my teeth in impotent despair.

HORACE

But it is folly to think by that way to come to it. They go, they come, they trot, they dance, but of death, never a word! All that is very fine, but then, when it comes either to themselves or to their wives, their children or friends, surprising them on a sudden and unprepared, what torments, what outcries, what rage and despair overwhelms them! Did you ever see any one so dejected, so changed, so bewildered? We must look to it earlier, and that bestial nonchalance, even though it should lodge in the head of a man of intelligence, which seems to me utterly impossible, sells us its merchandise too dear. Were it an enemy that could be avoided, I should advise borrowing the weapons of cowardice. But since that cannot be, since he will overtake you whether you be a runaway poltroon or a man of honour,

And death the coward slaves that fly
Pursues with steps as fleet,
Nor spares the loins and backs of those
Unwarlike youths who shun their foes, HORACE

and since no cuirass, however well-tempered, will cover you,

Though brass and steel encase the wary wight,
Death drags his head from forth his mask of mail,
PROPERTIUS

let us learn with firm foot to resist and fight him. And, to deprive him of the greatest advantage he has over us, let us first adopt a course quite contrary to the usual. Let us disarm him of his strangeness, let us become familiar and conversant with him, and keep nothing so frequently in our thoughts as death. At all times let us bring him before our imagination in his every shape. At the stumbling of a horse, at the fall of a tile, at the least prick of a pin, let us straightway ruminate: 'Well! and what if it had been death himself?' and thereupon stiffen and fortify ourselves. Amidst feasting and jollity let us ever repeat this refrain to remember our condition, and let us not be so carried away by our pleasures as not to remember, now and then, in how many ways our merriment is a mark for death, in how many ways he threatens to grip us. This the Egyptians did, who, in the midst of their banquets and at the height of their merriment, had the dry anatomy of a human corpse brought in, to serve as a warning to the guests.

Regard each day as if it were thy last;
The next day's joyful light thine eyes shall see,
And unexpected will more welcome be. HORACE

Where death is waiting for us is uncertain; let us await him everywhere. Premeditation of death is premeditation of freedom. He who has learned to die has unlearned to be a slave. The knowing how to die frees us from all subjection and constraint. There is no evil in life for him who has rightly understood that privation of life is no evil. Paulus Emilius, to a messenger sent by his prisoner, the wretched King of Macedon, to entreat him not to lead him in his triumph, replied, 'Let him make that request to himself'.

Indeed, if Nature lend not a hand, art and industry can hardly advance in any way. I am by nature not melancholic but a dreamer. Ever since I can remember, nothing has occupied my imagination more than death, yea, even in the most licentious season of my life,

> When gladsome spring my youthful eye rejoiced.
>
> CATULLUS

When in the company of ladies and at games, many a man has thought I was disturbed by inward digestion of some jealousy, or the uncertainty of some hope, the while I was meditating on someone or other who had been overtaken, a few days before, by a burning fever and by his end, and after leaving a similar entertainment, his head full of idle fancies, love, and a 'good time', as mine was then, and thinking that I was in the same parlous state.

> Brief is this fruit of joy to paltry man,
> Soon, soon departed, and thereafter, no,
> It may not be recalled.
>
> LUCRETIUS

Yet did not this thought wrinkle my brow any more than any other. It is impossible but we must at the outset feel the prickings of such imaginations, but by turning them over and over again in our minds, we may no doubt in the long run make them familiar. Otherwise I, for my part, should be in a perpetual fright and frenzy, for no man was ever more mistrustful of his life, no man ever counted less on its duration. Neither does my health, which hitherto has been with little interruption very robust, prolong, nor sickness curtail, my hope. Every minute I think may be my last, and this is my constant refrain: 'Whatever can be done another day can be done today.' Hazards and dangers bring us, indeed, little or no nearer to our end, and when we consider how many millions more remain and hang over our heads, not to speak of the calamity that seems most to threaten us, we shall find that, lusty or feverish, at sea or at home, in battle or in repose, it is equally near: *No man is more frail than another, no man more certain of tomorrow* (SENECA). To finish what I have to do before dying, were it but an hour's work, the longest leisure appears to me short.

The other day somebody, turning over my tablets, found a memorandum of something I wished to be done after my death. I told him, what was true, that being but a league's distance from my house, and healthy and robust, I had hastened to write it down on the spot, because I could not be certain even of reaching home. Continually brooding over my thoughts and turning them inwardly as I do, I am every moment about as prepared as I can ever be. And the unexpected coming of death can tell me nothing new.

We must be ever booted and ready to start, as far as

in us lies, and above all we must see to it that we have no business with any but ourselves;

> Why should we still project and plan,
> We creatures of an hour? HORACE

For that will keep us busy enough without any addition. One man will lament, not so much that he has to die, but that his death will interrupt the course of a fine victory, another that he has to quit before having married his daughter or arranged his children's education; one regrets losing the society of his wife, another that of his son, as the principal comfort of his life.

I am at this hour in such a condition, thank God, that I can quit whenever it shall please him, without any repining whatever, except it be for life, if the prospect of losing it happens to weigh me down. I disengage myself on all sides; my farewells are half taken, of all except of myself. Never did man more fully and absolutely prepare to quit the world and cut himself adrift from all things, than I propose to do. The deadest deaths are the soundest.

> Poor wretch, they say, one hostile hour hath ta'en
> Wretchedly from thee all life's many guerdons.
> LUCRETIUS

And the builder,

> The frowning battlements neglected lie,
> And lofty scaffolding that threats the sky.
> VIRGIL

A man should design nothing so far ahead, or at least with no such passionate intent to see it accomplished. We are born for action:

But when I die, would I might die in harness.

OVID

I agree that we should work and prolong the functions of life as far as we can, and hope that Death may find me planting my cabbages, but indifferent to him and still more to the unfinished state of my garden. I witnessed the death of one who, at his last gasp, incessantly lamented that Destiny was cutting the thread of a history that he had in hand, at the fifteenth or sixteenth of our kings.

They add not, 'yet no longer unto thee
Remains a remnant of desire for them'.

LUCRETIUS

We must throw off these vulgar and hurtful humours. Even as they laid out our cemeteries adjoining the churches and the most frequented parts of the city, in order, as Lycurgus said, to accustom the common people, the women and children, not to be scared at the sight of a corpse, and to the end that this continual spectacle of bones, tombs, and funeral processions might warn us of our condition;

A custom 'twas to cheer the guests
With bloody brawls and slaughter dire
Of men contending with the sword.
The dying fell among the cups
And splashed the board with plenteous gore;

SILIUS ITALICUS

and as the Egyptians, after their banquets, presented to the sight of the company a large image of death, while one called out, 'Drink and be merry, for such shall you be when you are dead'; so it has been my custom to have death continually not only in my mind, but on my lips. And there is nothing about which I am so desirous of gathering information, as the death of men, their words, their looks, their behaviour, nor any passages in history that I remark so attentively. It may be seen in the cramming of my book with examples that I have a particular fancy for this subject. If I were a maker of books I should compile a register, with comments, of different deaths. He who should teach men to die, would teach them to live. Dicearchus wrote one with a title of that kind, but to another and less profitable purpose.

I may be told that the reality so far exceeds our imagination that the best fencing is of no avail when it comes to the point. Let them say; premeditation without doubt gives one a great advantage. And then, is it nothing to go at least so far without disturbance and tremor? What is more, Nature herself lends us a hand and gives us courage. If the death be short and violent, we have no leisure to fear it; if otherwise, I am conscious that, as the malady gains on me, I naturally conceive a certain disdain of life. I find it much more difficult to digest this resolution to die when I am in good health, than when I am in a fever. As I become less strongly attached to the amenities of life, by reason of beginning to lose the enjoyment and pleasure of them, so do I look upon death with much less terror. That makes me hope that the farther I am removed from the former, and the nearer I approach to the latter, the more easily shall I become reconciled to the exchange. Even as I have experienced on several occasions that, as Caesar says, objects often appear larger at a distance than near at hand, so I have found that when in good health I had a much greater horror of sickness than when afflicted by it. The cheerful humour, the vigour and pleasure that I enjoy, make the other state appear so disproportionate to the present one, that in imagination I magnify those afflictions by one half, and conceive them to be heavier than I find them when they are on my shoulders. I hope that it will be the same in death.

Let us see, in these ordinary changes and declines that we suffer, how Nature hides from us the taste of our loss and decay. What remains to an old man of the vigour of his youth and his past life?

> Alas, in age how little joy of life!
>
> MAXIMIAN

Caesar, to a jaded and broken-down soldier of his guard, who came to him in the street to ask his leave to be put to death, looking at his decrepit appearance, humorously replied, 'You think then that you are alive?' Should we fall into this condition all of a sudden, I do not believe that we should be able to endure so great a change. But, led by the hand of Nature down a gentle and almost imperceptible slope, little by little, step by step, she rolls us into this miserable state, and makes us familiar with it, so that we feel not the shock when youth dies in us, which is, in truth and reality, a harder death than the complete death of a languishing life, than the death of old age, inasmuch as the leap from an evil existence to a non-existence is not so heavy as that from a pleasant and flourishing existence to a grievous and painful one.

A body that is bent and bowed has less strength to support a burden; so it is with the soul: it must be raised and straightened against the power of this enemy. For, as it is impossible for the soul to be at rest as long as the fear of him is on her, so, if she can once gain assurance, she may boast (a thing almost surpassing the power of man) that it is impossible that disquiet, torment, fear, even the least trouble, should dwell in her.

Nor hath the tyrant's menace skill
  His fixed resolve to shake;
Nor Auster, at whose wild command
  The Adriatic billows lash,
Nor Jove's dread thunder-launching hand.

HORACE

She is become mistress of her passions and lusts, mistress of indigence, shame, poverty, and all other of Fortune's harms. Let us gain this advantage, those of us who can: this is the true and sovereign freedom, which enables us to snap our fingers in the face of violence and injustice, and to laugh at prisons and chains;

'In a dungeon cell
I'll keep you bound with gyve and manacle.'
'A God will set me free whene'er I please.'
Meaning, methinks, Death as the God who frees –
Death that shuts up the sum of all our miseries.

HORACE

Our religion has no surer human foundation than the contempt of life. Not only the discourse of reason invites us to it, for why should we fear to lose a thing, which being lost cannot be lamented; and, since we are menaced by death in so many shapes, is it not a greater evil to fear them all than to endure one?

What matters it when it shall come to pass, since it is inevitable? To him who announced to Socrates that the thirty tyrants[9] had condemned him to death, he replied, 'And Nature, them'.

What folly to torment ourselves about passing into a state of exemption from all torment! As our birth brought us the birth of all things, so will our death bring us the death of all things. Wherefore it is as foolish to weep because a hundred years from now we shall not be alive, as to weep because we were not living a hundred years ago. Death is the origin of another life. So did we weep, so much did it cost us to enter into this life, so did we strip off our former veil on entering into it.

Nothing can be grievous that is but once. Is it reasonable to fear for so long a time of such brief duration? Long life and short life are by death made all one; for the long and the short are not in things that are no more. Aristotle tells us that there are little creatures on the river Hypanis that live but a day. The one that dies at eight o'clock in the morning dies in its youth, that which dies at five in the afternoon dies in its decrepitude. Which of us would not think it absurd to see this moment of duration put into the consideration of weal or woe? The greater or lesser duration of our lives, if we compare it with eternity, or yet with that of mountains, rivers, stars, trees, or even of some animals, is no less ridiculous.

But Nature compels us to it. 'Go out of this world, she says, as you entered into it. The same way you came from death to life, without fear or passion, return from life to death. Your death is of one piece with the order of the universe, it is of one piece with the life of the world.

9 Not the thirty tyrants, but the Athenians.

> We live as mortals by eternal give and take . . .
> And like to runners hand the lamp of life
> One to another.
>
> LUCRETIUS

'Why should I alter for you this beautiful disposition of things? Death is the condition of your creation, it is a part of you; you are flying from yourself. This being that you enjoy is equally divided between death and life. The first day of your birth starts you on the road to death as well as to life.

> The hour which gave us life begins our death.
>
> SENECA

> As we are born to die, our lots are cast,
> And our first hour disposeth of our last.
>
> MANILIUS

'Every day that you live you purloin from life; you live at the expense of life. The perpetual work of your life is to build up death. You are in death whilst you are in life; for you are after death when you are no more in life. Or, if you prefer it this way, you are dead after life, but dying while you live, and death handles the dying much more rudely than the dead, and more perceptibly and sharply.

'If you have made your profit out of life you are fed up with it; go your way satisfied.

> Why not,
> Even like a banqueter, depart the halls,
> Laden with life?
>
> LUCRETIUS

'If you have not known how to make the best of it, if it has been unprofitable to you, what matters it to you that you have lost it? To what end do you still desire to keep it?

Why seekest more to add – which in its turn
Will perish foully and fall out in vain? LUCRETIUS

'Life in itself is neither a good nor an evil; it is the scene of good and evil, as you arrange it. And if you have lived a day, you have seen all; one day is like all days. There is no other light, there is no other night. This sun, this moon, these stars, this order, are the very same that your ancestors enjoyed and that will rejoice your great-grandchildren:

No other saw our sires of old,
No other shall our sons behold. MANILIUS

'And if it comes to the worst, the distribution and variety of all the acts of my comedy are performed in a year. If you have taken heed of the swing of my four seasons, they embrace the childhood, the youth, the virility, and the old age of the world. It has played its part, and knows no other cunning but to begin again. It will be always the same thing.

Besides we're busied with the same device,
Ever and ever. LUCRETIUS

The year revolves and ay its steps retraces. VIRGIL

'I do not purpose to create for you any new pastimes:

For all I may devise or find
To pleasure thee is nothing: all things are
The same forever. LUCRETIUS

'Give place to others, as others have given place to you. Equality is the first part of equity. Who can complain of being comprehended where all are comprehended? So, live as long as you can, you shall by nothing shorten the time you are to be dead; it is all to no purpose: you will be as long in that state which you fear as if you had died at your nurse's breast:

> Therefore, O man, by living on, fulfil
> As many generations as you may:
> Eternal death shall there be waiting still.
>
> LUCRETIUS

'And yet I will place you in such a condition that you will have no cause to be displeased;

> Thou knowest not
> That in true death there is no second self
> Alive and able to sorrow for self destroyed,
> Or stand lamenting that the self lies there.
>
> LUCRETIUS

'Nor shall you so much as wish for the life that you so much regret;

> For no one then demands his self or being . . .
> Without desire of any selfhood more.
>
> LUCRETIUS

'Death is less to be feared than nothing, if there were anything less than nothing:

> Death is, then, to us
> Much less – if there can be a less than that
> Which is itself a nothing.
>
> LUCRETIUS

'Dead or alive, it concerns you not: alive, because you exist; dead, because you exist no more.

'No man dies before his hour. The time you leave behind you was no more yours than that which elapsed before you were born, and concerns you no more,

Look back:
Nothing to us was all fore-passed eld
Of time the eternal, ere we had a birth.

LUCRETIUS

'Wherever your life ends, it is all there. The profit of life is not in its length but in the use we put it to: many a man has lived long, who has lived little; see to it as long as you are here. It lies in your will, not in the number of years, to make the best of life. Did you think never to arrive at a place you were incessantly making for? Yet there is no road but has an end. And if society is any comfort to you, is not the world going the selfsame way as you?

And these, their life completed, follow you.

LUCRETIUS

'Do not all dance the same dance as you? Is there a thing that does not age with you? A thousand men, a thousand animals, and a thousand other creatures die at the same moment that you die:

No night a day, no dawn a night hath followed
That heard not, mingling with the small birth-cries,
The wild laments, companions old of death
And the black rites.

LUCRETIUS

'Why do you recoil, if you cannot draw back? You have seen men enough who were the better for dying, thereby escaping great miseries. But have you known of any who were the worse off? Hence it shows great simplicity to condemn a thing that you have proved neither in your own person nor in another's. Why dost thou complain of me and of destiny? Do we do thee any wrong? Is it for thee to govern us, or for us to govern thee? Though thy age be not yet accomplished, thy life is. A little man is an entire man as well as a big one: neither men nor their lives are measured by the ell.

'Chiron refused immortality, being informed of the conditions thereof by the god of time and duration himself, his father Saturn. Imagine, indeed, how much more grievous and insupportable everlasting life would be to man than the life I have given him. If you had not death you would eternally curse me for having deprived you of it. I have knowingly mingled a little bitterness with it, to prevent you, seeing the advantage of it, from embracing it too eagerly and unwisely. To keep you in that middle state, which I require of you, where you neither fly life nor again fly death, I have tempered both one and the other between sweetness and bitterness.

'I taught Thales, the first of your sages, that to live and to die are indifferent, which made him answer very wisely one who asked him why then he did not die, "Because it is indifferent".

'Water, air, earth, fire and the other members of this my edifice, are no more instruments of thy life than instruments of thy death. Why dost thou fear thy last day? It contributes no more to thy death than does every other day. The last step does not cause the lassitude: it declares it. All days journey towards death; the last arrives there.'

These are the good lessons of our mother Nature.

Now, I have often wondered how it is that in war the face of death, whether we see it in ourselves or in others, appears incomparably less dreadful than at home in our houses (if it were not so, an army would be made up of physicians and whiners); and that, although death is everywhere the same, we find much more assurance in villagers and people of humble condition than in others. I believe indeed that it is the dismal faces and the appalling ceremony with which we surround death that frighten us more than the thing itself: a quite new way of living, the cries of mothers, wives and children, a crowd of visiting friends numb and dazed with grief, and servants pale and blubbering, a chamber from which the sun is excluded, lighted by tapers, our bedside besieged by doctors and preachers; to sum up, nothing around us but horrors and bugbears. Behold us already shrouded and buried! Children are frightened even by friends, if they see them masked, and so are we. We must strip the mask from things and persons, which being removed, we shall see beneath it that same death which a varlet or simple chambermaid suffered the other day without any fear. Happy the death that leaves no time for all these ceremonious preparations!

One man's gain is another man's loss

Demades, an Athenian, condemned a man of his city whose trade it was to sell the necessaries for funerals, on the score that he demanded too much profit, and that this profit could only come to him by the death of many people. This judgment seems to be ill-grounded, inasmuch as no profit is made but at others' expense, and that by this reckoning profit of any kind must be condemned.

The tradesman thrives only by the extravagance of youth, the husbandman by the dearness of grain, the architect by the ruin of houses, the officers of justice by lawsuits and men's quarrels; even the honour and practice of ministers of religion depend on our death and our vices. No physician delights in the good health even of his friends, says the ancient Greek comic dramatist, nor does a soldier in the peace of his city; and so with the rest. And, what is worse, if each of us sounds his conscience, he will find that his inmost wishes are for the most part born and nourished at the expense of others.

Considering which, it has come into my fancy that Nature in this does not belie her general policy, for natural philosophers hold that the birth, nourishment, and increase of each thing is the alteration and corruption of another:

For change of anything from out its bounds
Means instant death of that which was before.

LUCRETIUS

Of different results of the same counsel

Jacques Amyot, Grand Almoner of France, one day told me this story to the honour of one of our princes (and ours he was deservedly, although of foreign origin),[1] that during our first civil war, at the siege of Rouen, this Prince had been warned, by the Queen-mother of the King, of an attempt that was to be made on his life; she particularly mentioned in her letters the person who was to carry out the design. This was a gentleman of Anjou, or of Maine, who with this end in view frequently visited the house of the Prince. He communicated this intelligence to no one, but, walking next day on the Mont Ste Catherine, from whence our battery played on Rouen (for it was at the time we were besieging it), with the aforesaid Lord Grand Almoner and another bishop at his side, he perceived the gentleman who had been denounced to him, and sent for him. When he came into his presence, he spoke to him thus, seeing him already turning pale and trembling at the alarms of his conscience: 'Monsieur So-and-so, you no doubt suspect why I wish to see you, and your face shows it. You have nothing to hide from me, for I am so well informed of your business, that you would only make things worse for yourself by trying to conceal it. You

1 The Duke François de Guise, of the house of Lorraine. The siege of Rouen took place in 1562: the Duke, who was on very friendly terms with Montaigne, was assassinated in the following year.

know very well such and such a thing (mentioning the ins and outs of the most secret circumstances of this conspiracy); fail not, on your life, to confess to me the whole truth of the plot.' When the poor man saw himself caught and convicted (for the whole plot had been discovered to the Queen by one of the accomplices), he could but join his hands and implore the Prince's pardon and mercy, and would have cast himself at his feet, but that the Prince prevented him, and continued as follows: 'Come hither; have I at any time done you an injury? Have I, in private feud, offended any of your kin? I have hardly known you three weeks; what reason could have induced you to attempt my death?' The gentleman replied, with trembling voice, that it was not for any private motive, but the general interest of his party's cause; and that he had been persuaded by some that it would be a very pious deed to extirpate, by any means whatsoever, so powerful an enemy to their religion. 'Now, continued the Prince, I will prove to you how much more humane is the religion I hold than that which you profess. Yours counsels you to kill me without being heard, though you have suffered no wrong at my hands; and mine commands me to pardon you, convicted though you be of having intended to murder me without reason. Get you gone, withdraw; let me see you no more; and if you are wise, you will henceforth choose better men to advise you.'

When the Emperor Augustus was in Gaul, he received certain information of a plot that was being brewed against him by Lucius Cinna; he decided on revenge, and to that end summoned a council of his friends for the next morning. But he passed the night between in great uneasiness of mind, considering that he was about to put to death a young man of good family and a nephew of the great Pompey, and in his trouble he turned various considerations over in his mind: 'What! said he to himself, shall it be ordained that I am to remain in a state of fear and alarm, and let my murderer meanwhile walk abroad at his pleasure? Shall he go quit, who is aiming at my head, which I have carried safe and sound through so many civil wars, so many battles by sea and land, and after having established the universal peace of the world? Shall he be absolved who has conspired not only to murder, but to sacrifice me?' (for the plot was to kill him in the act of sacrificing.) Then, after a short silence, he began again in a louder voice, and took himself to task: 'Why dost thou live, if so many people are interested in thy death? Shall there be no end to thy vengeances and cruelties? Is thy life worth all the evil that is done to preserve it?'

Livia, his wife, hearing him in his anguish, said to him: 'And will a woman's counsel be taken? Do as the physicians do, who, when the customary remedies are of no avail, try the contrary ones. You have hitherto gained nothing by severity: Lepidus has followed Salvidienus; Murena, Lepidus; Cepio, Murena; Egnatius, Cepio. Begin now and try how mildness and clemency will succeed. Cinna is convicted; pardon him; injure you henceforth he cannot, and it will be to your glory.' Augustus was well pleased to have found an advocate of his own mind, and having thanked his wife and countermanded his friends whom he had called in council, he commanded Cinna to be brought to him all alone. Having ordered all his attendants to leave his chamber, and bidden Cinna to be seated, he spoke to him in this wise: 'In the first place I ask you, Cinna, to hear me in peace: do not interrupt me; I shall give you time and leisure to reply. You know, Cinna, that having taken you, a prisoner in my enemies' camp, though you not merely became, but were born my enemy, I gave you your life, I put you in possession of all your goods, and made you in short so comfortable and well off, that the victorious are envious of the condition of the vanquished. I granted you the priestly office you asked of me, after refusing it to others whose fathers had always fought on my side. After so many obligations you have plotted to kill me.' To which Cinna exclaiming that he was very far from such a wicked thought: 'You do not keep your promise, Cinna, continued Augustus; you assured me that I should not be interrupted. Yes, you have conspired to kill me in such a place, on such a day, in such company and in such a manner.' And seeing him paralysed at these words and struck dumb, not on account of keeping his bargain to be silent, but with the weight of conscience: 'Why, he added, do you do it? Is it in order to be emperor? Truly the Republic is in a bad way, if I alone hinder you from coming to empire. You cannot even defend your house, and the other day you lost a lawsuit, thanks to the efforts of a mere freedman. What! can you use your resources to no better purpose than to attack Caesar? I will throw up the game, if it is I alone who obstruct your hopes. Do you think that Paulus, that Fabius, that the Cossii and the Servilii will tolerate you, not to speak of a great number of nobles, not only nobles in name, but who, by their virtue, are a credit to their nobility?' After much more to the same effect (for he spoke for more than two full hours), he said: 'Now go, Cinna; that life which I once gave you as to an enemy, I give as to a traitor and parricide; friendship shall commence from this day between us, and let us strive which of us shall show the better faith, I who have given you life, or you who have received it.' And thus he parted from him. Some time after this he gave him the consulship, complaining that he had not dared to ask for it. Ever afterwards he had in Cinna a firm friend, and was made by him sole heir to his estates.

Now, after this event, which befell Augustus in the fortieth year of his age, there was never any attempt or conspiracy made against his life, and he received a just reward for his clemency. But it did not so happen to our Prince, for his humane action could not save him from afterwards falling into the toils of a like treason.[2] So vain and unavailing a thing is human wisdom! and throughout all our plans, projects, and precautions Fortune is ever the mistress of events.

We call a physician lucky when he is successful in a case; as if his art were the only one that could not stand upon its own legs, and whose foundations were too weak to support it by their own strength, and as if it alone had need of the helping hand of Fortune in its operations. My opinion of the art of physic is as bad or as good as you please, for we have, thank God! no traffic together. My attitude towards it is quite the contrary to that of others; for I ever despise it indeed, but when I am sick, instead of becoming reconciled with it, I begin to hate and fear it as well; and to those who urge me to take physic I reply that they may wait

2 He was, after all, assassinated by a gentleman of Angoumois called Poltrot de Méré, and from the same motive.

at least until I am restored to health and strength, in order to be better able to support the effect and the danger of their potions. I allow Nature to work, and suppose her to be armed with teeth and claws to defend herself against the assaults that are made upon her, and to maintain this frame whose dissolution she fears. I fear lest, instead of assisting her, when she is at grips and struggling with disease, I might assist her adversary instead of her, and put fresh burdens on her shoulders.

Now, I say that not only in medicine but in several more certain arts, there is a good deal of luck. Why should we not attribute the poetic flights which ravish and transport their author out of himself to his good luck, since he himself confesses that they exceed his power and ability, and acknowledges them to proceed from something else than himself, and to be no more within his power than those extraordinary emotions and agitations of orators, which, as they say, impel them beyond their intention?

It is the same with painting, for it sometimes happens that touches escape from the brush of the artist that so far exceed his conception and his art as to excite his own admiration and astonishment. But Fortune still more evidently shows the share that she has in all these works, by the charm and beauty which enter into them, not only in spite of the intention, but without even the knowledge of the workman. A competent reader will often discover in the writings of others perfections other than the author intended or perceived, and lend them a fairer face and a richer meaning.

With regard to military enterprises, everyone knows how great a hand Fortune has in them. Even in our plannings and deliberations there must truly be mingled something of chance and good luck, for all that our wit can do is no great matter; the quicker and more acute it is, so much the weaker does it think itself to be, and so much the more does it distrust itself. I am of Sulla's way of thinking,[3] and when I closely examine the most famous exploits of war, I seem to see that they who conduct them only deliberate and take counsel as a matter of form, and leave the better part of their enterprise to Fortune; and, relying on her aid, at every turn go beyond the limits of all reason. There ensue, in their deliberations, accidental exhilarations and extraordinary fits of frenzy, which impel them most often to adopt a course that is apparently least founded on prudence, and which swell their courage beyond all reason. Whence it has come about that some of the great captains of old, to justify their foolhardy resolutions, declared to their soldiers that they were commanded by some inspiration, some sign or prognostic.

Wherefore, in the uncertainty and perplexity brought upon us by our inability to discern and choose the most proper course, by reason of the difficulties which the various accidents and circumstances of each thing bring along with them, the surest way, in my opinion, even though no other consideration should invite us to it, is to cast oneself on that side where there is most honesty and justice; and, when in doubt about the nearest path, to choose always the straight one; as in those two examples I have just cited, there can be

3 Sulla, according to Plutarch, 'disarmed envy by often commending his good fortune, and finally took the surname of Faustinus, the Fortunate'.

no doubt that it was more noble and generous in him who had received the offence to pardon it, than to do otherwise. If the former came to grief, it must not be put down to his good intention; nor do we know whether, had he adopted the contrary course, he would have escaped the end to which his destiny called him, and then he would have forfeited the glory of so humane an action.

In history we read of many men who were possessed by this fear, the greater part of whom followed the course of meeting and anticipating the conspiracies formed against them by vengeance and punishment, but I read of very few who benefited by this remedy: witness so many Roman emperors. He who finds himself in this danger must not put too much faith either in his power or his vigilance. For how difficult it is to guard ourselves against an enemy who puts on the mask of the most assiduous friend we have, and to know the inner thoughts and intentions of those who serve us! It is of no avail to have a guard of foreigners, and to be continually surrounded by a hedge of armed men; any man who disregards his own life always has the power of disposing of another's. And then, that continual suspicion which makes a prince distrustful of all the world, must be a strange torment to him.

Therefore it was that Dion, being advised that Callipus was watching his opportunity to put him to death, never had the heart to make further inquiries, saying that he would rather die than live in the misery of having to be on his guard, not only against his enemies, but against his friends. This attitude of mind was much more vividly and more undauntedly acted upon by Alexander. Having had information by letter from Parmenio that Philippus, his favourite physician, had been bribed by Darius's money to poison him, he gave the letter to Philippus to read, and at the same moment swallowed the potion he had brought him. Was not this to express a resolution that, if his friends desired to kill him, he was willing to give them an opportunity to do so? This prince is the supreme pattern of hazardous deeds, yet I know not whether in all his life he showed an act of more resolute courage than this, or a beauty of mind so illustrious from every point of view.

They who preach to princes so vigilant a distrust, under cover of preaching security, preach their ruin and shame. No noble thing can be done without risk. I know one who is by nature very spirited and enterprising, whose good fortune is every day marred by persuasions such as these: 'That he should keep himself closely surrounded by his friends; That he should give ear to no reconciliation with his old enemies; That he should stand aloof, and never trust himself to any stronger than himself, whatever promises may be made to him, whatever advantages he may see in that course.' I know another who has unexpectedly advanced his fortune by following quite contrary counsels.[4]

Courage, the reputation for which is so eagerly sought after, may, when the need arises, make as magnificent a show in a doublet as in a chain armour, in a cabinet as in the field, with arms pendent as with raised arm.

Caution so tender and circumspect is a deadly

4 This last sentence is supposed to refer to Montaigne's particular hero, Henry of Navarre, afterwards Henry IV of France.

enemy to lofty deeds. Scipio, in order to win over Syphax, was able to leave his army, abandoning the newly conquered and still doubtful country of Spain, and cross over into Africa in only two ships, to commit himself, in hostile territory, to the power of a barbarian king, to an unknown faith, without bond or hostage, under the sole security of his great personal bravery, his good fortune, and the promise of his high hopes. *Trust sometimes forces trust* (LIVY).

But in a life of ambition and glory it is necessary not to give way to suspicion, but to keep a tight rein upon it: fear and distrust draw and invite attack. The most mistrustful of our kings carried his point principally by voluntarily abandoning and committing his life and liberty into the hands of his enemies, thus showing his entire confidence in them, in order that they might place the same trust in him.[5] When his legions armed and mutinied against him, Caesar confronted them with the sole authority of his countenance and his proud words: he had so great confidence in himself and his fortune, that he felt no fear in abandoning and committing it to a seditious and rebellious army:

Upon a turfy mound unmoved he stood,
And, since he feared not, worthy to be feared.

LUCAN

But it is most true that this powerful assurance cannot show forth fully and naturally except in one who is not affrighted by the image of death, and by the worst that might in the end happen to him; for if it

5 A reference to the interview between Louis XI and Charles the Bold at Péronne in 1468.

appear tremulous, doubtful, and uncertain, in the service of an important reconciliation, it can effect nothing to any purpose. An excellent way to win the heart and goodwill of another is to submit to and trust him, as long as it is done freely and without the constraint of any necessity, and on condition that one brings to it a full and clear confidence, with a brow at least free from all doubt.

In my boyhood I saw a nobleman, the commandant of a large town,[6] hard put to it by the sedition of a furious populace. To quell this beginning of disturbance, he decided to leave a very secure shelter and place himself at the mercy of a mutinous mob; but it was his undoing, for he was miserably slain. But his mistake, I think, was not so much that for which he is usually blamed, namely, that he went out, as that he put on an air of meekness and submission, and attempted to lull the storm by obeying rather than by guiding, by entreaty rather than by remonstrance; and I believe that a gracious severity combined with an air of military command, assured and confident as befitted his rank and the dignity of his office, would have been attended with greater success, at least with more honour and seemliness. Anything is to be expected from that monster in a state of commotion sooner than humanity and gentleness; it is much more likely to be moved by fear and awe. I should have represented to him also that, having taken a resolution (to my mind brave rather than foolhardy) to cast himself, weak and in his doublet, into this tempestuous sea of madmen, he should have

6 This was M. de Monneins, governor of Bordeaux; the incident occurred in 1548.

swallowed the whole draught, and not have quitted the part he had assumed; whereas what happened was that, after he saw the danger near at hand, he began to bleed at the nose,[7] and the humble and wheedling mien he had so far put on was exchanged for one of terror: by charging his voice and eyes with consternation and penitence, and by trying, as it were, to scuttle away like a rabbit and hide himself, he inflamed and invited their fury.

A general muster of different armed troops was being discussed (these are the occasions of secret revenges, and nowhere can they be executed with greater safety). There were public and evident signs that it was not safe for certain men on whom devolved the chief and necessary duty of reviewing them. The matter being of weight and consequence, but difficult to decide, various proposals were put forward. My advice was that we should above everything show no sign of apprehension, but put in an appearance, and mix with the rank and file, with head erect and open countenance, and instead of cutting out anything (which was the chief purport of the other opinions), that we should, on the contrary, entreat the captains to command the soldiers to fire off fine and brave salvos in honour of the spectators, and not to spare their powder This pleased and gratified the suspected troops, and henceforth begat a mutual and wholesome confidence.[8]

The method of Julius Caesar I regard as the best that could be followed. In the first place, he tried by

7 Idiomatic; he 'got cold feet', as we should say.

8 This passage throws an interesting side-light on Montaigne's character, which has sometimes been described as 'unheroic'. A careful study of his life and work seems to show that he was undoubtedly a man of courage.

Of friendship

As I was considering the way in which a painter in my employment planned his work, I had a mind to imitate him. He chooses the fairest spots, the middle of each wall, for a picture that is elaborated with all his talent, and the vacant space around it he fills in with grotesques, that is to say, fantastic paintings whose only charm lies in their variety and extravagance.

And what are these essays but grotesque and monstrous bodies, pieced together of different members, without any definite shape, without any order, coherence, or proportion, except they be accidental?

Like a woman, lovely as a wish,
Tailing off into a loathsome fish. HORACE

In the second point indeed I go with my painter, but I fall short in the other and better part; for my talent is not such that I could presume to attempt a picture that is rich, finished, and formed in accordance with art. It has occurred to me to borrow one of Étienne de la Boëtie, which will cast a lustre on all the rest of this work. It is a dissertation to which he gave the name *La Servitude Volontaire*, but some who did not know this have since very appropriately renamed it *Le Contre Un*. He wrote it by way of essay in his early youth,[1] in

1 Montaigne originally added, 'having not yet reached the eighteenth year of his age.' At the end of this chapter he calls him a 'boy of sixteen'.

honour of liberty against tyrants. It has long been circulating among men of understanding, not without great and well-merited commendation, for it is elegant, and as full as can be. Yet it is far from being the best that he was capable of, and if, at the more mature age at which I knew him, he had adopted my plan of setting down his ideas in writing, we should see many rare things that would very nearly rival the writings of antiquity; for particularly in respect of natural gifts I know of no man who can compare with him. But he left behind him nothing besides this treatise (and it survived by chance, nor do I think he ever saw it after it left his hands), and a few memoranda on that Edict of January,[2] made famous by our civil wars, which will perhaps yet find a place elsewhere. These are all I have been able to recover of what he left (I, to whom, with such loving recommendation, when in the clutches of death, he bequeathed by will his library and papers), excepting the little volume of his works which I have already published.[3] And I am particularly obliged to this piece of work, since it was the medium of our first acquaintance. For it was shown to me long before I had set eyes on him, and first brought his name to my notice, thus paving the way to that friendship, which we cherished, as long as God willed it, so perfect and entire, that surely the like of it is seldom read of, and no sign of any such friendship is to be seen in the men of our day. It needs so many chances to build it up, that it

2 The Edict, issued in 1571, which granted the Huguenots the public exercise of their religion.

3 Containing translations of two minor works of Xenophon and Plutarch, and a collection of French poems; published in two volumes in 1571.

is much if Fortune can bring it about once in three centuries.

There is nothing to which Nature seems so much to have inclined us as to society. And Aristotle says that good lawgivers had more respect to friendship than to justice. Now the supreme point of its perfection is this. For, speaking generally, all those amities that are created and nourished by pleasure or profit, public or private needs, are so much the less noble and beautiful, and so much the less friendships, as they introduce some other cause and design and fruit into friendship, than itself.

Neither do the four kinds which antiquity knew, the natural, the social, the hospitable, and the venerean, either separately or conjointly, come up to the ideal friendship.

That of children to their fathers is rather respect. Friendship is kept alive by communication, which, by reason of too great disparity, cannot exist between them, and would haply conflict with natural duties. For neither can all the secret thoughts of the father be communicated to his son, in order not to beget an unseemly familiarity, nor can the admonitions and corrections, which are among the first offices of friendship, be administered by the son to the father. There have been nations where it was the custom for children to kill their fathers, and others where the fathers killed their children, to avoid their becoming at some time a hindrance to each other; and by the law of Nature the one depends on the destruction of the other. Some philosophers have been known to disdain their natural tie: witness Aristippus, who, being close pressed about the affection he owed to his children, as being come out of him, began to spit, saying that that had also come out of him, and that we also breed lice and worms. And that other whom Plutarch tried to reconcile with his brother: 'I do not think any the better of him, he said, for having come out of the same orifice.'

Truly the name of brother is a beautiful name, and full of affection, and on that model did he and I form our alliance.[4] But that intervention of worldly goods, those divisions, and the fact that the wealth of the one is the other's poverty, have a wonderful effect in softening and loosening the brotherly solder. Brothers having to conduct the progress of their advancement along the same path and at the same rate, they must of necessity often jostle and clash with one another. Moreover the agreement and the relation which beget those true and perfect friendships, why should they be found in natural brothers? The father and son may be of entirely different dispositions, and brothers too. He is my son, he is my kinsman, but he is sullen, ill-natured, or a fool. And besides, the more these friendships are imposed upon us by law and natural obligation, the less is there of our voluntary choice and freedom. And our voluntary freedom produces nothing more properly its own than affection and friendship. Not but that I have experienced on that side all that can possibly be experienced, having had the best father that ever was, and the most indulgent, even in his extreme old age; and one who from father to son was descended from a family famed and exemplary in this respect of brotherly concord:

4 They became *frères d'alliance*, and called each other 'brother'. So afterwards Mlle de Gournay became Montaigne's *fille d'alliance*.

Known
For loving-kindness father-like
To all his brothers shown.

HORACE

As to comparing it with our affection towards women, though it be born of our choice, we cannot do it, nor include it in this category. Its fire, I confess,

No stranger to the Goddess I,
Who blends with pain our bitter-sweet delight,

CATULLUS

is more active, fiercer, and more fervent. But it is a precipitate and volatile fire, fickle, and wavering, a feverish fire, subject to fits and returns, that holds us only by one corner. In friendship it is a general and universal warmth, tempered besides and equal, a constant and settled warmth, all gentleness and smoothness, with no sharp sting. What is more, in sexual love there is but a frantic desire for that which flies from us:

Like hunters that the flying hare pursue
O'er hill and dale, through heat and morning dew,
Which being taken, the quarry they despise,
Being only pleased in following that which flies.

ARIOSTO

As soon as it enters into the terms of friendship, that is to say into a conformity of wills, it flags and vanishes. Enjoyment destroys it, as having only a fleshly end and being subject to satiety. Friendship, on the other hand, is enjoyed in proportion as it is desired; it is bred, nourished, and increased only by enjoyment, as being spiritual, and the soul becoming refined by practice. During this perfect friendship those fleeting affections once found a place in me, not to speak of him, who only too clearly confesses them in his poetry. Thus I harboured those two passions, each known to the other, but to be compared, never! the first steadily soaring in proud and haughty flight, and disdainfully looking down upon the other going its way far, far below.

As concerning marriage, besides that it is a bargain to which only the entrance is free (its continuance being forced and constrained, and depending on something other than our will), a bargain moreover that is usually concluded to other ends, there supervene a thousand extraneous entanglements to unravel, sufficient to break the thread and disturb the course of a lively affection; whereas in friendship there is no traffic or business except with itself. Besides, to tell the truth, women are ordinarily not capable of responding to this communion and fellowship, the nurse of this sacred bond; neither does their soul appear firm enough to support the strain of so hard and durable a knot. And truly, if that were not so, if such a free and voluntary familiarity could be established, where not only the souls might have their complete enjoyment, but the bodies also shared in the alliance, in which the entire man was engaged, it is certain that the friendship would be the fuller and more perfect. But the sex has never yet, by any example, been able to attain to it, and, by common agreement of the ancient schools, is shut out from it.

And that other Greek licence is rightly abhorred by our moral conscience. For, there being, according to their practice, so necessary a disparity of ages and difference of services between the lovers, it no more answered sufficiently to the perfect union and harmony that we here require, than the other: *For what love is this of friendship? Why does no man love either a deformed youth, or a handsome old man?* (CICERO). For even the picture which the Academy draws of it will not belie me, I think, when I say this on its behalf: That this first frenzy inspired by the son of Venus in the heart of the lover at sight of a youth in his tender bloom, to which they allow all the insolent and passionate actions produced by an immoderate ardour, was simply founded on an external beauty, the false image of corporeal generation. For it could not be founded on the mind, the proof of which yet lay concealed, being but at its birth and before the age of budding; That if this frenzy took possession of a base heart, the means of its pursuit was riches, presents, favour in advancement to dignities, and such other base merchandise which one disapproves. If it fell on a more generous heart, the means of corruption were likewise generous: philosophical instruction, precepts to reverence religion, to obey the laws, to die for the good of one's country, examples of valour, wisdom, justice; the lover studying to render himself acceptable by the good grace and beauty of his soul, that of his body being long decayed, and hoping, by this mental fellowship, to establish a firmer and more durable contract.

When this courtship had its effect in due season (for that which they do not require in the lover, that he should bring leisure and discretion to his pursuit, they strictly require in the loved one, since he had to judge of an internal beauty, difficult to know and, being hidden, hard to discover), there was born in the loved one the desire of a spiritual conception by the mediation of a spiritual beauty. The latter was the main thing; corporeal beauty was accidental and secondary: quite the contrary to the case of the lover. For this reason they prefer the loved one, and aver that the gods also prefer him; and they greatly reprove the poet Aeschylus for having, in the love of Achilles and Patroclus, given the lover's part to Achilles, who was in the first and beardless bloom of youth, and the handsomest of the Greeks.

This general fellowship being established, the chief and more worthy partner in it exercising his functions and predominating, they say that there proceeded fruits very profitable to the private and public weal; that it constituted the strength of the countries where the custom prevailed, and the chief defence of equity and freedom: witness the salutary loves of Harmodius and Aristogiton. Therefore they call it sacred and divine. And, by their account, only the violence of tyrants and the cowardice of the people are inimical to it. In short, all that can be said in favour of the Academy is that it is a love terminating in friendship, which definition agrees well enough with that of the Stoics: *That love is the attempt to gain the friendship of one to whom we are attracted by beauty* (CICERO).

I return to my description of a more even and respectable kind of friendship. *They only are to be reputed friendships when the character is fortified and matured by age* (CICERO). For the rest, what we commonly call friends and friendship are no more than acquaintanceships and intimacies contracted by chance or for some advantage, by means of which our souls come together. In the friendship I speak of, our souls blend and melt so entirely, that there is no more sign of the seam which joins them. If I am pressed to say why I loved him, I feel that I can only express myself by answering, 'Because it was he, because it was I.'

There is, over and above my reason and all that I am able particularly to say, I know not what inexplicable power of fate, as mediator of this union. We sought one another before we met, from reports we had each heard of the other, which wrought upon our affections more than reports are, in reason, supposed to do; I believe by some heavenly ordinance. We embraced one another by our names. And at our first meeting, which chanced to be at a great feast and town gathering, we found ourselves so taken with one another, so well acquainted, so bound together, that from that moment nothing could be so close as we were to one another. He wrote an excellent Latin satire,[5] which is published, in which he excuses and explains the precipitancy of our mutual understanding, so suddenly come to perfection. Having begun so late, and with so little chance of a long duration (for we were both grown men and he several years my senior), our friendship had no time to lose; and it was not of the kind to conform to the regular pattern of mild friendships, which need all the precautions of a long preliminary intercourse. This one had no other model than itself, and can only be compared with itself. This is no one special consideration, nor two, nor three, nor four, nor a thousand: it is I know not what quintessence of all this

5 A didactic poem, rather than a satire in our sense of the word, of 332 lines, in which he admonishes his younger friend (by about two years), to be on his guard against the allurements of pleasure, to which Montaigne was in his opinion a little too much addicted.

mixture, which, having taken possession of my whole will, carried it to plunge and lose itself in his; which, having taken possession of his whole will, carried it to plunge and lose itself in mine, with a like hunger and emulation. I may truly say lose, reserving as we did nothing to ourselves, that was either his or mine.

When Lelius, in the presence of the Roman consuls, who, after Tiberius Gracchus was condemned, persecuted all those who had been in secret intelligence with him, came to ask Caius Blossius (who was his chief friend), what he would have done for him, he replied, 'Everything.' 'What means everything? answered Lelius; what if he had commanded you to set fire to our temples?' 'He would never have commanded that.' 'But supposing he had done so?' 'I should have obeyed him,' answered Blossius. If he was so perfect a friend to Gracchus as the historians say, he was not justified in offending the consuls by this bold and extreme confession, and should not have given up the assurance he had of Gracchus's intentions. Those however who accuse him of answering seditiously do not well understand this mystery, nor do they presuppose, as was the case, that he had Gracchus's will in his sleeve, both by his influence and knowledge. They were friends first, then citizens, more friends to one another than friends or enemies of their country, or than friends of ambition or sedition. Having wholly given themselves up to one another, they absolutely held the reins of one another's inclination; and if you suppose this team to have been guided by virtue and led by reason (without which it would be quite impossible to harness it), Blossius's answer was such as it should be. If their actions lost their handle, they were neither, according to my measure, friends to one another nor friends to themselves.

For the rest, this answer does not ring any more true than would mine if someone questioned me in this fashion: 'If your will commanded you to kill your daughter, would you kill her?' and I assented. For that would be no evidence of a consent to do it, because I am in no doubt with regard to my will, and just as little in regard to that of such a friend. All the arguments in the world cannot possibly dispossess me of the certainty I have of my friend's intentions and opinions. Not one of his actions could be reported to me, whatever aspect it might bear, but that I could immediately discover its motive. Our souls travelled together in such unity, they regarded each other with so ardent an affection, and with a like affection saw into the very depths of each other's hearts, that not only did I know his heart as well as my own, but I should certainly have trusted him in any matter concerning myself, sooner than myself.

I cannot allow those other common friendships to be placed in the same line with ours. I have as much knowledge of them as another, and of the most perfect of their kind, but I should not advise anyone to measure them with the same rule; he would be much mistaken. In those other friendships one has to walk with the bridle in one's hand, prudently and cautiously: the knot is not tied so tightly but that it will cause some misgiving. 'Love him, said Chilo, as if you had one day to hate him; hate him, as if you had to love him.' This precept, which is so abominable in this sovereign and commanding friendship, is of salutary use in the common and customary friendships, to which must be applied the saying that Aristotle was so fond of, 'O my friends! there is no friend.'

In this noble intercourse, good offices and benefits, the feeders of other friendships, deserve not even to be taken into account, by reason of the complete blending of our wills. For even as the love I bear to myself is not increased by the succour I give myself in time of need, whatever the Stoics may say, and as I feel no gratitude to myself for the service I do myself, so the union of such friends, being truly perfect, makes them lose the sense of such duties, and hate and banish from their minds these words that imply separation and distinction: benefit, obligation, gratitude, request, thanks, and the like. Everything being actually in common between them, wills, thoughts, opinions, possessions, wives, children, honour, and life, and their agreement being such that they are but one soul in two bodies, according to the very apt definition of Aristotle, they can neither lend nor give anything to one another. That is why the makers of laws, in order to honour marriage with some imaginary resemblance to this divine alliance, interdict all donations between husband and wife, meaning to infer therefrom that all should belong to each of them, and that they have nothing to divide and share out between them.

If, in the friendship of which I speak, one could give to the other, it would be the one who received the benefit that lays his friend under an obligation. For, as each of them studies above all to benefit the other, it is he who furnishes the matter and occasion that plays the liberal part, by giving his friend the satisfaction of doing that to him which he most desires.

When the philosopher Diogenes was in want of money he used to say that he redemanded it of his friends, not that he demanded it. And to show how that works in practice, I will relate a singular example from antiquity.

Eudamidas of Corinth had two friends, Charixenus a Sicyonian and Aretheus a Corinthian. When on his death-bed, being poor, and his two friends rich, he made his will after this manner: 'My legacy to Aretheus is that he maintain my mother and support her in her old age; to Charixenus, that he give my daughter in marriage, and provide her with as good a dowry as he is able to afford; and in case one of them chance to die I appoint his survivor to take his place.' They who first saw this testament laughed at it; but when the heirs were informed of it, they accepted it with a singular satisfaction. And one of them, Charixenus, dying five days later, leaving Aretheus at liberty to take his place, the latter supported the mother with great care, and of five talents he had in his estate, he gave two and a half as a marriage portion to his only daughter, and two and a half to the daughter of Eudamidas; and the two weddings took place on the same day.

This example is very complete, except for one objection, namely the number of friends For that perfect friendship of which I speak is indivisible: each one gives himself so wholly to his friend, that there remains to him nothing to divide with another; on the contrary he grieves that he is not double, triple, or fourfold, and that he has not several souls and several wills, to confer them all on the object of his love.

Common friendships are capable of being shared: we may love one for his handsome exterior, another for his easygoing manners, another again for his liberality; this one for his fatherly and that one for his brotherly ways, and so forth; but this friendship which possesses the soul and dominates it with absolute power, cannot possibly be split in two. If two at the same time entreated your assistance, to which of them would you hasten? If they required of you opposite services, how would you arrange it? If one of them imparted to you a secret that it would be useful for the other to know, how would you solve the difficulty?

The unique and paramount friendship dissolves all other obligations. The secret that I have sworn not to reveal to another, I may without perjury communicate to one who is not another: that is myself. It is miracle enough to divide oneself into two, and they know not the greatness of it who speak of dividing oneself into three. Nothing is extreme that has its like. And he who supposes that I can equally love each of two, and that they can love one another and me as much as I love them, makes a multiple brotherhood of a thing that is most one and united, and of which even one is the rarest thing in the world to find.

The sequel of that story agrees very well with what I was saying, for Eudamidas makes it a kindness and a favour to his friends to employ them for his needs. He leaves them heirs to his liberality, which consists in giving into their hands the means of benefiting him. And without doubt the power of friendship is much more richly evident in his action than in that of Aretheus.

In short, these are delights which are not to be imagined by one who has not tasted them; and therefore I highly honour the answer of a young soldier to Cyrus, who inquired of him what he would take for a horse that had just enabled him to win the prize in a race, and whether he would exchange it for a kingdom: 'No indeed, Sire, but I would willingly part with it to gain a friend, if I could find a man worthy of such alliance.' Not a bad answer, 'if I could find'; for it is easy to find men fit for a superficial acquaintance. But in the other kind, where we exhibit the very depths of our heart and make no reservations, truly all the springs of action must be perfectly clear and true.

In alliances that have but one end, we need only to provide against the imperfections which particularly concern that end. It matters little to me what religion my physician professes, or my lawyer. This consideration has nothing to do with the friendly offices that they owe me. In the domestic relations that arise between me and those who serve me, it is the same. I am little curious to know whether my footman is chaste, so long as he is assiduous. And I am less afraid to engage a muleteer who is a gambler, than one who is an idiot, or a cook who swears than an ignorant one. I do not meddle with telling people what they are to do in the world (there are plenty of others who do that); I only say what I do myself.

I do what pleases me, do thou the like.

TERENCE

With the familiarity of the table I associate amusement, and not wisdom; in bed, beauty comes before goodness; in serious conversation, ability, even should sincerity be wanting; and the like elsewhere.

As he who was discovered astride on a stick playing with his children begged the man who surprised him at it not to speak of it until he was himself a father, supposing that the affection that would arise in his heart would make him a fair judge of such actions; so I should wish to speak to people who have had experience of what I say. But knowing how far from common, nay how rare, is such a friendship, I have no expectation of finding a competent judge. For even the dissertations which the writers of antiquity have left us on the subject appear to me weak and flat in comparison with my own sentiments. And in this particular the reality surpasses even the precepts of philosophy:

Nothing, no, nothing on this earth,
Whilst I have reason, shall I e'er
With a true-hearted friend compare!

HORACE

The old poet Menander declared that man to be happy who had been able to meet with but the shadow of a friend. He was truly right in saying so, especially if he spoke from experience. For, in truth, when I compare all the rest of my life, although by the grace of God it has been spent in ease and comfort, and, saving the loss of so dear a friend, free from any grievous affliction, and in great tranquillity of mind; having been well compensated with my natural and original advantages, without seeking any others; when I compare all that, I say, with the four years which were granted me to enjoy the sweet companionship and society of that man, it is all smoke, a dark and wearisome night. From the day when I lost him,

The day which heaven hath willed to be
Sacred for evermore, but ever sad to me,

VIRGIL

my life has dragged on wearily, and the very pleasures which it offers me, instead of solacing me, redouble my grief for his loss. We were co-partners in everything, and it seems to me that I am robbing him of his share:

Nor is it just to taste of pleasure here
Till he return in safety to partake on't.

TERENCE

I was already grown so accustomed to being always and everywhere his second self, that I seem to be no more than a moiety:

Ah, since untimely fate hath snatched thee hence,
Thee, of my soul a part,
Why should I linger on, with deadened sense
And ever-aching heart,
A worthless fragment of a fallen shrine?
No, no, one day hath seen thy death and mine.

HORACE

In all my actions and dreams I miss him, as he would indeed have missed me. For as he infinitely surpassed me in all other virtues and talents, so he did in the duties of friendship.

Why blush that for a friend so dear we grieve,
Why stint our tears?

HORACE

But, brother, what with mirth was once so rife
Is turned to sadness by the timeless doom;
Dead with thy death is all that cheered my life,
And all our house is buried in thy tomb!

Gone are the joys that, whilst thou yet wert here,
Were by thy sweet affection fanned and fed,

All studies, all delights, that once were dear,
  I've banished from my soul since thou art dead.

Oh, is thy voice for ever hushed and still?
  O brother, dearer far than life, shall I
Behold thee never? But in sooth I will
  For ever love thee, as in days gone by.

CATULLUS

But let us give a little hearing to this boy of sixteen.

Having found that this work[6] has been since published, and with an evil intention, by those who seek to disturb and change the state of our government, without caring whether they improve it or not, and that they have mixed it up with some of their own scribblings, I have revoked my intention of inserting it in this place. And in order that the memory of the author may not be prejudiced in the eyes of such as cannot have had a real knowledge of his opinions and actions, I will inform them that this subject was handled by him in his early youth merely by way of an exercise, as a common theme that had been worn threadbare by a thousand other writers. I make no doubt that he believed what he wrote, for he was too conscientious to lie even in jest. And I know besides that, if he had had the choice, he would rather have been born in Venice than at Sarlac,[7] and with good reason. But he had another maxim, sovereignly imprinted on his soul, which was to obey and submit very religiously to the laws under which he was born. There never was a better citizen, nor one more

6 *La Servitude Volontaire*, mentioned at the beginning of the chapter.

7 Venice was then a republic; Sarlac or Sarlat in Périgord was La Boëtie's birthplace.

nterested in the tranquillity of his country, nor one nore hostile to the commotions and innovations of his ime. He would much rather have used his talents in uppressing them than in providing occasion for more nischief. His mind was moulded to a pattern of other ages than this.

Now, in place of that serious work I will substitute another, a product of that same season of his life, nore gallant and lively.

That we should soberly meddle with judging the divine ordinances

The true field and subject of imposture are things unknown, because, in the first place, mere strangeness induces belief; and moreover, as they do not come within our ordinary experience, we lose the means of combating them. For that reason, says Plato, it is much easier to satisfy people when speaking of the nature of the gods, than when speaking of the nature of men: because the ignorance of the hearers gives us a fine and wide range and every freedom to discuss hidden matters.

Whence it comes that nothing is so firmly believed as that of which we know least, and that there are no people so confident as those who entertain us with fictions, such as alchemists, prognosticators, astrologers, palm-readers, physicians, *id genus omne*. To whom I should like to join, if I dared, a pack of people interpreters and ordinary record-keepers of the designs of God, who profess to find out the causes of every event, to see into the secrets of the divine will and discover the incomprehensible motives of its works; and, although the variety and continual discordance of events drive them from corner to corner, from east to west, still persist in following their ball and with the same chalk paint black and white.

1 As in a tennis-court.

In a certain Indian nation they observe this commendable custom: When they have had the worst in a battle or encounter, they publicly ask pardon of the sun, which is their god, as if they had committed an unjust action: attributing their good or evil fortune to the divine reason, and submitting to it their own reason and judgement.

It is enough for a Christian to believe that all things come from God, to accept them with acknowledgement of his divine and inscrutable wisdom, taking them, however, as well meant, in whatsoever form they may be sent to him. But I disapprove the common practice of trying to confirm and bolster up our religion by the success and prosperity of our enterprises. Our faith has other foundations enough, without authorizing it by results; for when a people is accustomed to hear arguments which are so plausible and so much to their liking, there is a danger lest, when events turn to their disadvantage and contrary to their expectation, their faith be shaken. As in our present wars of religion, those who had the best of it in the engagement at La Rochelabeille, loudly rejoicing over this accidental success and regarding their good fortune as a certain approbation of their cause; when they afterwards came to excuse their misfortune at Montcontour and Jarnac, by saying that if they had not a people wholly at their mercy it was because they were being chastised and scourged by a fatherly hand, they make it quite clear that they are taking double payment for grinding one sack of corn, and blowing hot and cold with the same breath.[2] It would be better

2 At La Rochelabeille the Huguenots defeated the Catholics; in the other two engagements they were defeated. Jarnac came first, so that the word 'afterwards' is misleading.

to explain to them the true foundations of truth.

It was a fine naval victory that was won a few months ago against the Turks under the leadership of Don John of Austria;[3] but it has pleased God at other times to let us see other such, to our loss.

In short, it is a hard matter to reduce divine things to our scale, without their suffering waste. And he that would take upon himself to give reasons for Arius and Leo his Pope, the principal leaders of that heresy, dying, at different times, so similar and so strange a death (for they both, after withdrawing from the debate, with a pain in the bowels, to their closet, suddenly gave up the ghost), and declare that the divine vengeance was aggravated by the circumstance of the place, might very well add the death of Heliogabalus, who was also killed in a privy. But what about Irenaeus, who was involved in the same fate?

God, desiring to teach us that the good have something else to hope for, and the wicked something else to fear, than the fortunes and misfortunes of this world, controls and allots these according to his occult disposition, and deprives us of any occasion for foolishly explaining them to our advantage. And they deceive themselves who endeavour, by human reasonings, to make themselves out the better. They never score a hit with their rapier, but they get two in return. Saint Augustine proves it finely against his adversaries. It is a conflict that is decided by the weapons of memory rather than by those of reason.

3 By the combined fleets of Spain, Venice, and the Pope, on 7th October 1571, in the Gulf of Lepanto. It was in this engagement that the author of the immortal *Don Quixote* was seriously wounded.

We must be content with the light which it pleases the sun to communicate to us by its rays; and he who lifts up his eyes to receive more light into his body, let him not think it strange if, as a punishment for his overweeningness, he loses his sight. *For what man is he that can know the counsel of God? or who can think what the will of the Lord is?*[4]

4 Book of Wisdom 9:13, in the Apocrypha.

Of fleeing from pleasures at the price of life

I had indeed observed that most of the ancients agree on this point: That it is time to die when there is more evil than good in living; and that to preserve our life to our torment and discomfort, is to offend against the very laws of Nature, as the old precepts tell us:

> Or live without distress, or die in happiness.
> 'Tis good for us to die, when life brings infamy.
> O better far to die, than live in misery!
>
> *Gnomic poets*

But as for carrying contempt for death to such a degree as to make it a reason for withdrawing from the honours, riches, dignities, and other favours and blessings of Fortune, as we call them, as if Reason had not enough to do in persuading us to abandon them without thrusting this new charge upon her; I had never seen it either enjoined or practised, until that passage of Seneca fell into my hands, where, counseling Lucilius, a powerful personage and of great authority with the Emperor, to give up his life of pleasure and ostentation, and retire from worldly ambitions to a life of solitude and philosophic repose, to which Lucilius opposed some difficulties, he said: 'My advice is, that either you quit this life you are leading, or life altogether; I do indeed counsel you to follow the easier path, and to untie rather than cut the knot you have tied so badly, provided that you cut it, if it cannot be otherwise untied. There is no man so cowardly but that he would rather fall once for all than be always tottering.' I should have expected this advice to be conformable to the hard doctrines of the Stoics, but it is more strange that it should be borrowed of Epicurus, who writes in a similar vein and on a like occasion to Idomeneus.

Yet I think I have observed some sentiments of the same nature in men of our own religion, but expressed with Christian moderation. Saint Hilary, Bishop of Poitiers, that famous enemy of the Arian heresy, being in Syria, was informed that Abra his only daughter, whom he had left at home with her mother, was sought in marriage by the most eminent lords of the country, she being a beautiful, rich, and very well educated damsel in the flower of her age. He wrote to her (as we may see) that she should withdraw her affections from all those pleasures and advantages which were set before her eyes; that on his travels he had found a much greater and more worthy match, a bridegroom of much greater power and magnificence, who would bestow upon her gifts of robes and jewels of inestimable price. His design was to make her lose the appetite and use of mundane pleasures, and wed her wholly to God; but as the shortest and surest means to that end appeared to him to be the death of his daughter, he did not cease, by vows, prayers, and orisons, to beseech God to take her from this world, and call her to him. And so it happened, for soon after his return she departed from him, whereat he exhibited a singular joy.

This man seems to outbid the others, since from the very outset he has recourse to this means, which the others only adopt subsidiarily; and besides, it concerned his only daughter.

But I will not omit the end of this story, although it is not to the point. Saint Hilary's wife, having heard from him how by his will and design he had brought about the death of their daughter, and how much happier she was in being removed from this world than in being in it, conceived such a lively apprehension of the eternal and celestial beatitude, that she begged her husband most earnestly to do the same for her. And God having soon after taken her to him in response to their combined prayers, it was a death embraced with a singular and mutual contentment.

Of the custom of wearing clothes

Whatever I may be aiming at, I am obliged to force some barrier of custom: so carefully has she barred all our approaches! I was considering within myself in this chilly season, whether the fashion of going about quite naked, in those lately discovered nations, is a fashion imposed by the warm temperature of the air, as we say of the Indians and the Moors, or whether it is the original custom of mankind. Inasmuch as all things under heaven, as the holy word declares,[1] are subject to the same laws, men of understanding are wont, in considerations such as these, where we must distinguish the natural laws from those which have been invented, to have recourse to the general polity of the world, where there can be nothing counterfeit.

Now, all other creatures being fittingly provided with needle and thread, to maintain their being, it is really not to be believed that we alone should have been brought into the world in this defective and indigent state, in a state that cannot be maintained without foreign aid. So I hold that, as plants, trees, animals, all that lives, are by Nature equipped with sufficient covering to protect them against the injury of the weather,

And therefore almost all
Are covered either with hides, or else with shells,
Or with the horny callus, or with bark,

LUCRETIUS

1 Ecclesiastes 9:2, 3.

so were we; but, like those who with artificial light extinguish the light of day, we have extinguished our proper means with borrowed means. And it is easy to see that it is custom that makes impossible to us, what is not so: for among those nations that have no knowledge of clothes, there are some that dwell in much the same climate as we do; and moreover, the most delicate parts of us are those which are always uncovered, the eyes, the mouth, the nose, the ears; in the case of our peasants, as with our ancestors, the pectoral and ventral parts. If we had been born on condition of wearing farthingales and galligaskins, I make no doubt but that Nature would have armed with a thicker skin what she has exposed to the battery of the seasons, as she has done the finger-ends and the soles of the feet.

Why does this seem hard to believe? Between my habit of clothing and that of a peasant of my countryside there is a much greater distance than between his and that of a man who is clothed only in his skin.

How many men, especially in Turkey, go naked as a matter of religion! Somebody or other asked one of our beggars whom he saw in his shirt in the depth of winter, as merry as a grig and feeling the cold as little as many a man who is muffled up to the ears in sable, how he could patiently bear it. 'And you, sir, he replied, you have your face uncovered; now, I am all face.' The Italians tell a tale of, I think, the Duke of Florence's fool, that his master asking him how, being so poorly clad, he could bear the cold, which he himself was hardly able to do: 'Follow my recipe, he replied, and pile on all the garments you have, like me, and you will feel the cold no more than I do.' King Massinissa could not be induced, even in his extreme old age, to go with his head covered, were it ever so cold, stormy or rainy. The same is told of the Emperor Severus.

In the battles fought between the Egyptians and the Persians, Herodotus says that both he and others remarked that, of those who were left dead on the field, the skulls of the Egyptians were without comparison harder than those of the Persians, by reason that the latter always have their heads covered, first with biggins and afterwards with turbans, and the former are shaven from infancy and uncovered.

And King Agesilaus observed the habit, until his decrepitude, of wearing the same clothing in winter as in summer. Caesar, says Suetonius, always marched at the head of his army, and most often on foot, bareheaded, whether in sunshine or rain; and the same is said of Hannibal;

> Bareheaded then he braved the raging storm.
>
> SILIUS ITALICUS

A Venetian, who had long resided in the kingdom of Pegu, and has but lately returned from thence, writes that both the men and women of that country always go bare-foot, even on horseback, the rest of their body being clothed.

And Plato gives this wonderful advice, that, to keep the whole body in health, we should give the feet and head no covering but that which Nature has provided.

The man who, following our King, was chosen King of Poland,[2] and who is indeed one of the greatest princes of our age, never wears gloves, nor does he change, however severe the weather in winter, the

2 Henri III and Stephen Bathori.

bonnet he wears indoors. Just as I cannot go loose and unbuttoned, the labourers round about here would feel fettered if they had to button up. Varro contends that, when it was ordained that we should uncover in presence of the gods or the magistracy, it was rather for our health's sake, and to harden us against the inclemency of the weather, than upon the account of reverence.

And since we are on the subject of cold, and being Frenchmen accustomed to array ourselves in motley colours (not I myself, for like my father I seldom wear any but black or white), let me add, in another connexion, that Captain Martin du Bellay relates how, on the march to Luxemburg, he experienced so sharp a frost that the munition wine was cut with an axe or hatchet, and distributed among the soldiers by weight, and that they carried it away in baskets; and Ovid, as near as can be,

The frozen wines retain the vessel's shape,
Of which, instead of draughts, they pieces take.

The frosts are so severe at the mouth of the Palus Maeotides,[3] that at the same place where Mithridates' lieutenant had fought a battle, dry-footed, with the enemy and defeated them, when summer was come he again won a naval battle against them. The Romans suffered a great disadvantage, in the engagement they fought with the Carthaginians near to Placentia, in going to the charge with blood stiffened and limbs benumbed with cold; whilst Hannibal had distributed fire throughout his host to warm his soldiers, and each company was provided with oil, wherewith anointing

3 The Sea of Azov.

themselves they might render their sinews more supple and active, and encrust their pores against the blasts of air and the icy wind that was then blowing.

The retreat of the Greeks from Babylon to their own country is become famous on account of the hardships and discomforts which they had to surmount. One of them was that, being met in the mountains of Armenia by a terrible snowstorm, they lost all knowledge of the country and the roads; and, being thus suddenly besieged, they were a day and night without food, most of their cattle dead, many of themselves dead, many blinded by the driving hail and the dazzling snow, many crippled in their extremities, many stiff, paralysed and unable to move through cold, though in full possession of their senses.

Alexander saw a nation where they bury their fruit-trees in winter to protect them from the frost; and we may also see the same thing.

Apropos of clothing, the King of Mexico would change his raiment four times a day, never putting on the same again, using his cast-off clothing for his continual charities and rewards; and neither pot, nor dish, nor other kitchen or table utensil served more than once.

Of Solitude

We will not enter into a lengthy comparison between the active and the solitary life, and as for those fine words under which ambition and avarice take cover, 'That we were not born for our individual selves, but for the public', let us boldly appeal to those who are in the thick of the dance; and let them cudgel their conscience and ask themselves if on the contrary those positions, those offices, and that hurly-burly of the world are not rather sought after with a view to making private profit at the public expense. The evil means we adopt to push ourselves in these days very clearly show that the end cannot be worth much. Let us reply to ambition, That it is she herself that gives us a taste for solitude; for what does she shun so much as society? What does she seek so much as elbow-room? We may find opportunities anywhere for doing good or evil. However, if the saying of Bias be true, 'that the wicked are in a majority', or that of the Preacher, 'that there is not one good out of a thousand',[1]

> The just are rare, a race so small,
> The gates of Thebes would more than equal all,
> Or the seven mouths of Nile,
>
> JUVENAL

the danger of contact with the crowd is great. We

1 Ecclesiastes 7:28.

must either imitate the vicious or hate them. There is danger, both of resembling them because they are many, and of hating many of them, because they are unlike.[2]

And the traders who go to sea are right to take care that those who join the same ships are not dissolute, blasphemous, and wicked, regarding such company as unlucky. Wherefore Bias said humorously to his shipmates who, during a violent storm at sea, were calling on the gods for help: 'Be silent; let them not know that you are here with me.' And, in a more urgent case, Albuquerque, Viceroy in the Indies for Emmanuel, King of Portugal, when in extreme peril of shipwreck at sea, took upon his shoulders a young boy, to the sole end that, being partners in fortune, the child's innocence might serve him as a safeguard, and a recommendation to the divine favour to spare his life.

Not but that the wise man can live contented everywhere, and be alone even in a palace crowd; but if he has the choice, he will flee, he says, the very sight of it. He will endure, if need be, the former, but if it be left to him, he will choose the latter. He will not think himself sufficiently quit of vices, if he still has to contend with those of other men.

Charondas chastised as wicked men those who were convicted of keeping bad company.

There is nothing so unsociable and so sociable as man: the one by his vice, the other by his nature. And Antisthenes does not, in my opinion, give a satisfactory answer to that man who reproved him for

2 'But both courses are to be avoided; you should not copy the bad, simply because they are many, nor should you hate the many, because they are unlike you.' – SENECA, *Ep.*, VII.

associating with the wicked, when he said 'that physicians live indeed with the sick': for if they help to restore the sick to health, they impair their own by continually seeing and coming in contact with diseases.

Now the aim of all solitude, I take it, is the same, to live more at one's ease and leisure. But one does not always seek the right way. A man often thinks he has given up business, when he has only exchanged it for another. There is little less worry in governing a household than a whole state; whatever the mind is busied with, it gives itself entirely up to; and though domestic occupations be less important, they are no less importunate. Moreover, though we are rid of the court and the market-place, we are not rid of the chief vexations of our life:

> Ease and tranquillity of mind are due
> To plain good sense, not to a grand sea-view.
>
> HORACE

Ambition, avarice, irresolution, fear and the lusts do not leave us, though we have changed our country;

> Behind the horseman sits black care.
>
> HORACE

They will often follow us even into the cloister and the school of philosophy. Neither deserts, nor rocky caves, nor hair-shirts, nor fastings will rid us of them:

> The fatal shaft sticks in the wounded side.
>
> VIRGIL

Somebody said to Socrates that a certain man had not in any way been improved by his travels. 'I quite believe it, he replied; he took himself along with him.'

> Why quit home to find
> Lands warmed by other suns? Who, self-exiled,
> Leaves self behind?
>
> HORACE

If we do not at once unburden ourselves and our souls of the load that oppresses us, the motion will make it weigh more heavily: as a ship's cargo is less cumbrous when it has settled down. You do a sick man more harm than good by removing him to another place. The motion shakes the evil down into the sack; as stakes sink deeper and more firmly into the ground by being stirred and shaken. Wherefore it is not enough to get away from the people; it is not enough to change to another place: we must get away from the gregarious conditions that are within us; we must sequester and regain possession of ourselves.

> Can you for that exclaim, 'I've burst my chain'?
> No! for the struggling dog the rope may break,
> Yet as he flies it dangles from his neck.
>
> PERSIUS

We carry our fetters along with us: it is not full freedom; we still turn our eyes to that we have left behind; our fancy is full of it.

> Unless the breast be purged, what conflicts then,
> What perils, must bosom, in our own despite!
> O then how great and keen the cares of lust
> That split the man distraught! How great the fears!
> And lo, the pride, grim greed, and wantonness –
> How great the slaughters in their train! and lo,
> Debaucheries and every breed of sloth!
>
> LUCRETIUS

Our disease is rooted in our soul, and the soul cannot escape from herself;

> The soul is in fault, which never escapes from itself.
>
> HORACE

Therefore the soul must be brought back, and must retire within itself: that is the true solitude, which may be enjoyed in the midst of cities and kings' courts; but it is enjoyed more comfortably apart.

Now, since we are endeavouring to live alone, and to dispense with society, let us make our contentment to depend on ourselves; let us cut ourselves adrift from all the ties that bind us to others; let us so conquer ourselves as to be able to live really alone and then live contentedly.

Stilpo having escaped from the burning of his city, in which he had lost wife, children, and substance, Demetrius Poliorcetes, seeing him amidst the ruins of his home, with face unmoved by fright, asked him if he had not suffered loss. He replied, 'No; thanks to God, he had lost nothing of his.'[3] The same idea was expressed by the philosopher Antisthenes when he said wittily, 'That man should furnish himself with provisions that float on the water, then he might save them and himself from the shipwreck by swimming.'

Truly the sensible man has lost nothing, if he have himself. When the city of Nola was ruined by the barbarians, Paulinus, who was bishop of that place, having lost everything and being himself their

3 According to Seneca; but neither Plutarch nor Diogenes Laertius, when relating this anecdote, mentions the loss of wife and children. The Stoic Seneca exaggerates the resignation of the philosopher.

prisoner, prayed to God as follows: 'Lord, keep me from feeling this loss; for thou knowest that they have yet touched nothing of that which is mine.' The riches that made him rich, and the goods that made him good, were yet in their integrity. See what it is rightly to choose treasures that may be kept from injury, and to hide them in a place where no man comes, and which cannot be betrayed but by ourselves!

We should have wife, children, worldly goods, and, above all, health, if we can; but not be so strongly attached to them that our happiness depends on them. We must reserve a little back-shop, all our own, entirely free, wherein to establish our true liberty and principal retreat and solitude. In this retreat we should keep up our ordinary converse with ourselves, and so private, that no acquaintance or outside communication may find a place there; there to talk and laugh, as if we had neither wife, nor children, nor worldly goods, retinue or servants: to the end that, should we happen to lose them, it may be no new thing to do without them. We have a soul that can turn upon itself, that can keep company with itself; it has the wherewithal to attack and defend, to receive and give: let us not fear that in this solitude we shall stagnate in tedious idleness,

And seem a world with solitude around.

TIBULLUS

Virtue, says Antisthenes, is content with herself, without rules, without words, without deeds.

Of our customary actions there is not one in a thousand that concerns ourself. The man that you see scaling that wall in ruins, furious and beside himself, exposed to so many musket-shots; and that other, all scarred, pale and half-dead with hunger, determined to perish rather than open the gates to him, do you think they are there on their own account? For one, peradventure, whom they have never set eyes on, and who is quite unconcerned about their fate, and is all the time wallowing in idleness and pleasure.

This other, dirty, dripping from eyes and nose, that you see leaving his study after midnight, do you think he is searching among his books how to become a better, wiser, or more contented man? Not a bit of it. He will die or he will teach posterity the metre of a line of Plautus, or the correct spelling of a Latin word. Who is there that will not readily exchange health, tranquillity and life for reputation and glory, the most useless, worthless, and false coin in use? Our own death has not sufficiently frightened us; let us burden ourselves also with that of our wives, our children and dependants. Our own affairs have not given us sufficient anxiety; let us also torment and beat our brains over those of our neighbours and friends.

Good heavens! That a man
Should dote so much, or suffer anyone
To wind himself so close about his heart
As to be dearer to him than himself!

TERENCE

Solitude, I think, is more becoming and more reasonable in one who has given to the world the most active and vigorous period of his life, after the example of Thales.

We have lived enough for others; let us live for ourselves, at least this remaining bit of life. Let us bring back our thoughts and intentions to ourselves and our comfort. It is no small business to prepare securely one's retirement: it gives us enough to do without the intrusion of any other concerns. Since God gives us permission to arrange for our removal, let us prepare for it; let us pack up our belongings, take leave betimes of the company, and shake off those violent holdfasts that engage us elsewhere and estrange us from ourselves. We must undo those powerful bonds, and from this day forth we may love this and that, but be wedded only to ourselves. That is to say, let the rest be ours, but not joined and glued so firmly to us that it cannot be detached without taking our skin along with it, and tearing away a piece of us. The greatest thing in the world is to know how to belong to ourselves.

It is time to break our ties with society, since we can contribute nothing to it. And he who cannot lend must beware of borrowing. Our powers are failing us: let us withdraw them and concentrate them on ourselves. He who can transmute and turn upon himself the offices of friendship and fellowship, let him do so. In this fallen state which makes him useless, irksome, and troublesome to others, let him take care not to be troublesome to himself, as well as irksome and useless. Let him indulge and cherish, and above all govern himself, respecting and fearing his reason and his conscience to such a degree, that he cannot without shame make a false step in their presence. *For it is a rare thing to see one that sufficiently respects himself* (QUINTILIAN).

Socrates says[4] that the young should be instructed, that grown men should exercise themselves, in well-doing; that the old men should retire from all civil and

4 Not Socrates, but the Pythagoreans.

military employments, living at their discretion without being tied to any fixed office.

There are some natures that are more adapted than others to follow these precepts of retirement. Such as are of weak and slow apprehension, fastidious of taste and inclination, and reluctant to take service or office, whereof I am one, both by natural disposition and on reflection, will sooner comply with that advice than those active and busy minds that embrace all things, engage themselves everywhere, enter passionately into everything, who offer, who come forward and give themselves on all occasions. We should use those accidental opportunities that lie outside of us, so far as they are agreeable to us, but without making them our mainstay; they are not so: neither reason nor nature desires it.

Why should we, contrary to the laws of reason and nature, make our contentment subject to another's power? To anticipate, moreover, the accidents of fortune; to deprive ourselves of the good things we possess, as many have done from religious motives, and some philosophers in accordance with the dictates of reason; to be slaves to ourselves, to lie hard, to put out our eyes, throw our riches into the river, to court pain (either, as some do, to win the beatitude of another life by torturing ourselves in this, or, like others, to be safe from falling anew by standing on the lowest step), all such are acts of an excessive virtue. Let the strongest and most unbending natures make their hiding-place itself glorious and exemplary:

When no better I see,
Oh, the simple, the homely, the humble for me!
I'm a Stoic with nothing to tempt me. But say

Something rich or more toothsome shall
come in my way,
'They only are wise and live well, I protest,
Who in fine country-places their money invest.'

HORACE

I find difficulties enough without going so far as that. It is enough for me, while under Fortune's favours, to prepare for her disfavours, and to picture to myself, whilst I am well off, the ill that is to come, as far as my imagination can reach: just as we exercise ourselves in jousts and tournaments, and mimic wars, in the midst of peace.

I do not regard the philosopher Arcesilaus as less virtuous because he used vessels of gold and silver, as long as the condition of his fortune allowed him to do so; and I esteem him more highly for having used them moderately and liberally, than if he had done away with them.

I know how far our natural necessities extend, and when I see the poor man begging at my door, often more cheerful and healthy than myself, I can imagine myself in his place: I try to clothe my mind after his measure. And, thus running over all the other examples in my mind, although I may imagine death, poverty, contempt, and disease to be treading on my heels, I easily resolve not to stand in terror of what a meaner man than I accepts with so much patience. And I refuse to believe that a mean understanding can do more than a vigorous one, or that reason cannot attain the same results as habit. And knowing how unstable are these temporary blessings, I do not fail, whilst in the full enjoyment of them, to make it my sovereign request to God to make me content with myself and the good things I bring forth.

I see young men who, notwithstanding their robust health, keep a supply of pills in their trunks, to take when afflicted by a cold, which they fear the less for thinking that they have their remedy near at hand. This must we do; and, moreover, if we feel ourselves subject to a more serious malady, provide ourselves with drugs to deaden and relieve the part affected.

The occupation we should choose for such a life should be neither laborious nor tedious, otherwise our object in seeking retirement would be frustrated. That depends on the particular taste of each one: mine cannot in any way adapt itself to husbandry. They who love it should apply themselves to it with moderation,

And strive by outward circumstance to be
No more controlled, but make it bend to them.

HORACE

Agriculture is besides an occupation fit for slaves, as Sallust calls it. Some of its branches are more excusable, such as the care of gardens, to which, according to Xenophon, Cyrus was devoted, and a mean may be found between that abject and servile solicitude, that intense anxiety we see in men who are entirely immersed in it, and that extreme and rooted negligence that allows things to go to rack and ruin, that we may see in others:

Why marvel we if, whilst his soul,
Of body heedless, swept the pole,
Democritus allowed his beeves
Make havoc of his plants and sheaves? HORACE

But let us give ear to the counsel that the younger Pliny gives to his friend Caninius Rufus, on this matter of solitude: 'I counsel you, in the full and prosperous retreat wherein you are, to leave to your slaves the humble and sordid cares of managing your estate, and devote yourself to the study of letters, in order to derive something from them that shall be entirely your own.' He means reputation; he is of a like mind with Cicero, when he said he would employ his solitude and retirement from public affairs in acquiring by his writings an immortal life:

Is then your knowledge absolutely nought
Unless another know you have that knowledge?

PERSIUS

It seems only reasonable, when a man speaks of retiring from the world, that he should look outside of it. These people only half do it. They indeed arrange all their affairs for the time when they shall be no longer here; but, by a ridiculous contradiction, they still expect to reap the fruit of their action from the world on which they have turned their backs.

The idea of those who seek solitude from religious motives, filling their hearts with the certainty of the divine promises in the next life, is much more consistent with sanity. They keep God before their eyes, as an object infinite in goodness and power; there the soul has the wherewithal to satisfy its desires in all freedom. Pain and affliction come to them as a gain, being suffered for the acquisition of eternal health and gladness; death as a thing wished for, as a passage to so perfect a state. The asperity of their rules of discipline is at once made smooth by habit; and the carnal appetites are lulled and kept down by being denied, for nothing keeps them active but use and exercise. This prospect alone of another happily immortal life truly deserves that we should abandon the comforts and sweets of this our present life. And he who can really and constantly kindle his soul with the flame of that living faith and hope, builds himself in solitude a delicious and voluptuous life, transcending any other kind of life.

I am satisfied therefore neither with the end nor the means of that advice[5]: it still only means falling out of an ague into a burning fever.

Occupation with books is as laborious as any other, and as great an enemy to health, which should be the chief consideration. And we should not allow ourselves to be lulled to sleep by the pleasure we take in it: it is the same pleasure that ruins the economist, the miser, the voluptuary, and the man of ambition. The sages teach us often enough to beware of the treachery of our appetites, and to distinguish the true and entire pleasures from pleasures that are mixed and interlarded with more pain. For most of our pleasures, they say, caress and embrace us only to strangle us, like the thieves the Egyptians called Philistas.[6] And if the headache preceded the intoxication we should take care not to drink too much. But pleasure, to deceive us, walks before and conceals her retinue.

Books are pleasant companions, but if by associating with them we end by losing gaiety and health, our best possessions, let us leave them. I am one of those who believe that our enjoyment of them

5 Pliny's advice to Rufus.

6 *Philistas*, an error on the part of Montaigne or his printers for *Philetas*, as they were called by the Egyptians, according to Seneca.

cannot outweigh this loss. As men who, having long felt themselves weakened by some indisposition, at length place themselves at the mercy of physicians, and have certain rules of living prescribed to them by art, which are not to be transgressed: so he who retires, wearied and disgusted with everyday life, must model this retired life by the rules of reason, arrange and order it with premeditation and reflection. He must take leave of every kind of labour, in any shape or form, and flee, in general, the passions that hinder the tranquillity of body and soul,

> And choose the way that suits his humour best.
>
> PROPERTIUS

From husbandry, study, the chase, and any other pursuit he should get all the pleasure he possibly can, but beware of being drawn into them any further, where the pleasure begins to be a labour. He must reserve only so much business and occupation as is needful to keep him in breath, and save him from the evil consequences which the other extreme of slack and sleepy idleness brings with it.

There are sterile and thorny sciences, for the most part invented for public life; we must leave them to those who are engaged in the service of the world. For my part, I love such books as are either easy and entertaining, and that tickle my fancy, or such as give me comfort, and offer counsel in reordering my life and death;

> Sauntering silent through the healthful woods,
> In lonely reveries devising what
> May best engage a wise and good man's thought.
>
> HORACE

Wiser men, possessed of a strong and vigorous soul may create for themselves a wholly spiritual repose. I with my commonplace soul, have to bring my bodily advantages to my aid; and age having of late robbed me of those pleasures that were more to my fancy, I train and sharpen my appetite to those that remain and are more fitting to this later season. We must cling tooth and nail to the pleasures of life, which our years tear, one after another, from our hands:

> Pluck we life's sweets; tomorrow we shall be
> A little dust, a ghost, a gossip's tale.
>
> PERSIUS

Now, as to setting up glory as a goal, as Pliny and Cicero do, that is very far from my reckoning. The humour that is most incompatible with retirement is ambition. Glory and repose are two things that cannot lie in the same bed. As far as I can see, those two men have only their arms and legs out of the throng; their souls and intentions are more than ever in the thick of it:

> Dost thou in thy advancing years
> Cull dainty bits for others' ears?
>
> PERSIUS

They have only stepped back to take a better jump and to hurl themselves with a stronger impetus further into the crowd. Would you see how they shoot short by a grain's length? Let us counterbalance their advice with that of two philosophers,[7] of two very different sects, writing, the one to Idomeneus, the other to Lucilius, their friends, to induce them to give

7 Epicurus and Seneca.

up the management of public affairs and their high positions, and retire into solitude. 'You have hitherto, they say, lived swimming and floating; come now and die in harbour. You have given the first part of your life to light; give the other remaining part to the shade. It is impossible to give up your occupations, if you do not give up the fruits of them; therefore put away all care for reputation and glory. There is a danger lest the light of your past actions may dazzle you too much, and follow you even into your den. Quit with the other pleasures that which comes from others' approval; and as to your learning and talents, give yourself no concern about them: they will not lose their effect, if you yourselves are the better for them. Remember the man who, when he was asked to what purpose he took so much pains in an art which would come to the knowledge of few persons, replied: Few will suffice me; one, nay, less than one will suffice me. He spoke truly. You and a companion are a sufficient stage for one another, or you for yourself. Let the people be to you one, and let one be to you a whole people. It is a poor ambition to wish to extract glory from our idleness and hiding-place. We should do like those animals that remove the traces of their footsteps at the entrance to their lair. What you should concern yourself about is not that the world should talk about you, but how you should talk to yourself. Retire within yourself; but first prepare to receive yourself there: it would be madness to trust to yourself if you cannot govern yourself. There are ways of going wrong in solitude as well as in company. Until you have made yourself such that you dare not trip in your own presence, and until you are ashamed and stand in awe of yourself, – *let noble ideas be present to your mind* (CICERO) – keep ever before your mind Cato, Phocion, and Aristides, in whose presence the very fools would hide their errors, and appoint them controllers of all your intentions; should these get off the track, your reverence for those will set them right again. They will keep you in the way to be contented with yourself, to borrow nothing but of yourself, to keep your mind firmly fixed on definite and limited thoughts in which it may take pleasure; and, having understood the true blessings that one enjoys the more one understands them, to rest content with them, without any desire to prolong life and reputation.'

That is the counsel of true and natural philosophy, not of ostentatious and prating philosophy, like that of the first two.[8]

8 Pliny the younger and Cicero.

Of the inequality that is amongst us

Plutarch says somewhere that he does not find so great a difference between one animal and another as between one man and another. He is speaking of the perfections and internal qualities of the soul. In truth I can see such a distance between Epaminondas, as I imagine him, and certain men I know, I mean men capable of common sense, that I should be inclined to overbid Plutarch and say that there is more difference between this man and that man than between this man and that animal;

> Ye Gods, how much one man excels another!
>
> TERENCE

and that there are as many degrees in minds as there are cubits between here and heaven, and as innumerable.

But, speaking of the estimate of men, it is strange that, excepting ourselves, nothing is estimated but by its proper qualities. We praise a horse for its strength and speed,

> Is it not thus we praise the impatient steed,
> Whose easy triumph and transcendent speed
> Palm after palm proclaim – while victory
> In the hoarse Circus stands exulting by!
>
> JUVENAL

not on account of its harness; a greyhound for its swiftness and not its collar; a hawk for its wing and not for its jesses and bells. Why then do we not value a man for what is his? He has a great retinue, a fine palace, so much influence, so much income: all that is around him, not within him. You do not buy a cat in a bag. If you bargain over a horse, you remove its trappings, you see it bare and uncovered; or, if it is covered, as they were formerly shown to princes for sale, it is only as to the less important parts, that you may not waste your admiration on the beauty of its colour or the breadth of its crupper, but pay attention chiefly to its legs, its eyes and feet, which are the most useful parts,

> The custom is with princes not to buy
> A steed uncovered, lest they be deceived
> By crupper round, short head and ample chest
> Planted upon soft hooves and groggy legs.
>
> HORACE

Why, when estimating a man, do you estimate him all wrapped and muffled up? He exhibits only those parts which are in no wise his, and conceals from us those by which alone we may really judge of his value. It is the price of the sword you seek to know, not of the scabbard. You will perhaps not give a farthing for him when you see him stripped. We must judge him by himself, not by his attire. And, as one of the ancients[1] says very wittily: 'Do you know why you think him tall? You are counting in the height of his pattens.' The pedestal is no part of the statue. Measure him without his stilts: let him lay aside his riches and his honours, and show himself in his shirt. Has he a body equal to his functions, sound and active? What mind

1 Seneca.

has he? is it beautiful, capable, happily furnished with all its parts? Is it rich with its own store, or with that of others? has fortune nothing to do with it? Will his soul with open eyes face a naked sword? Does she care how life goes from her, whether by the mouth or by the throat? Is she sedate, even-tempered, contented? That is what we should consider, and thereby judge of the extreme differences that lie between us. Is he

The wise man, who
Can at all times himself subdue, –
Whom neither want, nor death, nor chains
Appal, – who manfully restrains
His appetites, nor cares to win
Titles or honours, and, within,
Himself self-centred and complete,
Life's chance and change can frankly meet –
Yea, front the heaviest blows of fate
With courage constant and sedate?

HORACE

Such a man is five hundred cubits above kingdoms and duchies; he is an empire in himself.

That man indeed is wise
Who his own fortune can devise. PLAUTUS

What more can he desire?

O not to see that nature for herself
Barks after nothing, save that pain keep off,
Disjoined from the body, and that mind enjoy
Delightsome feeling, far from care and fear!

LUCRETIUS

Compare him with the ruck of mankind, stupid, degraded, servile, unstable, and continually fluctuating in the storm of varying passions, which drive hir hither and thither, and entirely dependent on others there is a greater distance than between heaven an earth; and yet we are so blinded by custom, that w make little or no account of it; whereas, if we look at peasant and a king, a noble and a serf, a magistrate an a private individual, a rich man and a poor, ther immediately appears to our eyes an extreme disparity although they differ, in a manner of speaking, only i their breeches.

In Thrace the king was distinguished from hi people in a ludicrous and very exclusive way. He had religion to himself, a god all his own, whom it was nc meet for his subjects to worship: that was Mercury and he for his part disdained their gods, Mars Bacchus, and Diana.

Yet they are but coats of paint that make n essential difference. For, like the actors in a comedy you see them upon the platform putting on the airs c a duke or an emperor; but immediately after behol them again become wretched varlets and porters which is their true and original condition.

So the Emperor, whose pomp dazzled you i public,

> And (as ye may be sure)
> Big emeralds of green light are set in gold;
> And rich sea-purple dress by constant wear
> Grows shabby and all soaked with Venus' sweat;
>
> LUCRETIU

see him behind the curtain: he is nothing but a ordinary mortal, and perchance meaner than the leas of his subjects. *This one is inwardly happy; the other happiness is on the surface* (SENECA). He is moved b cowardice, irresolution, ambition, spite and envy, like any other man;

For hoarded treasures cannot keep
Disquietudes at bay,
Nor can the consul's lictor drive away
The brood of dark solicitudes, that sweep
Round gilded ceilings gay;

HORACE

and fear and anxiety hold him by the throat in the midst of his armies;

And of a truth man's dread, with cares at heels,
Fears not these sounds of arms, these savage swords,
But among kings and lords of all the world
Mingles undaunted, nor is overawed
By gleam of gold.

LUCRETIUS

Do fevers, the megrims, and the gout spare him any more than they do us? When old age weighs upon his shoulders, will the archers of his guard relieve him of it? When he is paralysed by the fear of death, will he be reassured by the presence of the gentlemen of his chamber? When he is in a jealous and capricious mood, will our bonnetings compose him? That bed-tester, all bloated with gold and pearls, has no virtue to allay the gripings of an acute colic:

Nor yet the quicker will hot fevers go
If on a pictured tapestry thou toss,
Or purple robe, than if 'tis thine to lie
Upon the poor man's bedding.

LUCRETIUS

The flatterers of the great Alexander made him believe that he was a son of Jupiter; one day, being wounded and seeing the blood flow from his wound, he said, 'Well, what say you? is not this a crimson and purely human blood? It is not of the thickness of that which Homer makes to flow from the wounds of the gods.' Hermodorus the poet had written some lines in honour of Antigonus, in which he called him son of the sun; but he contradicted him, saying: 'The man who empties my stool knows very well that I am nothing of the kind.'

When all is said he is but a man, and if he be of ignoble birth, the empire of the universe could not reclothe him.

Let maidens fly his smiles to greet,
And roses spring about his feet! PERSIUS

What if after all his soul be gross and stupid? Even pleasure and happiness are not felt without vigour and spirit.

Yet these all take their value from the mind
Of the possessor: he that knows their use
To him they're blessings; he that knows it not
To him misuse converts them into curses.
TERENCE

The blessings of fortune of every kind yet require the right sense to relish them. It is the enjoying, not the possessing, that makes us happy:

Nor house, nor lands, nor brass, nor golden store
Can of its fire the fevered brain relieve,
Or make the care-fraught spirit cease to grieve.
Sound, mind and body both, should be his health

To true account who hopes to turn his wealth.
Fortune nor home not more the man can cheer,
Who lives a prey to covetise or fear,
Than may a picture's richest hues delight
Eyes that with dropping rheum are thick of sight,
Or warm soft lotions soothe a gout-racked foot.

HORACE

He is a fool, his palate is blunt and dulled; he no more enjoys what he has than one with a cold in the head can appreciate the mellowness of Greek wine, or a horse the richness of the trappings that adorn it; just as, according to Plato, health, beauty, strength, riches, and everything we call good, are as great an evil to the unjust as they are a blessing to the just; and the evil contrariwise.

And then, where body and mind are in evil plight, what avail these external advantages, seeing that the least prick of a pin and suffering of the soul is enough to rob us of the pleasure of being monarch of the world? At the first twitch of the gout, in spite of his Sire and Majesty,

All bloated with silver, all bloated with gold,

TIBULLUS

will he not forget all about his palaces and his grandeurs? If he is in anger, will his princedom keep him from turning red or pale, from grinding his teeth like a madman? Now, if he be a man of parts and well-endowed by Nature, royalty will add little to his happiness:

Let your digestion be but sound,
Your side unwrung by spasm or stitch,
Your foot unconscious of a twitch;

Then could you be more truly blest,
Though you the wealth of kings possessed?

HORACE

he will see that it is all a snare and a delusion. Yea, he would peradventure agree with King Seleucus, 'That if a man knew the weight of a sceptre, he would not stoop to pick it up if he saw it lying on the ground.' He was thinking of the great and laborious charges incumbent upon a good king.

Truly it is no little thing to have to rule others, since ruling ourselves presents so many difficulties. As for commanding, which appears so smooth, I am strongly of opinion, considering the imbecility of human judgement and the difficulty of choice in things that are new and doubtful, that it is much easier and more pleasant to follow than to guide; and that it is very restful to the mind to have to keep to a beaten track, and to have itself alone to answer for:

So better far in quiet to obey,
Than to desire chief mastery of affairs
And ownership of empires. LUCRETIUS

Add to this that saying of Cyrus, that no man is fit to rule who is not better than those he rules.

But King Hiero, in Xenophon, says further, that in the enjoyment even of pleasures, kings are worse off than private individuals, inasmuch as the ease and facility rob them of the bitter-sweet sting we find in them.

Fat love and too much fulsome me annoys,
Even as sweet meat a glutted stomach cloys.

OVID

Do you think that the chorister-boys take a great pleasure in music? Satiety rather makes it tedious to them. Feasts, dances, masquerades, and tourneys delight such as seldom see them and have desired to see them; but to him to whom they are an ordinary fare they become stale and unpleasant. Nor do the ladies gratify him who has his fill of them. He who does not give himself time to be thirsty, can take no pleasure in drinking. The farces of the mountebanks delight us, but to the actors they are a drudgery. And that this is so we may see in the diversions of princes, to whom it is a great treat to be able sometimes to put on disguise, and stoop to a low and plebeian way of living:

It is the rich who relish best
  To dwell at times from state aloof;
And simple suppers, neatly dressed,
  Beneath a poor man's humble roof,
With neither pall nor purple there,
Have smoothed ere now the brow of care.

HORACE

There is nothing so clogging and so distasteful as abundance. What desire would not be repelled to see three hundred women at its disposal, such as the Grand Turk has in his seraglio? And what relish for sport and what form of it can that ancestor of his have retained who never went a-hunting without seven thousand falconers?

Moreover, I believe that this lustre of grandeur is attended with no small drawbacks in the enjoyment of the more delightful pleasures: the great are too much in the limelight and exposed to the public view. And, I know not for what reason, we expect them, more than we do others, to cover up and hide their errors. For what in us is indiscretion, in them the people deem to be tyranny, contempt and slighting of the laws; and, besides their proclivity to vice, it would seem that they take an additional pleasure in reviling public observances and treading them under foot. Plato, indeed, in his *Gorgias,* defines a tyrant as one who has a licence to do all that pleases him in a city. And often, for that reason, the public display of the vices offends more than the vice itself. Every man fears being spied upon and overlooked; princes, even as regards their demeanour and their thoughts, are under observation, since all the people think they have a right and an interest in judging them; besides that blemishes are magnified according to the eminence and brightness of the place where they are set: as a mole or wart on the forehead is more conspicuous than a scar in any other place.

For that reason the poets imagine the amours of Jupiter to be conducted under different disguises; of all the amorous adventures ascribed to him there is only one, it seems to me, where he appears in his majesty and grandeur.

But let us return to Hiero: he also tells of the many disadvantages he is sensible of in his kingship, in being unable to go about and travel in freedom, in being as it were a prisoner within the bounds of his country, and in finding himself encircled in all his actions by an importunate crowd. In truth, to see our kings all alone at table, besieged by so many talkers and strange onlookers, I have often been moved to pity rather than envy of them.

King Alphonso used to say that in this respect asses were better off than kings: their masters allow them to graze in peace, whilst kings cannot obtain that favour of their own servants.

And I have never been able to imagine why it should be so remarkable a convenience in the life of an intelligent man to have a score of people overlooking his close-stool; nor why the services of a man with an income of ten thousand pounds, or who has taken Casale or defended Siena, should be more convenient and acceptable than those of a good and experienced footman.

Princely advantages are quasi-imaginary advantages. Every degree of fortune has some semblance of principality: Caesar called all the lords in France who administered justice in his time, kinglets. Indeed, saving the title of 'Sire', we are coming very near to being kings. Consider, in the provinces remote from the court, taking Brittany as an example, the retinue, the vassals, the officers, the occupations, the services and ceremonies of a retired and homekeeping lord, brought up among his servants. And look at the flight of his imagination, than which there is nothing more regal. He hears speak of his master once in a year, as he might of the King of Persia, and only acknowledges him by some ancient cousinship of which his secretary keeps a record. In truth our laws are free enough, and the weight of sovereignty is hardly felt twice in a lifetime by a French nobleman. The real and actual subjection only concerns those of us who agree to accept it and who prefer to gain honours and riches by such service: for he who is content to live in obscurity by his own fireside, and is able to manage his house and family without quarrels and lawsuits, is as free as the Doge of Venice. *Slavery holds few; more hold fast to slavery* (SENECA).

But especially does Hiero emphasize the fact that he is deprived of all reciprocal friendship and comradeship, wherein consists the sweetest and most perfect fruit of human life. For what evidence of affection and goodwill can I extract from one who, willy-nilly, owes to me all his power? Can I make any account of his humble address and his courteous homage, seeing that it is not in his power to refuse them? The honour we receive from those who fear us is no honour: those respects are due to royalty, not to me.

The greatest good is this
Of royal power, that men are forced to praise
Their monarch's deeds as well as bear them.

SENECA

Do I not see that the wicked and the good king, he who is hated and he who is loved, are paid the same honour and respect, one as much as the other? The same outward show, the same ceremonies, attended my predecessor, and will attend my successor. If my subjects do not offend me, that is no evidence of any great affection: why should I take it in that sense, since they could not do so, even if they would? None follows me on account of any friendship that may exist between him and me: for no friendship can be knit where there is so little relation and correspondence. My elevation has placed me above human intercourse; there is too much disparity and disproportion. Their obedience is a posture and a habit: it is given to my fortune rather than to myself, to increase their own. All they say and do to me is but face-paint. Their freedom being bridled on all sides by the great power I have over them, I see nothing around me but what is covered and masked.

Julian the Emperor was one day praised by his courtiers for his good administration of justice: 'I might be puffed up with pride by this praise, he said, if it came from persons who would dare to condemn or disapprove my contrary actions, should I commit any.'

All the real advantages which princes enjoy are shared by men of mean fortune (it is for the gods to ride on winged steeds and feed on ambrosia): for their sleep and their appetites differ in no way from ours; their steel is of no finer temper than that with which we are armed; their crown shelters them from neither sun nor rain. Diocletian, who wore one so revered and fortunate, resigned it in order to retire to the joys of private life; and some time after, the urgency of public affairs requiring his return to resume his charge, he replied to those who were entreating him to do so: 'You would not attempt to persuade me to do this, if you had seen the beautiful order of the trees I have myself planted at home, and the fine melons[2] I have sown.'

In the opinion of Anacharsis the happiest state of government would be that in which, all other things being equal, precedence should be measured out to virtue, and the refuse to vice.

When King Pyrrhus was preparing to invade Italy, Cineas, his wise counsellor, desiring to bring home to him the vanity of his ambition, asked him: 'Well, Sire, to what end are you directing this great enterprise?' 'To make myself master of Italy,' he replied immediately. 'And then, continued Cineas, that being done?' 'I will pass over into Gaul and Spain,' said the other. 'And after that?' 'I will go and subdue Africa;

2 Diocletian said 'cabbages', but Montaigne had a particular weakness for melons.

and, at the end of it all, when I shall have brought the world under my subjection, I will take mine ease and live contented and happy.' 'In God's name! Sire, Cineas then retorted, tell me how it is that you are not at this moment, if you will, in that state? Why do you not at this very hour settle yourself in the state you say you aspire to, and save yourself all the labour and hazard you interpose?'

Because, of very truth, he hath not learnt
What the true end of getting is, nor yet
At all how far true pleasure may increase.

LUCRETIUS

I will close this passage with a line from an ancient writer which I think singularly fine and to the purpose:

Every man his own good fortune frames.

CORNELIUS NEPOS

Of sleeping

Reason commands us ever to walk along the same path, but not at the same pace; and, although the wise man should not permit his human passions to turn him from the right course, he may indeed, without prejudice to his duty, leave it to them to hasten or retard his steps and not plant himself like an immovable and impassive Colossus. Though Virtue herself should put on flesh and blood, I believe her pulse would beat more strongly when marching to an attack than when going to dinner: nay, it is necessary that she should be subject to emotion and heat. For that reason I have remarked as a rare thing to see great men, when engaged in the loftiest enterprises and the most important affairs, keep themselves so entirely in trim, as not even to curtail their sleep.

Alexander the Great, on the day assigned to that furious battle against Darius, slept so profoundly and so late in the morning, that Parmenion was obliged to enter his chamber, and, approaching his bed, call him two or three times by name to awaken him, the moment to go to battle being so urgent.

The Emperor Otho, having resolved to kill himself, on that same night, when he had settled his domestic affairs, divided his money among his servants, and sharpened the edge of a sword wherewith he intended to take his own life, staying only to know if each of his friends had retired in safety, fell into so sound a sleep, that his chamber-servants heard him snore.

The death of that Emperor has many points in common with that of the great Cato, and particularly that just mentioned: for, Cato being ready to make away with himself, whilst awaiting news to be brought to him whether the Senators whom he was sending away had evacuated the port of Utica, began to sleep so soundly that he could be heard breathing from the next room; and when the man he had sent to the port awakened him to tell him that the Senators were prevented by a storm from conveniently setting sail, he sent yet another, and, resettling himself in his bed, again began to slumber until the second messenger assured him of their departure.

We may also compare with that of Alexander his behaviour in that great and dangerous storm which threatened him through the sedition of Metellus the Tribune, when the latter insisted on publishing the decree recalling Pompey with his army to the city, on the occasion of Catiline's conspiracy; which decree Cato alone opposing, high words and violent threats passed between him and Metellus in the Senate. But it was on the next day that the matter was to be put into execution in the Forum, where Metellus, besides being favoured by the common people and by Caesar, then conspiring in Pompey's interest, was to appear accompanied by many alien slaves and desperate gladiators, Cato being fortified by his courage alone. His friends and relations and many worthy people were consequently in great anxiety about him, some of whom spent the night together without any desire to sleep, eat or drink, on account of the danger they saw threatening him; his wife and sisters especially did nothing but weep and fret in his house, whilst he, on the contrary, comforted everybody, and, after having supped in his usual manner, retired to his couch, and slept a very sound sleep till morning, when one of his fellow tribunes roused him to go to the skirmish.

The knowledge we possess of the greatness of this man's courage, throughout the rest of his life, may enable us to judge in all sureness that his conduct proceeded from a soul so far raised above such accidents, that he disdained to allow this one to cause him any more uneasiness than any ordinary event.

In the naval battle which Augustus won against Sextus Pompeius in Sicily, when on the point of entering into conflict, he was sunk in so deep a sleep, that his friends had to rouse him to give the signal for attack. This gave occasion to M. Antonius to reproach him afterwards, that he had not had the heart even to behold with open eyes the array of his army, and that he had not dared to appear before his soldiers, until Agrippa came to announce to him the victory he had gained over his enemies.

But as to the young Marius, who did still worse, for on the day of his last battle against Sulla, after having marshalled his army and given the word and signal for battle, he lay down to rest in the shade of a tree, and slept so heavily that he could hardly be awakened by the rout and flight of his own men, having seen nothing of the battle; they say it was because he was so extremely spent with fatigue and the want of sleep, that nature could hold out no longer.

On the subject of sleep, the physicians will determine whether it is so necessary that our life depends on it: for we hear indeed that King Perseus of Macedon, when a prisoner at Rome, was brought to his death by being prevented from sleeping; but Pliny instances cases of people who lived a long time without sleep. In Herodotus we read of nations where men sleep and wake by half-years.[1] And they who wrote the life of the sage Epimenides say that he slept for fifty-seven years on end.

1 Herodotus had it on hearsay, but declares positively that he does not believe it.

Of ancient customs

I would willingly excuse my countrymen for having no other rule and pattern of perfection but their own manners and usages, for it is a common weakness, not of the vulgar only but of practically all men, not to look beyond the ways they have been born to. I could understand the ordinary man, should he see Fabricius or Laelius,[1] regarding their looks and bearing as barbarous, since they are neither clothed nor fashioned according to our mode. But I do complain of his particular unwisdom in being so completely blinded and deluded by the authority of the fashion of the day as to be capable of altering his mind and opinion every month, if custom requires it, and of judging himself so diversely.

When it was the fashion to wear the busk[2] of the doublet as high as the chest, he would maintain with heated arguments that it was in its proper place; a few years after behold it slipping down as low as the thighs, then he laughs at the other fashion, finding it absurd and intolerable. The present fashion of dress makes him forthwith condemn the old so decidedly and unanimously that you might imagine it were

1 Meaning presumably the ancient Romans; the 1588 edition originally had *Scipio*, corrected to *Laelius*.
2 *Busc*, or *buste*: the long, small (or sharp-pointed) and hard-quilted belly of a doublet.

some kind of mania that makes his understanding thus turn heels over head. Our changes in this matter being so quick and sudden that the ingenuity of all the tailors in the world could not provide us with enough novelties, the despised fashions are very often bound to come into favour again, and these very same ones soon after fall into contempt; and one and the same thing will, with incredible levity and inconsistency, within the space of fifteen or twenty years, be the subject of two or three not only different but contrary judgements. Not one of us is so knowing but he will suffer himself to be hoodwinked into this contradiction, and both his outward and inward eyes to be insensibly blinded.

I will here scrape together a few ancient customs that I have in my memory, some of them resembling ours, others different; in order that, bearing in mind the continual variation in human things, our judgement concerning them may be clearer and more settled.

What we call fighting with rapier and cloak was already practised by the Romans, according to Caesar, who says: *they wrap their mantle around their left arms and draw their swords*. And even then he remarks on an uncivil custom in our country, which still prevails, namely that we stop travellers we meet on the road and oblige them to tell us who they are, and take it as an insult and an excuse for a quarrel if they refuse to answer.

At the baths, which the ancients took every day before meals, and which with them was as habitual as washing the hands is with us, they at first washed only their arms and legs; but afterwards they adopted the custom, which continued for centuries and in most countries of the world, of washing quite naked in water mixed with perfume; and they regarded it as evidence of great simplicity to wash in pure water. The most dainty and dandified perfumed their whole body three or four times a day. They often had all the hair of the body pulled out with tweezers, as the women of France have for some time been in the habit of treating their foreheads:

> From breast and thighs and arms you pluck
> the hair;
>
> MARTIAL

although they had unguents proper for that purpose:

> With unguents shines her skin, and chalk
> in acid steeped.
>
> MARTIAL

They loved to lie soft, and spoke of sleeping on a mattress as if it were a sign of endurance. They took their meals reclining on couches, in much the same posture as the Turks of our days:

> Then from his lofty couch Father Aeneas began.
>
> VIRGIL

And it is related of Cato the younger that after the battle of Pharsalia, being in mourning on account of the evil condition of public affairs, he always ate seated, and adopted a more austere mode of life.

They kissed the hands of the great as a mark of honour and affection; and friends saluted each other with a kiss, as do the Venetians:

> And kindest words I would with kisses mix.
>
> OVID

When saluting or proffering a request to a great person

they touched his knees. Pasicles the philosopher, brother of Crates, laid his hands on the genitals instead of the knee. When a man he was addressing rudely repelled him he replied: 'What, is not this yours as well as the knees?'

They ended their meals with fruit, as we do.

In the privy (that foolish squeamishness about words may be left to the women) they used a sponge; for which reason *spongia* is an indecent word in Latin; and this sponge was fastened to the end of a stick, as evidenced by the story of the man who, as he was being led along to be thrown to the beasts in presence of the people, asked permission to go and do his business, and, finding no other means of killing himself, thrust this stick and sponge down his throat and choked himself. After doing they used a piece of perfumed flannel:

At tibi nil faciam; sed lota mentula lana.[3]

MARTIAL

Where the streets met in Rome they placed vessels and small tubs for urinals:

And oft the innocent young,
By sleep o'ermastered, think they lift their dress
By pail or public jordan. LUCRETIUS

They used to take snacks between meals. In summer there were sellers of snow to cool their wine; and some there were who used snow in winter, their wine even then not being cold enough for them. The

3 Both the last two statements appear to be founded on insufficient evidence. In the quotation from Martial the correct reading seems to be *laeva* and not *lana*, and the line is variously interpreted.

great had their cup-bearers and carvers, and their buffoons to make them merry. In winter their food was served up on chafing dishes which were brought to the table; and portable kitchens were used, such as I have seen, which followed them about with all that was necessary for serving a meal.

> Keep for yourselves your ambulatory feasts,
> Ye epicures, for me they have no charms.
>
> MARTIAL

In summer they often had, in their lower rooms, fresh clear water flowing through pipes beneath them, in which was great store of live fish, which the guests would choose and catch with their hands, to be prepared according to the taste of each. Fish has ever had this privilege, and still enjoys it, that the great presume to know how to dress it; and it has indeed a more exquisite taste than flesh, at least to me.

But in every kind of magnificence, debauchery, effeminacy, and ingenuity in devising new and expensive pleasures, we are in truth doing our utmost to equal them; we have the will, which is as corrupt as theirs, but we have not the ability to succeed. We have not the power to compete with them either in their vices or their virtues, for both proceed from an intellectual vigour which was incomparably greater in them than it is in us; for the weaker a soul is, the less power has it to do either very well or very ill.

The high end with them was the middle.[4] The before and after, in writing and speaking, did not imply greatness, as is evident in their writings: they

4 Montaigne probably means that the guest of honour at a feast reclined on the middle couch of the *triclinium*.

will say Oppius and Caesar as often as Caesar and Oppius, and indifferently Me and Thee or Thee and Me. Which made me once note, in the life of Flaminius in the French Plutarch,[5] a passage in which the author, speaking of the jealousy between the Aetolians and the Romans for the glory of having won a battle in which they shared the victory, seems to attach some weight to the fact that in the Greek songs the Aetolians were mentioned before the Romans; unless there be ambiguity in the French words.

The ladies used to receive men in the vapour-baths, and even employed men-servants to rub and anoint them:

> A slave, his middle girt with apron black.
> Stands by while nude you revel in your bath.
>
> MARTIAL

They sprinkled themselves with some powder to suppress perspiration.

The ancient Gauls, says Sidonius Apollinaris, wore their hair long in front, whilst the back of the head was shorn: a fashion which is being revived in the effeminate and vicious usage of this age.

The Romans used to pay the boatman's fare as soon as they entered the boat, which we do not do till after returning to port:

> Thus while the mule is harnessed, and we pay
> Our fares, an hour in wrangling slips away.
>
> HORACE

The women used to lie on the side of the bed next the wall; this explains why Caesar was called *spondam*

5 That is to say, in Amyot's translation of Plutarch.

regis Nicomedis.[6] They took breath while drinking. They baptized their wine:

> What active boy from sparkling spring
> Water to soothe the heat will bring
> Of our Falernian wine? HORACE

And they also knew those rascally cunning looks of our lackeys:

> O Janus, whom no stork can peck behind,
> Whom none can mock by making asses' ears
> Or thrusting out a red derisive tongue
> As long as that of dogs in summer's heat.
> PERSIUS

The ladies of Rome and Argos wore white mourning as ours used to do, and would continue to do if they took my advice.

But there are whole books written on this matter.

6 For an explanation of this passage, see Suetonius's *Life of Julius Caesar*, § 49. The words there used are: *spondam interiorem regiae lecticae*, the inner side of the royal couch.

Of a saying of Caesar

If we would bestow a little consideration on ourselves now and then, and employ, in probing ourselves, the time we spend finding fault with others and prying into things that do not concern us, we should soon become conscious how all this fabric of ours is built up of weak and decaying pieces. Is it not a singular testimony of imperfection to be unable to fix our contentment on any one thing, and that even in desire and imagination it is beyond our power to choose what we stand in need of? This fact is well proved by the great contention which the philosophers have carried on from all times, that still endures and will endure for ever without agreement or solution, regarding the sovereign good of man.

> But whilst the thing we long for
> Is lacking, that seems good above all else;
> Thereafter, when we've touched it, something else
> We long for; ever one equal thirst of life
> Grips us agape. LUCRETIUS

Whatever it be that we know and enjoy, we feel that it does not satisfy us and we follow open-mouthed after things to come and unknown, inasmuch as those of the present do not satiate us; not that they have not, in my judgement, the power of satiating us, but that our hold upon them is infirm and ill-regulated:

For when he[1] saw that wellnigh everything
Which needs of man most urgently require
Was ready to hand for mortals, and that life,
As far as might be, was established safe,
That men were lords in riches, honour, praise,
And eminent in goodly fame of sons,
And that they yet, O yet, within the home,
Still had the anxious heart which vexed life
Unpausingly with torments of the mind,
And raved perforce with angry plaints, then he,
Then he, the master, did perceive that 'twas
The vessel itself which worked the bane, and all,
However wholesome, which from here or there
Was gathered into it, was by that bane
Spoilt from within.

LUCRETIUS

Our appetite is irresolute and uncertain: it can neither possess nor enjoy anything in the right way. Man, thinking that the fault lies in the thing he possesses, feeds on and fills himself with other things that he neither knows nor understands, on which he fixes his desires and hopes, holding them in honour and reverence; as Caesar says, *it happens by a common defect of nature, that we most trust and fear the things we have not seen, which are hidden and unknown to us.*

1 Epicurus.

Of prayers

I put forward shapeless and unresolved ideas, lik those who publish debatable questions for discussio in the schools, not to establish the truth, but to seek i And I submit them to the judgement of those whos concern it is to direct, not my writings and action only, but even my thoughts. Condemnation an approbation will be equally acceptable and profitabl to me, since I should hold it execrable if I sai anything, through ignorance or inadvertence, that contrary to the holy prescriptions of the Catholi Apostolic, and Roman Church, in which I am dying and in which I was born. And therefore, whilst eve submitting myself to the authority of their censur which has absolute power over me, I thus bold meddle with every kind of subject. As here.

I know not if I am wrong, but since, by particul favour of the divine goodness, a certain form of pray has been prescribed and dictated to us word for wor by the mouth of God, I have always thought that w ought to use it more commonly than we do. And, if might advise, I would have Christians say th *Paternoster,* if not exclusively, at least at all times: o sitting down and rising from table, on getting up an

1 The use of the present tense here appears odd, but it mu be remembered that Montaigne regarded death as beir ever present.

oing to bed, and on all particular occasions that are ssociated with prayer. The Church may amplify and iversify prayers, according to the need of our nstruction: for I know well that it is always the same ubstance and the same thing. But this one ought to ave the privilege of being continually in the mouths f the people. For it is certain that it says all that is ecessary and is very proper for all occasions. It is the nly prayer that I use on all occasions, and I repeat it ather than make a change. Whence it comes that I emember none so well.

It came into my mind just now to inquire how we ame to fall into that error of having recourse to God n all our designs and enterprises, and of calling upon im in every kind of need, and whenever our veakness requires support, without considering vhether the occasion be just or unjust; and of nvoking his name and power, whatever condition we nay be in, in whatever action we may be engaged, be never so vicious.

He is indeed our sole and unique protector, and is ll-powerful to succour us, but, although he deigns to onour us with this sweet fatherly kinship, yet he is as ist as he is good and powerful. But much oftener oes he exercise his justice than his power, and his avours are granted in accordance with the dictates of istice, and not according to our requests.

Plato, in his *Laws*, enumerates three kinds of belief ffensive to the gods: 'That there are no gods; That hey do not meddle with our affairs; That they refuse othing to our vows, offerings, and sacrifices.' The rst error, in his opinion, never remained unchanged n man, from his childhood to his old age. The two thers may remain persistent.

His justice and power are inseparable. In vain d we invoke his power in a bad cause. We must have clean soul, at least at the moment when we pray t him, free of all vicious passions, else we ourselve offer him the rods wherewith to scourge us. Instea of redressing our fault, we redouble it, by showing t one to whom we should sue for pardon, feelings ful of hatred and irreverence. Wherefore I am not in clined to commend a man who is so often an habitually on his knees, unless his actions immed iately preceding and following his prayers show evidence of some amendment and reform,

> If night and the Santonic hood disguise
> Thy form for some adulterous enterprise.
>
> JUVENA

And the state of mind of one who mingles piety wit an execrable life seems somewhat more damnabl than that of a man who is in conformity with himsel and in every way dissolute. Wherefore our Churc every day denies the grace of entry and fellowship t those of depraved morals who persist in any notoriou wickedness.

We pray as a matter of habit and custom, or, mor correctly speaking, we read or mutter our prayers. It i after all only a grimace. And I dislike seeing a ma cross himself three times at the Benedicite,[2] and a often at the Grace[2] (and I dislike it the more as it is sign I hold in reverence and continually use, eve when I yawn), and meanwhile employing every hou of the day in acts of hatred, avarice, and injustice. T the vices they devote an hour, and an hour to God, a

2 Grace before and after eating.

if it were a payment and settlement of accounts. It is wonderful to see actions so unlike following one upon the other with so even a tenor, that one can perceive no interruption and alteration, even upon the confines and transition from one to the other.

What an amazing conscience that must be which can be at ease, whilst harbouring under the same roof, in such peaceful and harmonious fellowship, both crime and judge!

A man whose head is unceasingly domineered by lechery, and who deems it to be most abominable in the divine sight, what can he say to God when he tells him of it? He pulls himself together, but immediately relapses. If the image of the divine justice and its presence did, as he declares, strike and chastise his soul, however short his repentance, his very fear would so often cast back his thoughts to it, that he would forthwith see himself become master of those vices which are habitual and inveterate in him.

But what of those who build their whole life on the fruit and emolument of a sin they know to be deadly? How many trades and professions have we not countenanced whose essence is vicious? And that man who, in confession to me, admitted that he had for quite an age professed and practised a religion which he regarded as damnable and which was at variance with his secret feelings, in order not to lose his credit and his honourable employments, how did he concoct that speech in his heart? With what words can such men converse on that subject before the divine justice? Their repentance consisting in a visible and manifest reparation, they lose the power of pleading it both to God and man. Are they so bold as to sue for pardon without making satisfaction and without repentance? I hold the first to be in the same case as the latter, but their obstinacy is not so easily overborne. These so sudden and violent contradictions and changes of mind which they feign before us savour to me of a miracle. They indicate a state of insoluble struggle.

How fanciful appeared to me the imagination of those who, of late years, were wont to accuse any man who gave evidence of an enlightened spirit, and yet professed the Catholic religion, of being a dissembler; and who thought they were doing him an honour when they maintained that, whatever he might say for appearance's sake, in his heart he could not but hold the reformed faith according to their measure! What a pitiful mania to think your position so strong, and to be convinced that it is impossible to hold the contrary faith! And still more pitiful to persuade oneself that a man so enlightened should put I know not what disparity of present fortune before the hopes and threats of eternal life! They may believe me. If anything could have tempted my youth, the ambition to share the risks and difficulties which accompanied this recent upheaval[3] would not have been the least motive.

It is not, I think, without good reason that the Church forbids the promiscuous, thoughtless, and indiscreet use of the divine and sacred songs which the holy Spirit dictated to David. We must not mingle God with our actions, except with a reverence and attention full of honour and respect. That voice is too divine to be used merely for the exercise of our lungs and to please our ears: it is from the conscience and

3 The Reformation.

not from the tongue that it should proceed. It is not consonant with reason that a shop-apprentice, with those empty and frivolous thoughts of his, should entertain and divert himself with such things.

Nor indeed is it reasonable to see the holy book of the sacred mysteries of our faith bandied about a hall or a kitchen. They were once mysteries; now they are sports and pastimes. So serious and venerable a study should not be taken up just by the way and in a hurry. It ought to be a premeditated and sober action, with which should always be associated that preface to our office, *Sursum corda,*[4] and in which even the body should so dispose its demeanour as to evidence a particular attention and reverence.

It is not all the world's study; it is the study of persons who are consecrated to it, who are called to it by God. The wicked, the ignorant, grow worse by it. It is not a story to tell, but a story to revere, to fear and adore. Absurd people they are who, because they have done it into the language of the people, think they have made it easy to be understood by the people! Is it only a question of words, if they do not understand all they find written? Shall I say more? By bringing the people this little step nearer to understanding, they remove them farther away from it. Pure ignorance, and complete dependence upon others, was much more salutary and wise than this vain and wordy knowledge, the nurse of presumption and foolhardiness.

I believe moreover that the liberty given to anyone to disperse so sacred and important a word in so many kinds of idioms is much more dangerous than it is profitable. The Jews, the Mohammedans, and almost

4 Lift up your hearts.

all others, are wedded to and revere the language in which their mysteries were originally conceived, and any alteration and change in them is forbidden; and that not without reason. Can we be sure that in the country of the Basques and in Brittany there are sufficient men of judgement to establish this translation into their own language? The universal Church has no harder and more solemn task than to decide this matter. In preaching and speaking the interpretation is vague, free, mutable, and piecemeal; so it is not the same thing.[5]

One of our Greek historians justly censured the age in which he lived, because the secrets of the Christian religion were scattered about the market-place and in the hands of the meanest artisans, so that anybody could talk and argue about them according to his lights, and holds that it should be a great shame to us who, by the grace of God, enjoy the pure mysteries of piety, to suffer them to be profaned in the mouths of the ignorant and vulgar, seeing that the Gentiles forbade Socrates, Plato, and the wisest men to investigate and speak of the things committed to the priests of Delphi. And he says, moreover, that the factions of princes are armed, in the matter of theology, not with zeal but with anger; that zeal partakes of the divine reason and justice, when guided by order and moderation; but that, when it is guided by human passion, it turns to hatred and envy and brings forth, instead of wheat and grapes, tares and nettles.

And rightly was it also said by that other, when counselling the Emperor Theodosius, that disputes are less likely to allay the schisms of the Church than

5 i.e., not the same thing as the text of the Scriptures.

to excite them, and to stir up heresies; that they should therefore flee all contentions and dialectical arguments, and frankly rely on the precepts and formulas of the faith established by the ancients. And the Emperor Andronicus, coming upon two great men in his palace engaged in a heated argument with Lopadius,[6] on some point of great importance to us, rated them and even threatened, if they continued, to throw them into the river.

Nowadays the children and women will lecture the oldest and most experienced on the ecclesiastical laws, whereas the first of Plato's laws forbids them to enquire into the reason even of the civil laws, which must be regarded as divine ordinances; and, though he allows the old men to confer among themselves and with the magistracy concerning them, he adds, 'provided it be not done in the presence of young and uninitiated persons'.

A bishop[7] has left in writing that at the other end of the world there is an island, called by the ancients Dioscorides, accommodatingly fertile in all kinds of fruits and trees, and with a healthful climate, the people of which are Christians, having churches and altars, adorned only with crosses without any other images; great observers of fasts and holidays, exact in paying their tithes to the priests, and so chaste, that no man may know more than one woman in his life. For

[6] It seems that Lopadius or Lopadia was the name of a lake, which Montaigne mistook for the name of a man.

[7] Osorius, Bishop of Silves, author of *De Rebus gestis Emanuelis regis Lusitaniae*, which Montaigne read in a French translation. The island is Socotra, in the Indian Ocean. With regard to the chastity of the men, all that was meant was that they were not polygamists.

the rest, so contented with their lot that, surrounded by the sea, they know not the use of ships, and so simple that of the religion they so diligently practise they understand not a word: a thing incredible to such as do not know that the pagans, who are such zealous idolators, know nothing of their gods but merely their names and statues.

The old beginning of *Menalippus*, a tragedy of Euripides, ran thus,

O Jupiter! for that name alone
Of what thou art to me is known.

I have also in my time heard people lament the fact that certain writings were purely human and philosophic, without any mingling of theology. Not without reason, however, we might say on the other hand, 'That the divine doctrine better keeps her rank apart as queen and mistress; That she should be first everywhere, and not subsidiary and suffragan; and That perhaps the examples used in grammar, rhetoric, and logic might more suitably be chosen elsewhere than from so sacred a matter, as well as the subjects for stage-plays, games, and public spectacles; That the divine arguments are treated with greater veneration and respect when by themselves and in their own style, than when coupled with human reasons; That the theologians more often commit the error of writing too humanly, than do the humanists that of writing too untheologically: philosophy, says Saint Chrysostom, has long been banished from the sacred schools as an unprofitable servant, and esteemed unworthy to look, even passing before the entry, upon the sanctuary of the holy treasures of celestial doctrine; That the human language has figures of speech on a lower level, and should not appropriate the dignity, majesty and authority of the divine eloquence.' I for my part permit it to speak, *in undisciplined language* (ST AUGUSTINE), of fortune, destiny, accident, good luck, bad luck, and the gods, and other phrases, in its own way.

I put forward human ideas, and my own, simply as human ideas, and considered separately, not as decreed and determined by divine ordinance, beyond doubt and dispute: as matter of opinion, not matter of faith; as the result of self-communings, and not of my faith in God, as boys show up their essays, not to instruct, but to be instructed; in a lay, not a clerical style, but still very religious.

And it might also be said, not without a show of reason, that the decree forbidding any but such as make express profession of religion to write about it, except very reservedly, would not lack some colour of utility and justice; and would perhaps command me among others to hold my peace.

I have been told that even those who are not of our persuasion forbid the use among themselves of the name of God in their ordinary conversation. They will not permit it to be used by way of interjection or exclamation, nor in giving evidence, nor for the purpose of comparison: wherein I think they are right. On whatever occasion we call upon God to accompany and assist us, it should be done seriously and religiously.

There is, I think, in Xenophon, a certain treatise in which he sets forth that we should pray to God less often, seeing that it is no easy matter for us to bring back our minds so often to that calm, chastened, and devotional state necessary for that purpose; otherwise our prayers are not only vain and unprofitable, but wicked. 'Forgive us, we say, as we forgive those who have offended us.' What do we mean by that except that we offer him our soul free from rancour and ill-will? Yet we invoke God and his assistance as an accomplice in our sins, and invite him to share our injustice:

> Which to impart you draw the gods aside.
>
> PERSIUS

The miser prays to him for the safe-keeping of his vain and superfluous treasures, the ambitious man for victories and the guidance of his ruling passion; the thief implores his aid in surmounting the dangers and difficulties that obstruct the carrying-out of his wicked designs, or thanks him for the ease with which he has been enabled to cut the throat of a traveller. At the foot of the house they intend to scale or blow up they make their prayers, with their hopes and intentions full of cruelty, lust, and greed.

> Well, just ask of
> Staius what you ask of Jupiter;
> He would say, 'By Jove, how dreadful!'
> May not Jove invoke himself so? PERSIUS

The Queen of Navarre, Margaret, tells a tale of a young prince (and, although she does not name him, his rank has made him recognizable enough), that, going to keep an amorous appointment to sleep with the wife of a Paris advocate, and his way taking him through a church, he never passed this holy place, going to or returning from his adventure, but he made his prayers and orisons. With his soul filled with that beautiful design, I leave you to judge for what purpose he employed the divine favour. And yet she cites this as a testimony of singular devotion.[8] But this proof does not stand alone to confirm our belief that women are hardly fit to treat theological matters.

A true prayer and a pious reconciling of ourselves to God cannot light upon an unclean mind, subject at the time to the domination of Satan. The man who calls God to his aid while leading a vicious life acts like the cut-purse who should call justice to his aid, or like those who call upon God to witness a lie.

In whispered tones we murmur guilty prayers.

LUCAN

There are few men who would dare to bring to the light of day the secret requests they make to God:

It is not everyone whose humble whispers
Within the shrines would bear the light of day.

PERSIUS

For that reason the Pythagoreans would have them made public and heard by all the world, that no one might ask any unseemly or unjust thing, like this man,

He first exclaims aloud, Apollo! Then
Into a whisper drops his voice again,
And mutters: O Laverna,[9] fair and bright,
Grant no suspicion e'er on me alight;
Make me to seem devout and just, and shroud
My frauds and follies in a friendly cloud.

HORACE

8 See the *Heptameron*, 3rd Day, novel 25. According to the story however, he prayed only on his return from the adventure.

9 Laverna was the patron goddess of thieves.

The gods cruelly punished the iniquitous vows of Oedipus by granting them. He prayed that his children might determine among themselves by arms the succession to his state. He had the misfortune to see himself taken at his word. We are not to ask that all things shall fall out according to our will, but in accordance with wisdom.

It would seem, indeed, as if the prayers we utter were a mere jargon, like those sacred and divine words which are used in sorceries and deeds of witchcraft; and as if we counted upon their efficiency depending on the form, the sound, and succession of the words, or upon our gestures. For with our souls full of lust, untouched by repentance or any new reconciliation with God, we offer to him those words that the memory suggests to the tongue, and hope by them to atone for our errors. Nothing is so kind, so indulgent, and so gracious as the divine law: she calls us to her, sinful and detestable as we are; she opens her arms and receives us into her bosom, however vile, filthy, and polluted we may be at present and in the future. But then, in return, we must look upon her with a favourable eye. We must receive this pardon with thankfulness, and, at least during the moment when we address her, our soul must be dissatisfied with its errors and at enmity with the passions which have driven us to offend her.

Neither the gods nor the good man, says Plato, accept the gift of the wicked.

The costliest sacrifice that wealth can make
From the incensed Penates less commands
A soft response, than doth the poorest cake,
If on the altar laid with spotless hands. HORACE

Of age

I cannot accept the way in which we fix the span of our lives. I have observed that the sages hold it to be much shorter than is commonly supposed. 'What! said the younger Cato to those who would prevent him from killing himself, am I now of an age to be reproached with yielding up my life too soon?' And yet he was but forty-eight years of age. He thought that age very ripe and well advanced, considering how few men reach it. And they who flatter themselves that such and such a term, which they call the natural course of life, gives promise of a few years beyond, might be justified, were they privileged to be exempt from the numerous accidents to which each of us, by a natural subjection, is exposed, and which may cut short the term they promise themselves.

What an idle fancy it is to expect to die of a decay of powers brought on by extreme old age, and to propose that as the term of our duration, seeing that that kind of death is the rarest of all, and most seldom reached! That death alone we call a natural death, as if it were contrary to nature to see a man break his neck by a fall, drowned in a shipwreck, suddenly snatched away by the plague or a pleurisy, and as if it were not our ordinary condition to be exposed to all such calamities. Let us not flatter ourselves with such fine words; we ought perhaps rather to call that natural which is general, common, and universal.

To die of old age is a rare death, singular and out of the ordinary, and hence much less natural than other deaths; it is the last and extreme kind of death: the further it is from us, the less it is to be expected. It is indeed the bourn beyond which we shall not go, and which the law of Nature has prescribed as a limit not to be overstepped; but it is a privilege she rarely bestows to let us live so long. It is an exemption she gives by special favour to one man in the course of two or three centuries, by releasing him from the crosses and difficulties she has cast in the way of this long career.

By this reasoning I have been led to regard the age which we have reached as an age which few people attain to. Since in the ordinary course of things men do not reach that stage, it is a sign that we are well advanced.

And since we have passed the usual limits, which are the true measure of our life, we must not hope to go much beyond. Having escaped so many occasions of death into which we see the world stumbling, we must acknowledge that the extraordinary and uncommon fortune which has kept us alive, is not likely to continue much longer.

It is a fault even in the laws to entertain this false idea: they will not allow a man to be capable of managing his affairs till he is twenty-five years of age; and he will be hard pushed to manage his life till then. Augustus cut off five years from the ancient Roman ordinances, and declared that a man was old enough at thirty to assume the office of a judge. Servius Tullius exempted the knights who had passed the age of forty-seven from the drudgery of war; Augustus released them at forty-five. To send men into retirement before they are fifty-five or sixty years of age seems to me not very reasonable. I should be of opinion that we should continue our professions and occupations as long as possible, for the public good; but I see a fault in the other direction, in that we are not set to business early enough. This emperor had been universal arbiter of the world at nineteen, and would have a man be thirty before he can give judgement about the position of a spout.

For my part, I consider that our minds are developed as far as they are likely to be at twenty and as promising as they can ever be. No mind that has not given evident earnest of its powers at that age, ever gave proof of them after. Then or never do the natural qualities and virtues exhibit the vigour and beauty that is in them:

If the thorn prick not at its birth,
Hardly will it ever prick,

as they say in the Dauphiné.

Of all the great human deeds, of whatever kind, that have come to my knowledge, I think I should have a longer task to enumerate those that have been performed, both in ancient and modern times, before the age of thirty, than after. Yea, often in the life of the same men.

May I not with full assurance say so of those of Hannibal and of Scipio, his great adversary? The better half of their lives was lived on the fame they acquired in their youth: great men afterwards, compared with all others, but by no means in comparison with themselves.

With regard to myself, I hold for certain that after that age both my mind and my body have lost rather than gained, and recoiled rather than advanced. It is possible that, in those who employ their time well, knowledge and experience grow with their years; but vivacity, quickness, firmness, and those other qualities which are much more our own, more important and essential, decay and languish.

Where already
The body's shattered by master-powers of age
And fallen the frame with its enfeebled powers,
Thought halts, tongue wanders, and the
mind gives way.

LUCRETIUS

Now it is the body that first surrenders to old age, now the mind; and I have seen a goodly number whose brains were enfeebled before their stomach and legs; and that is the more dangerous, as it is an infirmity that is little felt by the sufferer, and of obscure symptoms. For this once I complain of the laws, not that they keep us at work too late in life, but that they set us to work too late. Considering the frailty of our life, and to how many common and natural reefs it is exposed, we should not, in my opinion, allot so large a share at the beginning of it to idleness and to apprenticeship.

BOOK TWO

Of the inconsistency of our actions

They who make a practice of comparing human actions are never so perplexed as when they try to piece them together and place them in the same light, for they commonly contradict one another so strangely that it seems impossible they should have come out of the same shop. Marius the younger is now a son of Mars, now a son of Venus.[1] Someone said that Pope Boniface the Eighth entered upon his charge like a fox, behaved therein like a lion, and died like a dog. And who could believe that it was Nero, the very image of cruelty, who, when the sentence of a condemned criminal was brought to him to be signed in the usual way, exclaimed, 'Would to God that I had never learned to write!' So grieved was he in his heart to doom a man to death!

The world is full of such examples, nay, any man may provide such an abundance of them out of his own experience, that I sometimes wonder to see intelligent men at pains to sort the pieces, seeing that irresolution is, in my view, the most common and

1 'His martial intrepidity and ferocious behaviour at first procured him the title of the son of Mars, but his conduct afterwards denominated him the son of Venus.' – PLUTARCH, *Life of Marius*.

conspicuous defect of our nature: witness that famous line of Publilius the writer of low comedies,

> Poor is the plan that never can be changed.
>
> PUBLILIUS SYRUS

It seems reasonable to judge a man by the most ordinary acts of his life, but in view of the natural instability of our habits and opinions, I have often thought that even good authors are wrong in obstinately attributing to us a steadfast and consistent character. They hit upon a general feature in a man and arrange and interpret all his actions in accordance with this fanciful conception; and if they are unable to twist them sufficiently, set them down to dissimulation. Augustus has escaped them, for we see in this man, throughout the course of his life, so manifest, abrupt, and continual a variety of actions, that he has slipped through the fingers of even the most daring critics, and been left undecided. I find nothing more difficult to believe than man's consistency, and nothing more easy than his inconsistency. If we examine him in detail and judge of his actions separately, bit by bit, we shall most often find this true.

Throughout ancient history it would be difficult to choose a dozen men who have steered their lives in one certain and constant course, which is the principal aim of wisdom. For, to comprise it all in one word, as an ancient writer says,[2] and to embrace all the rules of life in one, is 'to wish and not to wish always the same thing. I will not vouchsafe to add, he says, provided the wish be right; for if it be not right, it is impossible it should be always the same.' I once learned indeed that

2 Seneca.

vice is no more than want of rule and moderation, and that it is consequently impossible to associate it with consistency. It is a saying attributed to Demosthenes, 'that the beginning of all virtue is consultation and deliberation; and the end and perfection, constancy.' If reason directed our course we should choose the fairest; but no one has thought of that:

> He scorns that which he sought, seeks
> what he scorned of late;
> He flows and ebbs, his whole life contradiction.
>
> HORACE

Our ordinary practice is to follow the inclinations of our appetite, to right, to left, up hill, down dale, as we are borne along by the wind of opportunity. We do not consider what we wish except at the moment of wishing it, and we change like that animal which takes its colour from what it is laid upon. What we have but now determined we presently alter, and soon again we retrace our steps: it is nothing but wavering and uncertainty;

> We are led as a puppet is moved by the strings.
>
> HORACE

We do not go, we are carried along, like things floating, now smoothly, now perturbedly, according as the water is angry or calm;

> We see them, knowing not
> What 'tis they want, and seeking ever and ever
> A change of place, as if to drop the burden.
>
> LUCRETIUS

Every day a new fancy; and our humours move with the changes of weather:

So change the minds of men, like days
That Father Jove sends down to earth,
To alternate 'twixt wet and fine.

HOMER

We waver between different minds; we wish nothing freely, nothing absolutely, nothing constantly. Should any man prescribe and establish definite laws and a definite policy in his own head, he would present throughout his life a shining example of even habits, an order and an unfailing relation of one action to another.

Empedocles remarked in the inhabitants of Agrigentum this discrepancy, that they abandoned themselves to their pleasures as if they were to die on the morrow, and that they built as if they were never to die.

The reason will be easily found, as we see in the case of the younger Cato; he who touches one note of the keyboard touches all: there is a harmony of sounds, all in perfect tune with each other, which is not to be mistaken. With us, on the other hand, the rule is: so many actions, so many particular judgements to be passed. The surest, in my opinion, would be to refer them to the nearest circumstances, without seeking any farther, and without drawing from them any other inferences.

It was told me, during the tumultuous times our poor State had to go through, that a young woman who lived quite near to where I then was, had thrown herself from a high window to avoid the forcible caresses of a poor knave of a soldier who was quartered in her house; the fall did not kill her, and, repeating the attempt on her life, she would have cut her throat with a knife, but was prevented; not however without inflicting a serious wound. She herself then confessed that the soldier had done no more than importune her with gifts, entreaties, and solicitations, but that she feared he would in the end proceed to violence. And all this, her words, her mien, and the blood which testified to her virtue, in the true manner of a second Lucretia!

Now I have heard, as a fact, that, both before and after, she was a wench not very difficult to come by. As the tale has it, 'Be as handsome and as fine a gentleman as you will, when you have failed in your pursuit, do not immediately conclude an inviolable chastity in your mistress; it does not follow that the muleteer will not find his opportunity.'[3]

Antigonus, having taken a liking to one of his soldiers, on account of his virtue and valour, ordered his physicians to attend him for a persistent internal malady which had long tormented him, and perceiving that after his cure he went much more coldly to work than before, asked him what it was that had so altered and cowed him. 'You yourself, Sire, he replied, by delivering me from the ill which made me indifferent to life.' A soldier of Lucullus, having been plundered by enemies, devised a bold stroke for his revenge; when he had retrieved his loss with interest, Lucullus, whose good opinion he had gained, tried to induce him, with the best persuasions he could think of, to undertake some risky business;

With words that might have stirred a
coward's heart.

HORACE

3 See the host's tale in Ariosto's *Orlando Furioso*, c. 28; La Fontaine's version of the same story, *Joconde*; or the *Arabian Nights* (Introd.).

'Employ, he replied, some wretched soldier who has been plundered;'

> Though but a rustic clown, 'he'll go
> Who's lost his money-belt,' he said; HORACE

and resolutely refused to go.

When we read that Mahomet having furiously rated Chasan, chief of his Janissaries, for allowing his line of troops to be broken by the Hungarians, and bearing himself like a coward in the battle; and that Chasan made no reply but, alone and just as he was with his weapon in his hand, rushed furiously into the first body of enemies that he met with, and was immediately overwhelmed; it was not so much a justification of his conduct as a change of mood, not so much natural prowess as a new spite.

Do not think it strange that the man who was so venturesome yesterday should prove such a poltroon on the morrow; either anger, or necessity, or company, or wine, or the sound of the trumpet had put his heart into his belly; it was not a courage thus formed by reason, but a courage stiffened by those circumstances; it was no marvel if other contrary circumstances made a new man of him.

These so supple changes and contradictions which we manifest have made some to imagine that we have two souls, others, that we have two powers which, each in its own way, accompany and stir us, the one to good, the other to evil, since so abrupt a diversity is not to be reconciled with a single subject.

Not only does the wind of accidents stir me according to its blowing, but I am also stirred and troubled by the instability of my attitude; and he who examines himself closely will seldom find himself twice in the same state. I give to my soul now one face, now another, according to the side to which I turn it. If I speak differently of myself, it is because I regard myself differently. All the contradictions are to be found in me, according as the wind turns and changes. Bashful, insolent; chaste, lascivious; talkative, taciturn; clumsy, gentle; witty, dull; peevish, sweet-tempered; mendacious, truthful; knowing, ignorant; and liberal and avaricious and prodigal: all this I see in myself in some degree, according as I veer about; and whoever will study himself very attentively will find in himself, yea, in his judgement, this discordance and unsteadiness. I can say nothing of myself absolutely, simply, and steadily, without confusion and mixture, nor in one word. *Distinguo* is the most universal member of my logic.

Though I am ever inclined to speak well of what is good, and rather to interpret favourably the things that are capable of such interpretation, yet such is the strangeness of our nature that we are often driven to do good, even by vice; if it were not that well-doing is judged by the intention alone.

Therefore a courageous deed ought not to imply a valiant man: the man who is really brave will be always so, and on all occasions. If valour were a habit, and not a sudden eruption, it would make a man equally resolute for all emergencies, the same alone as in company, the same in single combat as in a battle; for let them say what they will, there is not one valour for the pavement and another for the field. As bravely would he bear sickness in his bed as a wound in camp, nor would he fear death in his own home any more than in an assault. We should not see the same man charge with brave assurance into the breach, and afterwards worrying, like a woman, over the loss of a lawsuit or a son. When, though afraid of infamy, he bears up against poverty; when, though wincing at a surgeon's lancet, he stiffly faces the enemy's sword, the action is praiseworthy, but not the man.

Many Greeks, says Cicero, cannot look upon an enemy, and are brave in sickness. The Cimbrians and Celtiberians, quite the contrary: *For nothing can be consistent that has not reason for its foundation* (CICERO).

No valour could be more extreme in its kind than Alexander's; but it is of one kind only, and is not complete enough, nor universal on all occasions. Incomparable though it be, it has its blemishes. So it is that we see him so desperately disturbed by the slightest suspicions that his subjects may be plotting against his life, and carried away in his investigations to such violent and indiscriminate acts of injustice, and haunted by a fear that upsets his natural good sense. The superstition too with which he was so strongly tainted bears some likeness to pusillanimity. And the excess of his penitence for the murder of Clytus is also evidence of uneven temper.

Our actions are but a patchwork (*they despise pleasure, but are cowardly in pain; they are indifferent to fame, but infamy breaks their spirit*), and we try to gain honour by false pretences. Virtue will not be wooed but for her own sake, and if we sometimes borrow her mask for some other purpose, she will very soon snatch it from our face. When the soul is once steeped in it, the dye is strong and vivid, and will not go without taking the skin with it. Wherefore, to judge a man, we must long and carefully follow his traces. If constancy does not stand firm and wholly on its own foundation, *if the path of life has not been well considered and preconcerted* (CICERO); if changing circumstances make him alter his pace (I should say his route, for the pace may be accelerated or retarded by them), let him go: that man will go *A vau le vent* (down the wind), as the motto of our Talebot has it.[4]

It is no wonder, says an ancient writer,[5] that chance has so great a hold over us, since we live by chance. Unless a man has directed his life as a whole to a certain fixed goal, he cannot possibly dispose his particular actions. Unless he have an image of the whole in his mind, he cannot possibly arrange the pieces. How can a painter lay in a stock of colours, if he knows not what he is going to paint? No man draws a definite outline of his life, and we only think it out in details. The archer must first know at what he is aiming, and then accommodate his hand, his bow, the string, the arrow, and his movements, accordingly. Our plans go wrong because they have neither aim nor direction. No wind serves the ship that has no port of destination.

I cannot agree with those judges who, on the strength of seeing one of his tragedies, declared in favour of Sophocles, when accused by his son of being incapable of managing his domestic affairs. Nor do I hold with the conclusions arrived at by the Parians who were sent to reform the Milesians. Visiting the island, they remarked the best-cultivated lands and the best-kept country-houses, and made a note of

4 *Our* Talebot. Montaigne is probably referring to the Earl of Shrewsbury, who was killed quite near to his château of Montaigne. In the next chapter he refers to *our* Germans, meaning the German troops who were quartered in his neighbourhood.

5 Seneca.

their owners; and then, having called an assembly o the citizens in the town, they appointed these owner the new governors and magistrates, concluding that being careful of their private affairs, they would b equally careful of those of the public.

We are all made up of bits, and so shapelessly and diversely put together, that every piece, at every moment, plays its own game. And there is as much difference between us and ourselves, as between us and others. *Be sure that it is very difficult to be always the same man* (SENECA). Since ambition can teach a man valour, temperance, and liberality, yea and justice too since greed can implant in the heart of a shop apprentice, bred up in obscurity and neglect, the confidence to entrust himself, so far from the domestic hearth, to the mercy of the waves and angry Neptune in a frail bark; since it teaches also discretion and prudence; and since Venus herself can pu resolution and temerity into the boy who is still under the discipline of the rod, and embolden the heart o the tender virgin in her mother's arms,

With Love for guide,
Alone the maid steps o'er her prostrate guards,
And steals by night into the young man's arms;

TIBULLUS

it is not enough for a sober understanding to judge u simply by our external actions: we must sound the innermost recesses, and observe the springs which give the swing. But since it is a high and hazardous undertaking, I would rather that fewer people meddled with it.

Of drunkenness

The world is all variety and dissimilarity. Vices are all alike in that they are all vices; and that is perhaps how the Stoics understand it. But though they are equally vices, they are not equal vices. And it is not to be believed that he who has crossed the bounds

> Beyond the which no right path can be found,
>
> HORACE

a hundred paces, is in no worse condition than he who has gone but ten; nor is it to be believed that sacrilege is no worse than the theft of a cabbage out of our garden:

> Nor can right reason prove the crime the same
> To rob a garden, and, by fear unawed,
> To steal by night the sacred things of God.
>
> HORACE

In this there is as great diversity as in anything else.

It is dangerous to confuse the order and the measure of sins. The murderer, the traitor, and the tyrant would get off too easily. It is not in reason that they should soothe their conscience with the excuse that some other man is idle, or lascivious, or less assiduous in his devotions. Every man weighs down his neighbour's sin, and makes light of his own. Even our teachers often range them badly, in my opinion.

As Socrates said that the principal office of wisdom

is to distinguish between goods and evils, we others, the best of us being ever in a state of sin, should say the same of the knowledge which distinguishes the different sins; for, unless it be very exact, the virtuous and the wicked will remain confounded and undistinguished.

Now drunkenness, among the others, appears to me a gross and brutish vice. In others the mind has more share: in some vices there is something we may call generous. Some are blended with knowledge, diligence, valour, prudence, skill, and refinement, but drunkenness is all of the body and the earth. And the only nation in the present day among whom it is held in honour is at the same time the grossest. The other vices impair the understanding: this overturns it, and dulls the body.

When the strong wine has entered into man . . .
There follows then a heaviness of limbs,
A tangle of the legs as round he reels,
A stuttering tongue, an intellect besoaked,
Eyes all aswim, and hiccups, shouts and brawls.

LUCRETIUS

The worst state of man is when he loses the knowledge and control of himself. And among other appropriate things they say that, just as must, seething in a vessel, drives all the lees from the bottom to the top, so does wine, in those who have drunk to excess, uncork the most intimate secrets.

You make the sage forget his care,
His bosom's inmost thoughts lay bare,
And drown his solemn-faced pretence
Beneath your blithesome influence. HORACE

Josephus tells us how he wormed out the secrets of a certain ambassador sent to him by the enemy, by making him drink too much. And yet Augustus, though he confided his most private affairs to Lucius Piso, who conquered Thrace, was never mistaken in him; nor was Tiberius in Cossus, to whom he disburdened himself of all his plans; and yet we know them both to have been so addicted to wine, that they had often to be carried drunk out of the Senate-house.

> His veins were swelled with wine of yesterday.
>
> VIRGIL

And Cimber, who was often intoxicated, was as confidently entrusted with the design of killing Caesar, as Cassius, a water-drinker; as to which he made the witty reply: 'What, I carry a tyrant, who am unable to carry my wine!' We see our Germans, drenched with wine, remembering their quarters, their watchword, and their rank.[1]

> Though soaked in wine and reeling drunk,
> No easy task it is to vanquish them. JUVENAL

I could not have believed in a drunkenness so profound, so dead and senseless, if I had not read the following in history: that Attalus, having invited to supper, with intent to put a singular indignity upon him, that same Pausanias who, for the same reason afterwards killed Philip, King of Macedon (a king whose fine qualities testified to his upbringing in the house and company of Epaminondas), made him drink so much that he could senselessly abandon his

1 Our Germans; that is, the foreign mercenaries encamped in his neighbourhood during the civil wars.

beauty, as any hedge-side drab might do her body, to the muleteers and a number of low-born slaves of his household.

And I have been told by a lady whom I hold in singular honour and esteem, that near Bordeaux, towards Castres, where she has her house, a woman of the village, a widow of chaste repute, feeling the first inklings of pregnancy, told her neighbours that she might think she was with child if she had a husband; but when from day to day her suspicion grew into evident certainty, she went so far as to authorize the priest to announce from the pulpit that, if any man should avow himself privy to the deed, she promised to pardon and, if he approved, marry him. A young labourer in her service, emboldened by this proclamation, declared that he had found her one holiday so much under the influence of wine, so fast asleep, and in so indecent a posture by her fireside, that he had been able to ravish without awakening her. They are still living as man and wife.

It is certain that in ancient times this vice was not greatly decried. Several philosophers even touch upon it very tenderly in their writings, and some of the Stoics even advise an occasional excess in wine, even to intoxication, in order to relax the mind.

They say in this too, Socrates the wise,
And great in virtue's combats, bore the prize.

CORNELIUS GALLUS

Cato, the censor and corrector of others, has been blamed for hard drinking:

And even old Cato's worth, we know,
Took from good wine a nobler glow. HORACE

One of the reasons why Cyrus, so renowned a king, claimed to be a better man than his brother Artaxerxes, was that he was a much better drinker. And among the best regulated and governed nations this drink test was very prevalent. I have heard Silvius, an eminent Paris physician, say that to keep the digestive powers from becoming sluggish, it is a good thing, once a month, to prod and rouse them up by this excess, lest they should grow dull.

And we read that the Persians discussed their most important affairs after wine.

My taste and constitution are more hostile to this vice than my reason. For, besides that I am inclined to bow to the authority of the ancients, I certainly look upon it as a weak and stupid vice, but less hurtful and mischievous than the others, which almost all, and more directly, offend public society. And if, as they hold, we cannot take any pleasure but at some cost to ourselves, I am of opinion that this vice costs our conscience less than the others, besides that it is not difficult to get at and to satisfy: a consideration not to be despised.

A man, well advanced in years and dignity, said to me that he counted this among the three main comforts that remained to him in life. And where can a man more justly expect to find comfort than in the natural pleasures? But he looked at it from the wrong point of view. Delicacy and a careful choice of wines is to be avoided. If your pleasure depends upon your drinking to please your palate, you condemn yourself to the penance of sometimes drinking an unpalatable sort. Our taste should be freer and more easily pleased: a good toper should have a less delicate palate. The Germans will drink almost any wine with equal pleasure, their object being to pour it dow rather than to taste it. They have the better bargair Their pleasure is more copious and near at hand.

Secondly, to drink after the French fashion, at th two meals and in moderation, is to restrict to narrowly the favours of the god. It needs more tim and more application. The ancients spent whol nights in this practice, often extending their potation to the following day. So we should establish our habit on a broader and firmer basis.

I have seen a great lord of my time, a man who ha done great things and earned fame by his successe who drank, without any effort and in the course of hi ordinary meals, seldom less than twenty bottles c wine. And on leaving off was only too wary an knowing, as we knew to our cost.

The pleasure which we account worth while in th course of our life, should take up more of our tim Like the shop-assistant and the labouring man w should neglect no opportunity to drink, and have th desire always in our mind. It seems to me that we ar every day curtailing the indulgence of it; and that th luncheons, snacks, and collations which I rememb in my boyhood, were much more frequent and usu in our houses than they are now. Can it be that i some things we are in the way of improvemen Truly, no. But the fact is that we are much mor given to lechery than our fathers. These are tw occupations that thwart one another in their vigou On the one hand, lechery has weakened ou stomachs, and, on the other, sobriety helps to mak us more spruce and more wanton in the exercis of love.

Wonderful are the tales I have heard my fath

elate of the chastity of the times in which he lived. He was well qualified to speak of it, being well fitted, both by nature and training, for intercourse with ladies. He spoke little and well, and his language was besides sprinkled with picturesque expressions derived from books written in the vulgar tongues, especially Spanish; and among the Spanish his usual reading was that which they call *Marcus Aurelius*.[2]

He bore himself with a pleasing, humble, and very modest gravity. He was singularly careful of neatness and propriety in his person and dress, whether mounted or on foot. He was wonderfully punctilious in keeping his word; conscientious and scrupulous in general to the point of superstition.

For a man of low stature he was very strong, with an upright and well-proportioned figure. Of a pleasing countenance, and a complexion inclining to brown. Nimble and excelling in all kinds of gentlemanly exercises. I still remember seeing some canes filled with lead, with which they tell me he used to exercise his arms when training to throw the bar or the stone, or for fencing; as well as shoes with leaded soles, to make him lighter for running or leaping. Of his vaulting they remember little wonders. I have seen him, when past sixty, putting our agility to shame by

The vulgar tongues, i.e., the modern languages, as distinct from Latin. *The Golden Book of Marcus Aurelius* was the best-known work of Antonio de Guevara (1490–1545), an historical romance based on the life of that Emperor which, in North's translation, became extremely popular in England. The style resembles what we call Euphuism, which has also been called Guevarism. We see reflections of it in Shakespeare, especially in *Love's Labour's Lost*.

leaping into the saddle in his furred gown, making th round of the table on his thumb,[3] and scarcely eve mounting the stairs to his room without taking thre or four steps at a time.

In the matter I am speaking of he declared that i the whole of a province there was scarcely one woma of quality with an evil reputation. He would tell c strange intimacies, especially his own, with hones women, quite above suspicion. And he solemnl swore of himself, that he was a virgin when h married. Yet he had taken part for a considerabl period in the wars beyond the mountains, of which h has left a journal written in his own hand, giving a the details of what happened there, both of genera interest and concerning himself in particular.

He consequently married when he was well on i years, at the age of thirty-three, in the year 1528, o his way home from Italy. Let us return to our bottles.

The discomforts of old age, which has need of som support and refreshment, might reasonably beget i me a desire for this faculty of drinking. For it is, w might say, the last pleasure that the course of year robs us of.

The natural heat, so the good fellows say, begins i the feet: that concerns infancy. From thence it mount to the middle regions, where it long takes root an produces, in my opinion, the only true pleasures of th

3 This feat has greatly exercised the commentators, some c whom suggest impossibilities. What Montaigne reall meant must be left to conjecture.

4 A humorous variant of a favourite phrase of Rabelais *revenons à nos moutons*, which occurs in the old farce c *Maître Pathelin*.

bodily life. The other pleasures are comparatively dormant. Towards the end, like a rising and exhaling vapour, it arrives at the gullet, which it makes its final resting-place.

I cannot, however, understand how a man can prolong the pleasure of drinking beyond his thirst, and forge in his imagination an artificial and unnatural appetite. My stomach could not go to those lengths: it has enough to do to deal with what it takes for its need. By disposition I care not to drink except after eating, consequently my last draught is almost always the biggest.

And since in old age our palate is thickened with phlegm or depraved by some ailment, wine tastes the better if our pores are washed and opened; at least it rarely happens that I really relish the first draught.

Anacharsis wondered at the Greeks drinking from larger glasses at the end than at the beginning of their meals; they did it, I imagine, for the same reason that the Germans do it, who then begin their drinking contests.

Plato forbids the use of wine by children before they are eighteen years of age, and intoxication before the age of forty. But after they have passed that age, he orders them to take a pleasure in it, and to mingle copiously with their convivialities the influence of Dionysus, the kind god who restores cheerfulness to men and youth to the aged, who softens and melts the passions of the soul, as iron is melted by fire. In his *Laws* he declares these convivial gatherings to have their use, provided there be a master of the feast to enforce rule and restraint; intoxication being, he says, a good and certain test of every man's nature, and at the same time calculated to put heart into the elderly and give them a delight in dancing and music: wholesome pleasures which they dare not indulge in when sober. He adds that wine is capable of making the soul mellow and the body healthy.

He approves, however, the following restrictions, in part borrowed from the Carthaginians: That no wine be drunk on warlike expeditions; That every judge and magistrate abstain from it when about to enter on his duties, and before discussing public business; That we shall not spend the day over it, a time due to other occupations, nor the night which we have reserved for procreation.

It is said that the philosopher Stilpo, weighed down by old age, purposely hastened his end by drinking his wine unmixed. A like cause, but not of his own design, also extinguished the vital spark of the philosopher Arcesilaus, when broken by old age.

But it is an old and absurd question, 'Whether the soul of the wise man is of a nature to yield to the strength of wine?'

Should we lay siege to wisdom's stronghold?

HORACE

To what absurdity are we not driven by our self-conceit! The best-regulated soul in the world is hard put to it to keep her feet, and to guard against being thrown to earth through her own weakness. Not one in a thousand is erect and sober for an instant in life. And it may be doubted if, in her natural state, she can ever be so. But if she be steadfast she will attain to the highest state of perfection; provided, I mean, that she be subjected to no shock, which may happen in a thousand ways.

Much good did Lucretius, that great poet, get from

his philosophy and his strength of mind, when behold him maddened by a love-philtre! Do you think that Socrates could not be floored by a fit of apoplexy, as well as any porter? Some, under the influence of a malady, have even forgotten their own names, and a slight wound has turned the judgement of others topsy-turvy. Let him be as wise as he will he is after all a man, and what can be imagined more crazy, more miserable, and insignificant? Wisdom does not master our natural disposition:

Sweats and pallors spread
Over the body, and the tongue is broken,
And fails the voice away, and ring the ears;
Mists blind the eyeballs, and the joints collapse, –
Aye, men drop dead from terror of the mind.

LUCRETIUS

He has to blink his eyes when threatened by a blow; he has to quake like a child on the brink of a precipice, Nature having reserved to herself those slight marks of her authority, which are proof against our reason and stoic virtue, to teach man his mortality and frailty. He turns pale with fear, red with shame: a sharp attack of the colic will make him, if not shout with despair, at least utter a broken and muffled groan:

From human ills he shall not be exempt.[5]

TERENCE

The poets, who invent all things to suit their

5 *Humani a se nihil alienum putet*: a perversion, to suit the context, of the well-known line, *Homo sum; humani nil a me alienum puto*, 'I am human, and interested in everything human.'

humour, dare not even acquit their heroes of the weakness of tears:

> Weeping he speaks, and gives his fleet the rein.
>
> VIRGIL

Let it be enough if a man curbs and moderates his inclinations, for it is not in him to banish them. Even our Plutarch, so perfect and excellent a judge of human actions, seeing Brutus and Torquatus kill their children, begins to doubt whether virtue could go to such lengths, and whether those men were not rather stirred by some other passion. All actions exceeding the ordinary bounds are liable to a sinister interpretation, seeing that we cannot appreciate what is above us any more than what is beneath us.

We may leave aside that other sect that openly professes a proud spirit,[6] but when, even in that sect which is regarded as the more effeminate,[6] we hear these braggings of Metrodorus: *I have anticipated and caught you, Fortune; I have cut off every access, so that you cannot reach me* (Cicero); When Anaxarchus, lying in a stone trough by command of Nicocreon, tyrant of Cyprus, and belaboured to death with an iron mallet, cries unceasingly, 'Strike, break; it is not Anaxarchus but his shell that you are pounding'; When we hear our martyrs, in the midst of the flames, crying to their tyrant, 'This side is sufficiently roasted; slice it, eat it, it is well done; begin on the other side'; When we hear that boy in Josephus, his flesh torn to pieces by biting pincers, and pierced by the bodkins of Antiochus, still defying him and crying with a firm and assured voice, 'Tyrant, you are wasting your

6 The Stoics and the Epicureans, respectively.

time, I am still at my ease; where is that pain, where are those tortures you threaten me with? Is this all you can do? My fortitude pains you more than your cruelty does me. O poor weakling! you are giving way, and I am growing stronger; make me complain, make me yield, if you can; put heart into your satellites and executioners: see, they are losing courage, they cannot stand it; arm them, stir them up!' When we see all this, we must truly admit that there is some derangement, a sort of frenzy in these souls, how holy soever.

When we come to these stoic outbursts: *I had rather be mad than voluptuous*, a saying of Antisthenes; When Sextius tells us that he would rather be fettered with pain than with sensuality; When Epicurus tries to think he is caressed by his gout, and, refusing health and repose, defies his ills with a gay heart; and when, despising the less acute pains, disdaining to battle and struggle with them, he wishes and calls for others more violent, more painful, more worthy of him,

No more
He heeds such timid prey, but longs to hear
The tawny lion, issuing with a roar
From forth the lofty hills, or front the
foaming boar,

VIRGIL

who will not conclude that these are outbursts of a courage thrown off its balance?

Our soul cannot from her seat reach to such a height. She must quit it and rise, and, taking the bit between her teeth, forcibly carry her man so far, that he will afterwards be astounded at his own deeds. So, in the exploits of war, the generous soldier is often impelled in the heat of combat to deeds of so perilous a nature that, having come to himself, he is the first to be struck with amazement.

And so the poet is often rapt in admiration of his own work, no longer recognizing the track along which he ran so fine a race: in him also we call it madness and frenzy. And as Plato says that in vain does a sober-minded man knock at the door of poetry so Aristotle says that no mind of any eminence is free from a tinge of madness. And he is right in calling madness every transport, however admirable, that transcends our reason and judgement; seeing that wisdom is a well-ordered government of our soul carried out with measure and proportion, for which she is responsible to herself.

Plato argues thus: 'that the power of prophecy is above us; that we must be beside ourselves when we exercise it: our sober senses must be clouded either by sleep or by some malady, or lifted from its place in a heavenly rapture.'

Of conscience

Travelling one day, my brother the Sieur de la Brousse and I, during our civil wars, we met with a gentleman of good presence. He was of the opposite faction to ours, but I had no inkling of it, for he pretended to be other than he was; and the worst of these wars is that the cards are so shuffled, your enemy being distinguished from you by no apparent mark, either of language or demeanour, having been brought up under the same laws and customs, and breathing the same atmosphere, that it is difficult to avoid confusion and disorder. This consideration made me afraid, for my own part, of meeting our troops in a place where I was not known, lest I might be placed in the predicament of telling my name or perhaps of incurring some worse danger. As it had befallen me before; for, in a misunderstanding of that kind, I lost both men and horses, and among others a page of mine, a young Italian of gentle birth, whom I was carefully bringing up, was miserably killed; in him died a very fair youth and of great promise.

But this man, every time we met with mounted men or passed through a town that held with the King, was so desperately afraid and looked so dead, that I at length guessed that it was his conscience that was giving him so much alarm. The poor man seemed to fear that the secret intentions of his heart could be read through his disguise and in spite of the crosses on his cassock. So wonderful is the power of conscience! It makes us betray, accuse, and fight against ourselves, and, for want of outside testimony, witness against ourselves.

> The tortured mind is struck by invisible scourges.
>
> JUVENAL

This tale is in the mouth of children: Bessus, a Paeonian, rebuked for having wantonly knocked down a sparrow's nest and killed the young, said that he had good reason to do so, because these fledglings would keep on accusing him falsely of the murder of his father. This parricide had hitherto lain secret and unknown, but the Furies, conscience's avengers, made him who was to bear the penalty of it bring it to the light of day.

Hesiod amends the saying of Plato, 'that punishment follows close on the heels of sin'; for he says, 'it is born at the same instant as the sin'. He who expects punishment, suffers it; he who has deserved it expects it. Wickedness forges torments against itself:

> He suffers most who plans the evil deed;
>
> *Proverb quoted by* AULUS GELLIUS

as the wasp stings and hurts others, but herself most for she loses her sting and power for ever;

> And in the wound lays down her very life.
>
> VIRGIL

The Spanish fly has something about it which, by a contrariety of nature, acts as an antidote to its own poison. So, while we take a pleasure in vice conscience at the same time breeds a contrary displeasure which torments us, both waking and sleeping, with many painful reflections:

> For many, often babbling in their dreams,
> Or else in sickness raving, have been known
> To drag to light of day long-hidden crimes.
>
> LUCRETIUS

Apollodorus dreamt that he was being flayed by the Scythians, then boiled in a cauldron, and that his heart was murmuring: 'I am the cause of all these thy woes.' No hiding-place will serve the wicked, says Epicurus, for they cannot be sure of being hid, whilst their conscience discovers them to themselves:

> This is the first revenge: himself being judge
> No guilty man will ever be acquitted.
>
> JUVENAL

As conscience fills us with fear, so does it also fill us with assurance and confidence. And I may say that I have walked in many perils with a much firmer step by reason of the secret knowledge I had of my own will and the innocence of my intentions:

> As a man's conscience is, so hope within
> Or fear prevails, according to his deeds.
>
> OVID

Of numerous examples three may suffice, of the same man: Scipio, being one day arraigned before the Roman people on a serious charge, instead of excusing himself or flattering his judges, said: 'It will become you well to sit in judgement on the head of the man by whose means you have power to judge the whole world!' And on another occasion, instead of pleading his cause, all the answer he made to the imputation cast upon him by a tribune of the people was: 'Come, my citizens, let us go and give thanks to the gods for the victory they granted me over the Carthaginians upon such a day as this;' and behold him striding off to the temple with the whole assembly and the accuser himself at his heels!

And when Petilius, instigated by Cato, demanded of him an account of the money that passed through his hands in the province of Antioch, Scipio, having come into the Senate for that purpose, produced the book of accounts which he had under his toga, wherein he said his receipts and disbursements were accurately entered. But, being required to give it into the hands of the registrar, he refused, saying he would not have this shame put upon him, and with his own hands, in the presence of the Senate, he tore it in pieces. I do not believe that a cauterized soul could have counterfeited such assurance. He had a heart too big by nature and his lot had been cast in too high a place, says Livy, that he should play the part of a criminal and stoop so far as to defend his innocence.

The invention of tortures is a dangerous invention; they seem to be a test of endurance rather than of truth. He who can endure them conceals the truth as well as he who cannot. For why should pain rather make me confess what is, than force me to say what is not? And, on the other hand, if the man who has not done what he is accused of has the patience to suffer these tortures, why should not the guilty man have that patience, being offered so fair a reward as life?

I believe that the idea underlying the use of torture is the power of conscience. For in the guilty man conscience would seem to assist the rack to make him confess his guilt, and to weaken him; and on the other hand to fortify the innocent man against the torture. To tell the truth, it is a practice fraught with uncertainty and danger. What would we not say, what would we not do, to escape such cruel pains?

> Pain will force the innocent to lie.
>
> PUBLIUS SYRUS

The effect is that the man whom the judge has put to the torture, that he may not die innocent, is made to die both innocent and tortured. Thousands and thousands have, by means of torture, loaded their heads with false confessions. Among these I place Philotas, considering the circumstances of Alexander's accusations against him, and the progress of his tortures.

And yet it has been said that it is the least evil that weak human nature has been able to invent. Very inhumanly, however, and very little to the purpose, to my mind.[1]

Many nations, less barbarous in this respect than the Greeks and Romans who call them so, esteem it cruel and horrible to torture and pull a man to pieces for a crime of which they are still in doubt. How can he help your ignorance? Are you not unjust when, because you will not kill him without cause, you do worse than kill him? That that is so, consider how often he would rather die without cause than undergo that ordeal which is more painful than the execution, and which often by its ruthlessness anticipates the execution and accomplishes it.

I do not know whence I had this story, but it exactly reflects the conscience of our justice. A village woman accused a soldier before an army-general, a great lover

1 The '*question*' was not abolished in France till 1789.

of justice, of having snatched from her little children the little broth that she had left to sustain them with, the army having pillaged all the villages round about. Of proof she had none. The general, after charging the woman to take good heed to what she was saying, since if she lied she would be guilty of false witness, and she still persisting, he commanded the soldier's stomach to be opened to find out the truth of the matter. And the woman was found to be in the right. An instructive sentence![2]

2 The story is to be found in Froissart, iv. 87. The general was Bajazet I, Turkish Sultan (fourteenth century).

Of rewarding honour

They who write the life of Augustus Caesar observe this point in his military discipline, that he was wonderfully free of gifts to those who deserved them, but that he was just as sparing of mere rewards of honour. And yet he himself had all the military honours showered upon him by his uncle before he had ever been in war.

It was a pretty idea, and has been accepted in most of the governments of the world, to institute certain empty and valueless marks as an honour and reward of virtue, such as wreaths of laurel, oak, and myrtle, a garment fashioned in a certain way, the privilege of riding through the town in a coach or of being preceded by a torch by night, some particular seat in the public assemblies, the prerogative of bearing certain surnames and titles, a certain distinction in the coat of arms, and similar things, which have prevailed and still prevail in different degrees according to the notions prevalent in different nations.

We have for our share, like several of our neighbours, the orders of knighthood which have been founded for this purpose alone. It is in truth a very good and profitable custom to find means of recognizing the worth of men of distinction and eminence, and to please and satisfy them by payments which are no charge on the public and cost the Prince nothing. And there is good reason and justification for what has always been known by long experience in ancient times, and was formerly observed among ourselves, namely, that people of quality were more jealous of such rewards than of those which were attended by gain and profit. If with the prize, which should be purely one of honour, are mingled wealth and other advantages, this mingling, instead of augmenting its value, lessens and degrades it.

The order of Saint Michael,[1] which has so long been held in repute with us, had this advantage above all others, that it was accompanied by no other advantage. With the result that formerly there was no office or rank, of whatever nature, to which the nobility aspired with so great longing and desire as this order, and no quality that carried with it more respect and dignity: since virtue is more inclined to aspire to and embrace a reward that is purely due to it alone, and is attended by glory rather than profit. For indeed other gifts have not the same dignity, seeing that they are bestowed for all kinds of reasons. With money we pay for the services of a valet, the assiduity of a courier, for dancing, vaulting, speaking, and the meanest offices that we receive: nay, even vice is paid for, flattery, pandering, treachery. It is small wonder if virtue is less ready to desire and receive this kind of common coin, than that which is proper and peculiar to it, and altogether noble and generous. Augustus was right to be more sparing and niggardly of this than of the other, seeing that honour is a privilege that derives its chief essence from its rarity; and virtue the same:

1 It must be remembered that Montaigne was a knight of this order.

If you think none are bad, then how
can one be good?

MARTIAL

We do not particularly commend a man for his care in rearing his children, since that is an ordinary action, however right it may be; no more do we admire a tall tree in a forest of tall trees. I do not think that any citizen of Sparta took any credit to himself for his valour, for that was a universal quality in that nation; and he gloried as little in his contempt of riches, and his fidelity. No reward accrues to a virtue, however great, that has passed into a custom; and I know not withal whether we should ever call it great if it were common to all.

Since therefore these distinctions are only prized or esteemed because few enjoy them, it only needs to be lavish of them to bring them to naught. Even though there might be more men deserving our order than there were in former times, yet there was no need to lower it in estimation. And it may easily be that more are deserving of it; for there is no virtue that so easily spreads as military valour.

There is another virtue, true, perfect, and philosophic, of which I do not speak (and I use the word in our acceptation), very much greater and fuller, which is a strength and assurance of soul that equally despises all kinds of adverse fortunes, equable, uniform, constant, of which ours is but a very poor reflection. Use, education, example, and habit can do all that they will in establishing this I speak of, and easily make it common, as the experience afforded by our civil wars has made manifest enough. And if any man could unite us at this hour, and rouse up the whole of our nation to one common enterprise, our old military reputation would again flourish as before.

It is very certain that this order was in times past not bestowed as a reward of virtue alone; it looked further. It was never a payment of a gallant soldier, but of a leader of renown. The quality of obedience did not merit so honourable a wage. In former times they required a more universal expert knowledge of warfare, comprising the most and the greatest qualities of a soldier – *the qualities of a soldier are not the same as those of a general* (LIVY); and that he should be besides of a rank befitting so great a dignity. But, as I say, though more men should be found worthy of it than formerly, it should not be for that reason more freely bestowed; and it would have been better to fall short in not bestowing it on all to whom it was due, than to lose for ever, as we have recently done, the advantage of so useful an institution.

No man of spirit deigns to plume himself on what he has in common with many; and the men of today who have least merited this reward make more show of disdaining it, in order thereby to be ranked with those who have been wronged by the unmerited diffusion and degradation of this distinction which was their particular due.[2]

Now to expect, by obliterating and abolishing this order, immediately to renew and restore to honour an institution of the same kind, is to expect a thing not likely to occur in so licentious and sick a period as the present one; and it may happen that the latest[3] will

2 It seems that the Order of St Michael came to be called '*le collier à toutes bêtes*'.

3 The Order of the Holy Ghost, instituted by Henri III in

incur, from its very initiation, the disadvantages which have just ruined the other. The rules for the distribution of this new order would need to be extremely tightened and restricted, if it is to enjoy any consideration; and this tumultuous period is not capable of being kept under a short and steady rein. Besides that, before this can be brought into repute, it is necessary that the memory of the first, and the contempt into which it has fallen, should pass away.

This might be a fitting occasion to discuss valour, and how this virtue differs from others; but as Plutarch has often touched upon this theme, it would be a vain meddling in me to repeat here what he has said on the subject. But it is worthy of consideration that our nation has given to valour (*vaillance*) the first rank among the virtues, as indicated by its name, which comes from *valeur* (worth); and that, according to our usage, when we say of a man that he is very worthy (*qu'il vaut beaucoup*), that he is a worthy man (*un homme de bien*), in the style of our court and our nobility, it means no other than that he is a valiant man (*un homme vaillant*), somewhat after the Roman fashion; for with them the general appellation of virtue (*virtus*) takes its etymology from strength.[4] The proper and only and essential place for the nobility in France is in the military profession.

It is probable that this was the first virtue that

1578. It appears from Brantôme that Montaigne's fears were only too well justified.

4 Montaigne evidently means that *virtus* is derived from *vis*, strength, which seems not far from the truth, although modern etymologists derive it from *vir*, man.

manifested itself in man, and gave to one man an advantage over another, enabling the strongest and bravest to become master of the weaker, and acquire a particular rank and reputation; wherefore it was dignified in speech with that honourable name. Or perhaps it was that among the very warlike nations the prize and the most worthy appellation was given to the quality that was most familiar to them.

In the same way our passion and the feverish solicitude we have for the chastity of our women has brought it about that when we speak of 'a good woman' (*une bonne femme*), 'an honest and virtuous woman' (*une femme d'honneur et de vertu*), we mean in fact no more than a 'chaste woman' (*une femme chaste*); as if, to keep them to that duty, we were indifferent to all the others, and left them a free rein to commit any other fault, on condition that they never commit this.

Of the affection of fathers for their children

To Madame d'Estissac

Madame, if strangeness and novelty, for which things are usually prized, do not save me, I shall never come off with honour out of this foolish undertaking;[1] but it is so fantastic an idea, and so out of the common, that that itself will perhaps enable it to pass. It was a melancholy humour, and consequently a humour very inimical to my natural disposition, brought about by the brooding solitude into which I was plunged a few years ago, that first put into my head this idle fancy of meddling with writing. And then, finding myself empty and totally destitute of any other matter, I offered myself for the subject-matter of my essays. It is the only book of its kind in the world, wildly and extravagantly planned. So there is nothing noteworthy in this business but its oddness; for the best craftsman in the world would have been baffled to shape a matter so mean and unsubstantial in such a way as to deserve consideration.

Now, Madame, having decided to draw a lifelike portrait of myself, I should have neglected an important feature if I had failed to depict upon it the honour I have ever paid to your deserts. And I wished to declare it explicitly at the head of this chapter, the more so as among your other good qualities the love

1 Of writing the Essays, or perhaps, of portraying himself.

you have shown to your children ranks among the first. One who knows at what age you were left a widow by Monsieur d'Estissac, your husband, the great and honourable proposals that have been made to you, which are as many as have been made to any lady of your condition in France, the constancy and fortitude with which you have sustained, through so many years and so many thorny difficulties, the burdensome conduct of their affairs, which have driven you about from one corner of France to another, and still hold you besieged, the happy guidance you have given them by your wisdom alone or your good fortune, will readily agree with me that there is no more conspicuous example of maternal affection to be seen in our days than yours.

I thank God, Madame, that it has been so well applied; for the great promises that your son, Monsieur d'Estissac,[2] gives of himself, are a sufficient guarantee that, when he comes of age, you will reap the obedience and gratitude of a very good son. But since, by reason of his boyish years, he has not been capable of noticing the many and very great services for which he is beholden to you, I wish, if these writings should one day fall into his hands, when I shall no longer have the mouth and speech to express it, that he should receive from me this very true testimony, which will be still more strongly evidenced by the good results which, if it please God, will make him feel that there is not a gentleman in France who owes more to his mother than he; and that he cannot in future give a more certain proof of his goodness

2 Young M. d'Estissac, with several others, accompanied Montaigne on his travels in 1580.

and virtue, than by his acknowledgement of the same.

If there be a real law of Nature, that is to say any instinct that is universally and permanently rooted in animals and men (which is not beyond dispute), I may say that, in my opinion, next to the anxiety for self-preservation and avoiding what is harmful, which is possessed by every animal, the affection which the begetter has for his offspring takes the second place. And, because Nature seems to have recommended to us this affection, looking to the extension and advance of the successive parts of this her machine, it is not to be wondered at if the love of children towards their parents, since it goes backwards, is not so great.

To which may be added that other Aristotelian consideration, that the man who benefits another loves him better than he is loved by the other; and that he to whom a thing is owing loves better than he who owes. Every artisan loves his work better than he would be loved by the work if it had feeling; since being is a thing to be cherished, and being consists in motion and action. Wherefore everyone in some sort lives in his work. He who benefits another does a beautiful and worthy deed; he who receives, only a useful one.[3] Now the useful is much less to be loved than the beautiful. The beautiful is stable and permanent, affording him who has exercised it a constant gratification. The useful is easily lost and escapes, nor is the memory of it

3 The benefited person stands to the benefactor in the relation of a work to the artist, and is regarded with feelings of affection. The benefactor associates an idea of the beautiful with the recipient of his good deeds; the other associates with him only an idea of the profitable. – ARISTOTLE, *Nicomachean Ethics*.

either so fresh or so pleasing. Those things are most dear to us that have cost us most; and it is more difficult to give than to take.

Since it has pleased God to endow us with some capacity for reason, in order that we may not, like the beasts, be slavishly subject to the common laws, but rather that we should adapt ourselves to them by exercising our judgement and free will, we ought indeed to yield a little to the simple authority of Nature, without being tyrannically carried away by her; reason alone should guide our inclination.

As for me, my tastes are strangely blunted to those propensities which arise in us without the direction and mediation of our judgement. For example, on the subject I am speaking of, I cannot understand that passion for dandling scarcely born infants that have neither motion of soul nor recognizable shape of body, by which they can make themselves lovable. And I never willingly tolerated their being nursed in my presence.

A true and well-regulated affection should spring and increase as we come to know them; and then, if they are worthy of it, the natural propensity walking side by side with reason, we should cherish them with a truly paternal love; and, if they be not worthy, use the same judgement, ever submitting to reason, notwithstanding the force of Nature. Very often it is the other way, and we are generally more excited by the kickings, the silly, playful childish movements of our infants, than we are later by their grownup actions; just as if we loved them for our pastime, as if they were apes and not human beings. And many a man will liberally supply his children with toys who will be closefisted when it comes to incurring the least necessary expense after they have come to years of discretion. Nay, it would seem as if the jealousy we feel on seeing them make their appearance in society and enjoy life when we are about to quit it, makes us more close and reserved towards them. It vexes us to see them tread on our heels, as if to solicit us to depart. And if that is what we fear, since it is in the order of things that they cannot really be and live but at the expense of our being and our life, we should not meddle with being fathers.

For my part I think it cruelty and injustice not to receive them into a share and partnership of our goods, and admit them as companions in the understanding of our domestic affairs when they are capable of it; and not to retrench and restrict our comforts in order to provide for theirs, since we have begotten them to that end. It is not right that an old, broken-down, half-dead father should enjoy alone, in his chimney-corner, resources that would suffice for the advancement and maintenance of several children, and suffer them meanwhile to waste their best years for want of means to push themselves in public service and the notice of their fellow-men.

They are driven to the desperate course of seeking, by any means however wrong, to provide for their needs. In my time I have seen several young men of good family so addicted to larceny that no correction could turn them from it. I know one, well-connected, to whom, at the request of a brother of his, a very honourable and brave gentleman, I once spoke to that purpose. He answered me and confessed quite bluntly that he had been driven into that mire by the rigour and avarice of his father; but that now he was so accustomed to it that he could not keep out of it. He had just been caught pilfering the rings of a lady whose levee he, with many others, had been attending.

His case put me in mind of the story I had heard of another nobleman, who from the time of his youth had become so accustomed and so expert in this pretty business that, when he afterwards came into possession of his own property, although resolved to give up this traffic, if he happened to see something he had need of in a shop he was passing, he could not keep his hand from stealing it, on pain of having afterwards to send and pay for it. And I have seen several so habituated and hardened to this vice, that even among their fellows they would commonly purloin things they intended to give back.

I am a Gascon, and yet there is no vice I am so little skilled in as that. I hate it rather more by natural disposition than I condemn it in words. I do not, even in desire, deprive another of what is his. This province is indeed decried a little more in this repect than the other parts inhabited by the French people. Yet we have on divers occasions in our day seen men of good family in other provinces in the hands of justice, convicted of many horrible robberies.

I fear that for this disorder the avarice of fathers must in some sort be held responsible. And if they should answer me as a very sensible nobleman once did, 'that he saved up his money, not to derive any other use and enjoyment from it except to make himself honoured and sought after by his people; and that, age having deprived him of all other powers, it was his only remaining remedy for maintaining his authority in his family, and preventing his falling into contempt and disdain with all the world' (and indeed not only old age, but every kind of feebleness, according to Aristotle, is the promoter of avarice); that is something. But it is the physic for a disease of which the birth should be prevented.

A father is indeed miserable who holds the affection of his children only through the need they have of his assistance, if that may be called affection. He should make himself worthy of respect by his virtue and abilities, and worthy of love by his kindness and gentle manners. Even the ashes of a rich matter have their price; and we have been accustomed to hold in respect and reverence the bones and relics of persons of honour.

No old age can be so decrepit and musty in a person who has lived an honourable life, but it should be revered, especially by his children, whose minds he should have trained to their duty by reason, not by want and the need that they have of him, nor by harshness and compulsion:

He greatly errs who thinks a father's rule
Can be upheld with more stability
By stern, unbending measures than
By any loving kindness. TERENCE

I condemn all harsh measures in the bringing-up of a tender soul that is being trained for honour and freedom. There is a something that savours of slavishness in severity and compulsion; and I hold that what cannot be done by reason, by wisdom and tact, can never be done by force. I was brought up in that way. They tell me that in all my early childhood I did not taste the rod but twice, and very gently. I owed the same treatment to the children I have had. I lost them all as infants in their nurses' arms; but Leonor, an only daughter who escaped that misfortune, has reached the age of six years or more, without our ever employing for her guidance and for the chastisement of her childish faults (her mother's indulgence readily conforming thereto), any but words, and very gentle ones. And if I should be disappointed in my hopes of her, there are other causes enough to blame, without condemning my educational methods, which I know to be right and natural. I should in this respect have been much more scrupulous with boys, who are not so much born for service, and of a freer condition. I should have loved to make their hearts big with free and noble sentiments. I have never known any other effect of the rod but to render the soul more cowardly and more deceitfully obstinate.

Do we wish to be loved by our children? Would we take from them all occasions to desire our death (although no cause for so dreadful a desire can be either right or excusable – *no crime is founded on reason* (LIVY))? Let us reasonably furnish their lives with what is in our power. To do that we should not marry so young that our age will be almost confounded with theirs. For this inconvenience plunges us into many great difficulties. I refer specially to the nobility, who are of a leisurely condition, living, as they say, on their rents only. For in other classes where they have to earn their living, the plurality and company of children are an additional resource to the household, and so many new tools and instruments wherewith to grow rich.

I married at thirty-three, and concur in Aristotle's opinion, who is said to have recommended thirty-five. Plato would have nobody marry before thirty; but he rightly ridicules those who perform their connubial functions after fifty-five, and condemns their brood as unworthy to live and be fed.

Thales gave the truest limits, who as a young man replied to his mother who was urging him to marry, 'that it was too soon', and, when he was getting on in years, 'that it was too late'. We must deny opportuneness to every inopportune action.

The ancient Gauls[4] regarded it as a highly blameworthy action to have had knowledge of a woman before the age of twenty, and recommended especially those men who desired to be trained for warfare to preserve their virginity till they were well on in years, since courage is enfeebled and diverted by intercourse with women.

But married to a young and beauteous bride,
His courage melted in her sweet embrace;
And, in his babes now placing his chief pride,
Sad o'er the risks of war the sire and
husband sighed.

TASSO

Greek history observes of Jecus of Tarentum, of Chryso, of Astylus, Diopompus and others that, to keep their bodies in vigour and serviceable for the races in the Olympic games, for wrestling and other such exercises, they denied themselves, as long as there was need, any kind of sexual act.

Muley-Hassan, King of Tunis, the same whom the Emperor Charles the Fifth restored to his estates, upbraided the memory of his father Mahomet, for his frequent intercourse with women, calling him slack, effeminate, a child-maker.

4 The Germans, according to Caesar.

In a certain region of the Spanish Indies the men were not permitted to marry until after they were forty; and yet the girls were allowed to marry at ten.

For a gentleman of thirty-five it is too soon to make way for his son of twenty: he is yet able to cut a good figure both in warlike expeditions and at the court of his prince. He has need of all his resources, and he ought certainly to share them, but not to the extent of neglecting himself for another. And such a man may rightly make use of the answer that fathers usually have on their lips: 'I have no desire to undress until I go to bed'.

But a father, stricken with years and infirmities, barred by his weakness and poor health from the ordinary society of his fellow-men, wrongs himself and his family by brooding unprofitably over a great hoard of wealth. He has come to that state when, if he is wise, he will wish to strip, not to his shirt, but to a nice warm nightgown, to go to bed. The remaining pomps, for which he has no further use, he should willingly bestow on those to whom, by the order of Nature, they should belong. It is only right that he should leave to them the enjoyment which Nature denies him: otherwise he is surely moved by envy and malice.

The finest act of the Emperor Charles the Fifth was that, in imitation of some of the ancients of his own calibre, he had the discretion to see that reason sufficiently commands us to strip when our gowns become a burden and a hindrance, and to go to bed when our legs fail us. He resigned his possessions, his greatness, and his power to his son, when he felt himself failing in the strength and firmness necessary to conduct his affairs with the glory he had hitherto acquired.

Set free betimes the ageing nag, before
He strains his flanks, a laughing-stock for fools.

HORACE

This fault in a man of not being able to know himself betimes, and of being insensible to the impotence and the great changes that old age naturally brings with it, both to body and soul, affecting both equally, in my opinion (if indeed it does not affect the soul by more than half), has ruined the reputation of most of the great men of the world. I have in my time seen and intimately known persons of great authority who, as could very easily be seen, had strangely declined from that former efficiency which I knew of by the reputation they had thereby acquired in their best years. I could heartily, for the sake of their honour, have wished them comfortably retired to their homes, freed from public and military occupations which were grown too heavy for their shoulders.

I was at one time intimate with the family of a gentleman, a widower and very old, but still of a sufficiently green old age. This man had several marriageable daughters and a son already old enough to cut a figure: his house was in consequence burdened with many expenses and strange visitors. This gave him little pleasure, not only on the score of economy, but still more because, by reason of his age, he had adopted a manner of life far removed from ours. I said to him one day, rather boldly according to my wont, that it would be more befitting in him to yield place to us younger folk and leave his principal house (for this one alone was well situated and furnished) to his son, and retire to a neighbouring estate of his, where his repose would be undisturbed since he could not otherwise avoid our troublesome company, seeing the condition of his children. He afterwards took my advice and was the better for it.

I do not mean to say that we should give ou property up to them by means of a bond which canno be recalled. I, who am old enough to play this part would resign to them the enjoyment of my house and property, but with liberty to repent, if they should give me occasion. I should leave them the use thereof because it would be no longer convenient to me, bu would reserve to myself as much as I thought good o the management of affairs in general, having ever been of opinion that it must be a great satisfaction to an aged father, himself to put his children in the way o managing his affairs, and to have the power, during hi lifetime, of controlling their behaviour, giving them instruction and advice according to the experience he has of them, and of personally directing the ancien honour and order of his house in the hands of hi successors, and so make himself responsible for the hopes he may conceive of their future conduct.

And to this end I would not fly their company: would observe them near at hand and join, as far a my age would permit, in their mirth and thei pastimes. If I did not live in the midst of them (which I could not do without trespassing on their gatherings by reason of the peevishness of my old age and the exigencies of my infirmities, and without beside straining and breaking through the regularity of the habits and mode of living that I should then have adopted), I would at least live near them in a corner o my house, not the most showy, but the most comfortable.

I would not live like a certain Dean of Saint Hilary at oitiers whom I saw a few years ago, reduced to so reat solitude by his distressful melancholy that, at the ime when I entered his chamber, he had not moved a tep out of it for twenty-two years. And yet he was uite free and easy in his movements, his only ailment eing a cold in the stomach. Hardly once a week ould he permit anyone to come in to see him; he kept imself ever shut up in his room alone, except that a alet brought him food once a day; but he only came n and went out. His occupation consisted in walking o and fro, reading some book (for he had some slight nowledge of letters), obstinately resolved moreover n dying in this routine, as he did soon after.

I would endeavour, by kindness and familiarity, to ultivate in my children a strong and unfeigned ffection and goodwill towards myself. In well-born atures this is easy to win; for if they be furious brutes, hich our age produces in profusion, they should be ated and shunned as such.

I dislike the custom of not allowing the children to se the name of father, and expecting them to address im as if he were a stranger, as being more respectful; s if Nature had not usually provided us with ufficient authority. We call Almighty God Father, nd scorn to have our children call us so. I have re-ormed this error in my family.[5]

The last words appear to have been added by the literary executors. In this respect Montaigne must have followed the example of King Henri IV who 'did not wish his children to call him Monsieur, a name which seems to make strangers of them and is a mark of subjection, but Papa, a name full of love and tenderness'.

It is also foolish and wrong not to admit them t familiarity with their fathers when they are grown up and to try to maintain towards them an austere an scornful gravity, hoping thereby to keep them in aw and obedience. For that is a very futile pretence which makes fathers distasteful and, what is worse ridiculous to their children. They are in possession o youth and vigour, and consequently enjoy the good will and favour of the world; and receive with mocker those fierce and tyrannical looks of a man who has n longer any blood in his heart or his veins: regula scarecrows in a hempfield!

Even though I could inspire fear I would much rather inspire love.

There are so many kinds of faults in old age; there i so much helplessness; it is so fit a mark for contempt that the best thing we can gain is the love and affection of our family; command and fear are no longer ou weapons.

I have known one who in his youth had been kep under very strict control. Having come to man' estate, although in the best possible health, he strikes he bites, he swears: the most tempestuous master in France. He wears himself out with cares and vigilance It is all an amusing comedy, which his family even conspires to keep up. Of his storeroom and cellar, na of his purse too, others have the greater enjoyment whilst he guards the keys of them in his pouch as they were more precious to him than his eyes. Whils he is pleased with the economy and niggardliness o his table, in divers corners of his house there is nothin but dissipation, gambling and waste, attended with amusing tales of his vain choler and his parsimony Everyone is on guard against him. If by chance an wretched servant becomes attached to him, he immediately becomes an object of suspicion, a feeling at which old age is of itself ready to bite. How many times he has boasted to me how well he kept his people in hand, and of the strict obedience and reverence they paid him, and what a clear insight he had into his affairs!

Alone he knows not what goes on about him.

TERENCE

I know of no man who is better qualified, both by nature and training, to uphold the mastery than he, and yet he has fallen off from it like a child. Wherefore I have picked him out from amongst several I know in that condition, as the best example.

This might form the theme of a scholastic dispute, 'whether he is best thus or otherwise'. In his presence all bow and submit to him. They allow his fancied authority to run its course, without ever resisting it. They testify their assent, they fear him, they respect him, to his heart's content. Does he dismiss a servant? He packs up his bundle, and behold him gone! But only out of his sight. The steps of old age are so slow, its senses are so blurred, that he will continue to live and serve in the same house for a year without being perceived. And when the time is ripe, there will come letters from a distance, supplicating, cringing, full of promises to do better, on the strength of which he is received back into favour. Does Monsieur carry out some transaction or send some message they do not like? They suppress it and soon after invent reasons enough to excuse the lack of execution or of an answer. No letters from outside being first brought to him, he sees only those which it suits their convenience that he should know. If by any chance he gets hold of them, being accustomed to rely on a certain person to read them to him, this man will on the spur of the moment invent what suits him, and often pretend that so-and-so, who is abusing him in this same letter, is asking his pardon. In short, he sees his own affairs only in a purposely arranged reflection, to himself as satisfactory as they can make it, in order not to arouse his anger and ill-humour. I have seen, in various forms, enough of these household managements, carried on consistently for long periods, with very similar results.

Women have ever a propensity to disagree with their husbands. They will seize with both hands any pretext to thwart them; the first excuse serves them for a full justification. I have known one who robbed her husband wholesale, in order, as she told her confessor, to give fatter alms. Don't you believe in such charity! No management of affairs seems to them sufficiently worthy of consideration if it proceeds from their husband's concession. They must needs usurp it, either by cunning or insolence, and always offensively, to lend it grace and authority in their eyes. When, as in the case I speak of, it is against a poor old man and for the sake of the children, then they grasp at this pretext, and triumphantly make it serve their passion; and, as if they were ordinary slaves, readily intrigue against his rule and authority. If there are grown-up and stalwart sons, they also presently suborn, either by force or favour, both steward and receiver, and all the rest of them.

Such as have neither wife nor sons do not so easily fall into this misfortune, but at the same time they are more cruelly and shamefully treated. Cato the elder said in his time, 'so many slaves, so many enemies'. Consider whether, seeing the difference in purity between his age and ours, he did not intend to forewarn us that 'wife, sons and servants are so many enemies to us.'

It is well for decrepit age to be provided with the sweet blessings of want of perception and ignorance and easy credulity. If we took the bait, how should we fare, especially in such an age as this where the judges who have to decide our quarrels are usually partisans of the young, and interested ones? Even though I see no evidence of cheating, I am at least quite aware that I could be easily taken in.[6]

And can one ever sufficiently declare the value of a friend, and what a different thing friendship is in comparison with these civil ties? Even the reflection of it which I see in animals, so unpolluted, how religiously I respect it!

If others cheat me I do not at least cheat myself into thinking I have the power to prevent it, or cudgel my brains to acquire that power. My own bosom is a refuge from such treacheries; not that I am a prey to uneasy and disturbing cares, but rather from a determination to divert my thoughts.

When I hear of someone's predicament, I do not waste my thoughts on him. I immediately turn my eyes on myself, to see how it is with me. All that concerns him touches me. His experience is a warning to me, and puts me on my guard in that direction. Every day

6 In a manuscript note, afterwards cancelled, but just decipherable, we may read: 'Three and four times happy is he who can trust his pitiable old age to a loving hand.' It has been conjectured that the words were cancelled by some other person and not by Montaigne.

and every hour we say of one another what we should more properly say of ourselves, if we could turn our thoughts on ourselves as well as let them rove to others.

And many authors in this way prejudice their own cause by heedlessly rushing upon the cause they attack, and hurling shafts at their enemies which may with greater effect be hurled back at them.

The late Monsieur the Maréchal de Montluc, having lost his son, who died in the island of Madeira, a brave gentleman indeed and of great promise, when speaking to me of it, greatly stressed, among other regrets, the grief and heartache he felt because he had never opened himself out to him; and that by always putting on the stern looks of a parent, he had lost the opportunity of really knowing and appreciating his son, and also of declaring to him the deep love he bore him, and the well-merited opinion he had of his virtue. 'And that poor boy, he said, never saw me but with a sullen and scornful countenance, and is gone with the belief that I was never able to love and esteem him as he deserved. For whom did I reserve the revealing of this singular affection I had for him in my soul? Was it not he that should have had all the pleasure and all the recognition of it? I forced and tormented myself to keep up that empty mask, and have thereby lost the pleasure of his intercourse and of his affection at the same time; for his feelings to me must have been very cool, having never met with anything but harshness and tyranny on my part.'[7]

7 Madame de Sévigné remarks, in a letter to her daughter, that she could never read this passage without tears. 'My word! she adds, how full of good sense is this book!' Blaise de Montluc, who died in 1577, was one of the greatest

This lament appears to me reasonable and well-rounded: for, as I know by too certain experience, here is no consolation in the loss of our friends so weet as that which is given us by the knowledge that ve withheld nothing from them, and that we were in erfect and entire communion with them. [O my riend! am I the better off for having tasted this riendship, or am I the worse off? Truly I am much etter off; my sorrow for him is a comfort and an onour to me. Is it not a pious and a pleasing service n my life to be for ever mourning him? Can there be ny satisfaction equal to this bereavement?][8]

I am as open with my family as I can be, and very eadily signify to them the state of my feelings towards hem and my opinion of them, as I do to everybody. I asten to reveal and make myself known to them, for do not wish to be misunderstood, or thought either etter or worse than I am.

Among other peculiar customs of our ancient Gauls was this, according to Caesar, that sons did not nake themselves known to their fathers, nor dare to ppear in their company in public, until they began to ear arms; as if to signify that it was now time for their athers to admit them to their familiarity and cquaintance.

I have observed yet another error of judgement in

---

military leaders of the time; very brave but very sensual and very cruel, especially towards the Protestants.

A reference to his great friend, Étienne de la Boëtie, who died of the plague in 1563. See the chapter *On friendship.* In the 'Bordeaux MS' this passage, except the first three words, is heavily crossed out, it has been supposed by some other hand than Montaigne's.

some fathers of my day, who, not content with having during their own long life, deprived their children of the share they should naturally have had in their fortunes, leave their wives after them with the same control over their whole property, and with authority to dispose of it at their pleasure. And I have known a certain lord, one of the first officers in our kingdom, who, having in prospect, by right of succession, an income of more than fifty thousand crowns, died in want and overwhelmed in debts, although he was over fifty years of age, whilst his mother, in her extreme old age, was still in the enjoyment of all his property by the will of his father, who for his part had lived till nearly eighty. That appears to be anything but reasonable.

However, I think it is of little advantage to a man in good circumstances to seek a wife who burdens him with a large settlement; there is no outside debt that brings more ruin to a house. My ancestors have generally been of this opinion, and have very fitly acted upon it, as I too have done.

But they who would dissuade us from marrying a rich wife, in the fear of her being less tractable and grateful, are mistaken, since we might lose some real advantage on so frivolous a conjecture. It costs an unreasonable woman no more to override one reason than another. They love themselves most when they are most in the wrong. They are allured by injustice just as good women are allured by the honour due to their virtuous actions; and the richer they are, the more sweet-tempered are they, just as the more beautiful they are, the greater pride do they take in their chastity.

It is right to leave the administration of affairs to the

mother as long as the children are not, according to the laws, old enough to undertake the charge; but that father has brought them up very badly who cannot expect them to be wiser and more efficient, when they have reached that age, than his wife, considering the ordinary weakness of the sex.

Yet it would in truth be more contrary to nature to make the mother dependent on the discretion of her children. She should be liberally provided with the means to keep up her state according to the standing of her house and her age; the more so as want and necessity are much more unsuitable and harder to bear for a woman than a man. I would rather lay this burden on the children than on the mother.

As a general rule the soundest distribution of our property after death is, in my opinion, a distribution according to the custom of the country. The laws have considered the matter better than we; and it is better to allow them to err in their choosing, than rashly to run the risk of miscarrying in ours. The property is properly speaking not our own, since, by a civil prescription and apart from ourselves, it is destined for certain successors. And, although we have some liberty to go outside the law, I hold that we must not, without great and very apparent reason, deprive one of what is his by fortune, and what common justice entitles him to. And it is an abuse of this liberty, and contrary to reason, to make it serve our own frivolous and private whims.

My lot has been kind to me in not offering me occasions to tempt me, and to divert my inclination to follow the usual and lawful practice.

I know of some on whom a long succession of attentions and good services is mere waste of time: a word taken ill is enough to blot out the merit of ten years. Fortunate is he who has the opportunity to oil their humour at this last crossing over! The last action carries the day; not the best and most frequent services, but the most recent and the most present, do the trick. Those are men who trifle with their last wills as we do with apples and rods in the case of children, to reward or punish every action of those who pretend an interest in them. It is a thing of too far-reaching consequence and too much importance to be thus trotted out at every moment; and in which wise men take their stand once for all, having regard to reason and public observance.

We lay these male substitutions too much to heart.[9] And we expect a ridiculous eternity for our names. We also attach too much weight to vain conjectures regarding their future which their childish minds suggest. Perhaps it might have been an injustice to dispossess me of my rank for being the dullest and most leaden-minded, the slowest and most unwilling at my lessons, not only of all my brothers, but of all the boys in my province, whether in mental or bodily exercises. It is foolishness to sift us in that extraordinary way on the faith of prognostics which so often turn out deceptive. If it is permissible to violate the rule and correct the choice which the destinies have made of our heirs, it may be done with more likelihood of reason in consideration of some extraordinary and abnormal physical deformity, some

9 And yet Montaigne at his death shared the same weakness, in leaving his estates and name to the youngest of his male descendants; which proceeding led to a lawsuit which was only settled two centuries later.

persistent and incorrigible blemish that, according to us who are great admirers of beauty, is likely to do serious harm.

The amusing dialogue between Plato's lawgiver and his citizens may dignify this discussion. 'What, they say, when they feel that their end is near, may we not dispose of our own to whom we please? Ye gods! how cruel that it shall not be lawful for us, according as we have been served by our friends in our sickness, our old age and our affairs, to give them more or less at our own pleasure!' To which the lawgiver replies in this fashion: 'My friends, seeing that you are no doubt soon to die, it is difficult for you both to know yourselves and to know what is yours, according to the Delphic inscription.[10] I, who make the laws, maintain that neither do you belong to yourselves, nor does that belong to you which you enjoy. Both your goods and you belong to your family, both past and future. But still more do your family and your goods belong to the public. Wherefore, if some flatterer in your old age or your sickness should unseasonably solicit you, or if you should be impelled by some passion to make an unjust will, I will guard you against them. But, having regard to the general interest of the city and that of your family, I will establish laws and make you understand, what is only reasonable, that private interests should yield to the interest of the community. Go your way quietly and cheerfully whither human necessity calls you. It is for me, who regard not one thing more than another, and who, as far as I am able, look after the general interest, to take

10 'Know thyself.'

charge of what you leave behind you.'

To return to my theme, it appears to me, I know not why, that women ought by no means to have the mastery of any kind over men, except the natural mastery of a mother; unless it be for the punishmen of those who, led by some passionate mood, have voluntarily submitted to them. But this does no concern those elderly women of whom we are speaking. It is the reasonableness of this consideration which made us so ready to enact and give force to tha law, which no one ever set eyes on, by which women are debarred from succeeding to the crown o France;[11] and there is hardly a sovereignty in the world where it is not pleaded, as in our case, by probable reasons which authorize it; but Fortune ha given it more credit in some places than in others.

It is dangerous to leave to their judgement the disposal of our succession according to the choice they will make of the children, which is at all time unjust and capricious. For those unruly appetites and morbid tastes which they have at the time of thei pregnancy, they have at all times in their soul Commonly we see them devoted to the weakest and most puny, or to those, if they have such, who are stil hanging on their neck. For, not having sufficient force of reason to choose and embrace those who deserve it they are more likely to be carried away where the impressions of nature are most left to themselves; like animals who know their young only as long as they hang on to their teats.

Moreover it is easily seen by experience that thi natural affection, to which we give so much authority

11 Known as the Salic Law.

has very slender roots. For a very small gain mothers every day allow their children to be torn from their arms, in order to take charge of ours; we make them abandon their own to some wretched nurse to whom we are not willing to commit ours, or to some goat, forbidding them not only to suckle their own, whatever danger these may thereby incur, but even to give any care to them, that they may devote themselves entirely to the service of ours. And in most of them we soon see, begotten by habit, a bastard affection more vehement than the natural, and a greater solicitude for the preservation of the foster-children than of their own.

And, speaking of goats, it is common in my neighbourhood to see the women of the village, when they are unable to nurse the children from their own breast, calling in the aid of goats. And I have at this moment two lackeys who never drew woman's milk longer than a week. These goats are very quickly trained to come and feed these little ones, to recognize their voice when they cry and run up to them. If any other but their nurseling is brought to them, they will refuse to feed it; and the child in like manner will refuse to take milk from any other goat. The other day I saw one from whom they had taken away his goat, because his father had only borrowed her from one of his neighbours; he could never take to the other that was brought to him, and died, doubtless of hunger. Animals change and bastardize their natural affections as readily as we.

I believe that when Herodotus tells us that, in a certain district in Libya, the men and women mingle indiscriminately, but that the child, when able to walk, will find out its father in a crowd, natural inclination guiding its first steps, there must b frequent mistakes.[12]

Now, when we consider this simple reason fo loving our children, namely that we have begotte them, for which reason we call them our secon selves, there is, methinks, a very different kind o production proceeding from us which is no les worthy of consideration. For that which we engende by the soul, the fruit of our mind, our heart and ou abilities, is brought forth by a nobler part than that o the body, and is more our own; in this generation w are father and mother at the same time. These cost u much dearer and bring us more honour, if there is an good in them. For the worth of our other children i much more their own than it is ours, the share w have in them being very small; but of these all th beauty, all the charm and value are ours. For tha reason they represent us and reflect us much mor vividly than the others.

Plato adds that these are immortal children tha immortalize, nay that deify, their fathers, as in the cas of Lycurgus, Solon, Minos.

Now, history being full of examples of tha common affection of fathers to their children, i seemed to me not inappropriate to pick out one o two of this kind.

Heliodorus, that good bishop of Tricea, chos rather to forfeit the dignity, the profit, and the devou life, of so venerable a prelacy, than to sacrifice hi daughter, a very pretty daughter that still lives, who i

12 Montaigne seems to have misread Herodotus, who say that the man is reputed to be the father whom the chil most resembles.

perhaps however a little too curiously and too wantonly tricked out for the daughter of a churchman and a priest, and in too erotic a fashion.[13]

There was one Labienus at Rome, a man of great worth and authority, who, amongst other qualities, was eminent in every branch of literature. He was, I think, son of that great Labienus, the chief of the captains who served under Caesar in his Gallic war, and who afterwards, having joined the party of the great Pompey, conducted himself so valorously in that conflict, until Caesar defeated him in Spain. This Labienus of whom I am speaking, was an object of jealousy to many, on account of his great qualities, and, as seems likely, counted among his enemies the imperial courtiers and favourites of his day, on account of his independence and his antagonism, inherited from his father, to tyranny, with which we may well believe that his books and other writings were coloured. His adversaries prosecuted him before the Roman authorities, and succeeded in having several of his published works condemned to be burned. It was with him that this new example of penalty was begun, which was afterwards continued against several others at Rome, of punishing with death even writings and studies. As if there were not enough occasions and objects on which to exercise cruelty without bringing in things that Nature has exempted from all feeling and suffering, such as our reputation and the products of our mind, and without

13 Meaning the love-tale of *Theagenes and Chariclea*. It seems that Heliodorus was elected to the bishopric on condition that he burned his novel, but preferred to sacrifice the dignity.

applying corporal punishments to teachings and the monuments of the Muses!

Now Labienus could not endure this loss or survive this progeny, so dear to him: he had himself conveyed and shut up alive in the tomb of his ancestors, thus providing for his suicide and burial at the same time. It would be difficult to show a more vehement paternal affection than that. Cassius Severus, a man of great eloquence and his intimate friend, seeing his books being burned, exclaimed that by the same sentence they should have condemned him to be burned alive with them, seeing that he carried and preserved in his memory all that they contained.

The like misfortune befell Cremutius Cordus, accused of having praised Brutus and Cassius in his books. That base, servile, and corrupt Senate, who deserved a worse master than Tiberius, condemned his writings to the flames. He was content to bear them company in death, and killed himself by abstaining from food.

The good Lucan, having been condemned by that scoundrel of a Nero, in the last moments of his life, when his blood was wellnigh spent from out the veins of his arms, which at his request his physicians had lanced to bring on death, and when the cold had seized his extremities and was approaching his vital parts, the last thing he had in his memory was some of the lines from his poem on the Battle of Pharsalia, which he recited; and he died with these last words on his lips. What was this but a tender and fatherly leave-taking of his children, resembling the adieux and close embraces with which we part from ours when we die, and the result of that natural inclination which recalls to our memory, in these last moments, the things we have held most dear in life?

Can we believe that Epicurus, who, being tormented at his death, as he said, by an acute colic, found his sole consolation in the beauty of the teachings he left to the world, would have felt the same satisfaction in a number of well-born and well-brought-up children, if he had had them, as he had in the production of his pregnant writings, and that, if he had had the choice between leaving behind him a misshapen and ill-born child and a foolish and absurd book, he would not have chosen, and not he alone but any man of like genius, to incur the first misfortune rather than the other? It would perhaps have been an act of impiety in Saint Augustine (to take an example), if, it being proposed to him to bury either his writings, from which our religion gathers such abundant fruit, or his children, in case he had any, he had not rather chosen to bury his children.[14]

And I do not know that I would not much rather have begotten a perfectly shaped child by intercourse with the Muses than by intercourse with my wife.

To this child, such as he is, what I give I give purely and irrevocably, as one gives to the children of one's body. The little good I have done him is no more at my disposal: he may know many things that I no longer know, and hold from me what I have not retained, and what I should have to borrow of him as from a stranger, if I had need of it.[15]

If he is richer than I, I am wiser than he.

14 Saint Augustine had a son, as he tells us in his *Confessions*, 'the child of his sin', whom he called Adeodatus, 'Not-God-given'.

15 Montaigne is of course speaking of his Essays.

There are few men devoted to poetry who would not be prouder to be the father of the *Aeneid* than of the handsomest boy in Rome; and who would not more easily suffer the loss of the latter than of the former. For, according to Aristotle, of all craftsmen the poet is especially the one who is most in love with his work.

It is difficult to believe that Epaminondas, who boasted of leaving no other posterity but daughters who would one day do their father credit (meaning the two noble victories which he had gained over the Lacedemonians), would willingly have consented to exchange them for the most gorgeously handsome women in all Greece; or that Alexander and Caesar ever desired to be robbed of their great and glorious exploits of war, for the advantage of having sons and heirs, however perfect and accomplished they might be.

Nay, I doubt much whether Pheidias, or any other eminent sculptor, would so much desire the preservation and continuance of his natural children as he would that of an excellent statue, which with prolonged labour and study he had perfected according to art. And as to these furious and wicked passions with which fathers have sometimes been kindled for their daughters, or mothers for their sons, the same is also found in this other kind of parenthood: witness what they relate of Pygmalion, who, having built up the statue of a woman of singular beauty, fell so madly and desperately in love with his work, that to gratify his infatuation the gods had to inspire it with life:

The ivory yields,
Softening beneath his fingers; nor retains
Its rigid hardness.

OVID

Of cruelty

I imagine virtue to be something else and something more noble than the propensity to goodness that is born with us. The well-born and naturally well-regulated mind follows the same path, and produces the same actions as the virtuous mind. But virtue somehow rings too great and is too active to allow itself, by a happy disposition, to be meekly and calmly led in the train of reason. The man who, by reason of a meek and easy-going nature, despises injuries received, does a very fine and praiseworthy thing. But he who, provoked and stung to anger by an injury, arms himself with the arms of reason against that furious desire for revenge, and, after a great struggle, masters it in the end, without doubt does a great deal more. The former does well, the latter acts virtuously. The first action might be called good, the other, virtuous. For the name of virtue, I think, presupposes difficulty and contradiction, and cannot be exercised without opposition. It is for that reason perhaps that we call God good, mighty, liberal and just, but we do not call him virtuous. His works are altogether natural and effortless.

Of the philosophers, not only Stoics, but even Epicureans – (for in putting the former on a higher level than the latter I follow the common practice, which is wrong, in spite of the sly witticism with which Arcesilaus answered a man who taunted him with the fact that many men passed from his school to the Epicurean, but never the other way. 'I can quite believe it: cocks are often made capons, but capons are never made cocks.' For, in truth, in strength of mind and austerity of opinions and precepts the Epicurean sect in no wise yields to the Stoic. And it was a Stoic who, more honest than those disputants who, to combat Epicurus and load their own dice, make him say things he never contemplated, twisting his words awry, and, usurping the grammarian's licence, argue into his language a different meaning and a different belief to that which they knew he had in his mind and showed in his morals, said that he gave up being an Epicurean upon this consideration among others, that he found their road too lofty and inaccessible; *and they who are called lovers of pleasure, being in fact lovers of honesty and justice, cultivate and practise all the virtues* (CICERO)); – of the Stoic and Epicurean philosophers, I say, there are some who decided that it was not enough to have the soul in good trim, well-regulated and well-disposed to virtue. It was not enough that we should be resolute in word and deed, and beyond the reach of Fortune; but we should also seek occasions to be put to the proof. They think that we should go in quest of pain, indigence and contempt, in order to fight them and keep our souls in breath: *Virtue provoked is greatly strengthened* (SENECA).

That is one of the reasons why Epaminondas, who was also of a third sect,[1] refuses the wealth that Fortune gives into his hands by very lawful means, in order, he says, to have to battle with poverty; and in

1 The Pythagorean.

these straitened circumstances he held on to the last.

Socrates, I think, put himself upon a much ruder trial, keeping for his exercise his wife's bad temper; which is to fence with the button off.

Metellus, having, alone of all the Roman senators, taken upon him, by dint of his virtue, to resist the violence of Saturninus, tribune of the people at Rome, who tried by might and main to pass an unjust law in favour of the plebeians, and having thereby incurred the dreadful penalties that Saturninus had provided for such as refused, talked with those who, in this extremity, were walking with him in the Forum, in these terms: 'To do an ill action is too easy and too base; to do a good one that involves you in no danger, is quite common: but it is the proper duty of a virtuous man to do great and good things, though he risks everything by it.'

These words of Metellus very clearly set forth what I desired to make out, that virtue declines the company of facility; and that that easy and gentle incline down which are guided the regular steps of a good natural disposition is not the way of true virtue. She asks for a rugged and thorny path; she would have either outside difficulties to wrestle with, like those of Metellus, by means of which Fortune delights to break the speed of her career, or internal difficulties that our inordinate appetites and the imperfections of our nature place in her way.

So far my way has been smooth. But at the end of this discussion this fancy comes into my mind that the soul of Socrates, which is the most perfect that has come to my knowledge, should be, according to my reckoning, a soul little deserving of commendation. For I cannot conceive this man to have been besieged by any vicious lusts. I cannot imagine any difficulty or constraint in the way of his virtue. I know his reason to have been so powerful a mistress over him that she would never have allowed a vicious appetite even to arise in him. I have nothing to set against a virtue so sublime as his. I seem to see her marching with a victorious and triumphant step, in state and at her ease, without hindrance or disturbance. If Virtue can shine only through the conflict of contrary desires, shall we therefore say that she cannot dispense with the help of vice, and that to vice she owes it that she is held in honour and repute? What should we say of that noble and generous Epicurean voluptuousness, which makes such a show of tenderly cherishing Virtue in its bosom, and there makes her frolic, giving her disgrace, fevers, poverty, death, and tortures, for toys to play with? If I take it for granted that perfect Virtue is known by her combating and patiently enduring pain, by bearing up against the attacks of the gout without being thrown off her balance; if I allow hardships and difficulties to be her necessary aim: what shall we say of the virtue raised to such a pitch as not only to despise pain but to rejoice in it, and to feel tickled by the pangs of a violent colic, which is that which the Epicureans have established, and of which many of them by their actions have given us very certain proofs? As have many others who, I find, have actually exceeded even the rules of their teaching.

Witness the younger Cato. When I see him dying and plucking out his bowels, I cannot be satisfied with simply believing that his mind was then wholly free from distress and horror; I cannot believe that he merely maintained that attitude which the rules of the Stoic sect prescribed, calm, impassive, emotionless;

there was, it seems to me, in the virtue of this man too much sap and virility to stop there. I believe that without doubt he felt a sensual pleasure in an action so noble, and that he felt a greater satisfaction in it than in any other action of his life: *He departed this life, rejoicing in having found a motive for leaving it* (CICERO).

I am so far advanced in that belief that I begin to question whether he would have wished to be robbed of the opportunity of so heroic an achievement. And, if I were not held in check by consideration of the goodness which made him espouse the public interest more than his own, I could readily fall in with this opinion, that he was grateful to Fortune for having put his virtue to so noble a test, and for having favoured that brigand[2] in treading under foot the ancient freedom of his country. I seem to read in that action I know not what exultation in his soul, and the expression of an extraordinary pleasure and manly voluptuousness, when she considered the nobility and sublimity of his deed:

Embracing death with desperate ferocity, HORACE

not goaded by any hope of fame, according to the popular and effeminate opinion of some, for that is too mean a consideration to touch a heart so generous, so haughty and so unbending; but by the beauty of the thing in itself, which he, who worked the springs of it, discerned much more clearly and in its perfection than we are able to do.

I am pleased to find that philosophy decided that a deed so heroic would not have been in keeping with any other life than Cato's, and that his alone was fitted

2 Caesar.

to end in that way. Therefore he enjoined, in accordance with reason, both his son and the senators who accompanied him to provide otherwise for themselves. *Cato, whom Nature had endowed with an incredible strength of soul, and who, ever following the path he had traced for himself, had by habit strengthened the firmness of his character, was bound to die rather than look upon the face of a tyrant* (CICERO).

Every death should correspond with its life. We do not become different for dying. I always interpret a death by its life. And if anyone tells me of a death, brave in appearance, annexed to a feeble life, I maintain that it is produced by a feeble cause, in keeping with the life.

Must we then say that the easiness of this death, and that facility which he had acquired through the strength of his soul, should abate anything from the splendour of his virtue?

And what man whose brain is ever so little tinged with the true philosophy can be satisfied with imagining Socrates merely free from fear and emotion when prison, fetters and condemnation fell to his lot? And who does not discover in him, not only courage and confidence (for that was in his nature), but also I know not what new satisfaction, and a gay cheerfulness in his last words and actions?

By that thrill of pleasure that he feels when scratching his leg after his irons were removed, does he not betray a like joy and delight in his soul at being unfettered of past discomforts, and prepared to enter into a knowledge of the things to come?

Cato will pardon me, if he please; his death is more tragic and more strained, but this one is somehow still more beautiful.

Aristippus said to one who was lamenting his death, 'May the gods send me one like it!'

We see in the souls of these two men[3] and their imitators (for I very much doubt whether they had their equals) so perfect a habituation to virtue, that it passed into their nature. It ceases to be a laborious virtue, or the result of the precepts of reason, to keep to which the soul needs to brace itself; it is the very essence of their soul, it is its natural and ordinary course. They rendered it such by long practice in the precepts of philosophy, lighting upon a rich and fine nature. The vicious passions which arise in us can find no door of entry into them. The strength and rigidity of their soul stifles and extinguishes the lusts as soon as they begin to stir.

Now I think there is no doubt that it is a finer thing to prevent, by a sublime and divine resolution, the birth of temptations, and so to train oneself to virtue that the very seeds of vice are rooted out, than by main force to stop their progress, and, after being taken unawares by the first stirrings of the passions, to arm oneself resolutely to arrest their progress and vanquish them; and that this second power is still finer than to be simply furnished with an easy and compliant nature, which has a natural distaste for vice and debauchery. For this third and last degree seems indeed to make a man innocent, but not virtuous; free from ill-doing, but not sufficiently capable of well-doing. To which may be added that this condition is so near to imperfection and weakness that I do not quite know how to recognize and distinguish their confines. The very names of

3 Socrates and Cato.

goodness and innocence are, for that reason, in some sort words of contempt. I can see that some of the virtues, such as chastity, sobriety and temperance, may be due to feebleness of body. Fortitude in face of dangers (if it must be called fortitude), contempt of death, patience in misfortunes, may often be found in a man through his being unable to rightly calculate such mishaps, and to conceive their nature. Thus, want of apprehension and dullness sometimes counterfeit valorous actions. And I have often chanced to hear a man praised for a thing that deserved blame.

An Italian lord once spoke as follows in my presence, to the discredit of his nation: that the subtlety of the Italians and the vivacity of their imagination were so great, that they foresaw the dangers and accidents that might befall them so far ahead, that it should not be thought strange if they were often seen in war to look to their safety, even before they had clearly seen the peril of it; that we French and the Spaniards, who were not of so fine a grain, are more reckless, and that we must be made to see the danger with our own eyes and touch it with our hands before we take the alarm, and that then we lose all control; but that the Germans and Swiss, who are heavier and coarser, have not the sense to recover their bearings, and hardly even when they are crushed under the blows.

This was perhaps only spoken in jest. Yet it is very true that in the business of war the novice very often hurls himself into hazards with much greater want of consideration than he does after having burned his fingers in it:

Well I knew
How potent was the new-born pride in arms,
And a first onset's all-entrancing spell.

VIRGIL

That is why, in judging a particular action, we must consider many circumstances, as well as the whole man by whom it is performed, before we give it a name.

To say a word about myself. I have sometimes known my friends to call prudence in me what was due to chance, and to regard something as being won by courage and patience which was won by thought and judgement; and to apply to me one name instead of another, sometimes to my advantage, sometimes to my detriment. After all, so far am I from having attained to that first and most perfect degree of excellence where virtue becomes a habit, that I have hardly even given any proofs of the second. I have not made any great efforts to bridle the desires by which I have been importuned. My virtue is a virtue, or, to speak more correctly, an innocence that is casual and accidental. If I had been born with a more unruly disposition, I am afraid I should have been in a pitiable way. For I have not experienced much steadfastness in my soul to resist passions, if they were ever so mild. I am unable to cherish quarrels and conflicts in my bosom. Hence I cannot be greatly beholden to myself for being free from many vices:

And if some trivial faults, and these but few,
My nature, else not much amiss, imbue,
Just as you wish away, yet scarcely blame,
A mole or two upon a comely frame,

HORACE

I owe it to my fortune rather than to my reason. To her I owe that I am descended from a race famous for honesty, and that I am the son of a very good father. I know not whether he has passed on to me something of his character, or whether perhaps the home examples and my good education in childhood have insensibly contributed to it, or else whether I was born so:

> Whether 'neath Libra's aspect I was born
> Or the dread Scorpion's, of the natal hour
> The stormier influence, or of Capricorn,
> Who sways the Western wave with tyrant power;
>
> HORACE

but so much is true that I have a natural horror of most of the vices.

The answer which Antisthenes gave to one who asked him what was the best apprenticeship, 'Unlearn evil', seems to be rooted in this idea.

I hold them in horror, I say, with so natural and so inborn a persuasion, that this same instinct or impression with regard to them that I imbibed from my nurse I have preserved without any occasion having arisen to make me alter it; nay, not even my own reasonings, which, through having deviated from the beaten path in many things, might easily give me a licence to do what my natural inclination makes me hate.

I will tell you something that may appear monstrous, but yet I will tell it: the effect of that is that in many respects there is more order and restraint in my morals than in my opinions; my sexual appetites are less dissolute than my reason.

Aristippus was so outspoken in favour of pleasure and wealth, that all philosophy rose up in revolt against him. But as to his morals, Dionysius the tyrant having offered him three fair young girls to choose from, he replied that he chose all three, for that Paris had got into trouble for preferring one over her companions. But, having taken them to his house, he dismissed them untasted.

When his servant, who was following him, complained that the money he was carrying was too heavy, he ordered him to throw away so much as he found burdensome.

And Epicurus, whose teachings are non-religious and non-ascetic, was very devout and laborious in his way of living. He writes to a friend of his that he lives only on coarse brown bread and water, and entreats him to send him a little cheese, in case he has a mind to make a sumptuous repast. Can it be true that, in order to be thoroughly good, we must be so by an occult, natural and universal quality, without law, without reason or example?

The excesses in which I have found myself involved are, thank God, not of the worst kind. I have indeed condemned them in myself as they deserved, for my judgement has not been infected by them. On the contrary, I blame them more rigorously in myself than in another. But that is all, for after all I offer too little resistance to them and am apt to incline too much to the other side of the scales, except that I moderate them and prevent them mixing with other vices. For they most generally keep together and become interlocked, in one who is not on his guard. Mine I have cut down and forced to be as single and simple as I could make them;

Outside of that no vices I indulge. JUVENAL

For, as to the theory of the Stoics, who say, 'The wise man acts, when he does act, by all the virtues together, although there be one more apparent, according to the nature of the action (and herein the comparison with the human body might serve them in some degree, for anger cannot work without the aid of all the other humours, although anger may predominate); if from thence they would draw a like inference, that when the sinner sins, he sins by all the vices together, I am not so simple as to believe them, or I do not understand them; for in effect I feel the contrary. Those are minute, unsubstantial subtleties, with which philosophy sometimes busies itself.

Some vices I am addicted to, but others I fly as much as any saint could do.

The Peripatetics, besides, reject this indissoluble connexion and union; and Aristotle maintains that a wise and just man may be both intemperate and incontinent.

Socrates confessed to those who discovered in his physiognomy a certain inclination to vice that that was in truth his natural propensity, but that he had corrected it by discipline.

And the intimate friends of the philosopher Stilpo used to say that, though naturally fond of wine and women, he had by study become very abstemious in respect of both.

The good that is in me I owe, on the other hand, to the accident of my birth. I owe it neither to law, to precept nor to any other apprenticeship. The innocence that is in me is a natural innocence; there is little of vigour in it, and no artifice.

Among other vices, I cruelly hate cruelty, both by nature and reason, as the worst of all the vices. But ıen I am so soft in this that I cannot see a chicken's .eck wrung without distress, and cannot bear to hear ıe squealing of a hare between the teeth of my .ounds, although the chase is a vehement pleasure.

They who have to combat voluptuousness are fond f employing this argument, to prove that it is wholly icious and contrary to reason: 'That when it is at its ighest pitch, it masters us to such a degree that eason can have no access.' And they instance the eeling we experience in intercourse with women,

When now
Their bodies have sweet presage of keen joys,
And Venus is about to sow the fields
Of woman;

LUCRETIUS

ı which they think that the pleasure carries us so far eyond ourselves that our reason cannot then erform its office, being crippled by the ecstasy of leasure.

I know that it may be otherwise, and that we may ometimes, by force of will, succeed in that same ıstant to bring back our mind to other thoughts. But needs to be deliberately strained and stiffened. I now that it is possible to master the violence of that leasure, and I know it from personal experience. For have not found Venus so imperious a goddess as ıany men, and those more chaste than I, testify to er being. I do not regard it as a miracle, as does the ueen of Navarre in one of the tales of her *Ieptameron* (which is a pretty book for its matter), nor s a thing of extreme difficulty, to pass whole nights, ith every opportunity and in all freedom, with a ng-desired mistress, keeping the word one has pledged her to be satisfied with kisses and simpl contact.

I think the example of the chase would be more t the point. Though the pleasure be less, we are mor carried away by it and more liable to surprises, ou reason, taken unawares, having no time to prepare fc and resist the onslaught, when, after a long quest, th quarry suddenly starts up and appears in a plac where perhaps we least expected to see it. This shoc and the eagerness of the hue and cry so strike ou senses that it would be hard for those who love th kind of sport to withdraw their thoughts, at th moment, elsewhere.

And the poets make Diana triumph over the torc and arrows of Cupid:

> Who, mid such sports, does not forget his woes
> And all the cares of love? HORACE

To come back to my subject, I have a very tende compassion for others' afflictions, and could readil weep for company, if I were able to shed tears on an occasion. Nothing draws my tears except tears, nc only real ones but of whatever kind, feigned or paintec The dead I can hardly pity, and I should rather env them; but I very greatly pity the dying.

The savages who roast and eat the bodies of the dead do not scandalize me as much as they wh persecute and torture the living. I cannot even loo upon executions of the law, however reasonable the may be, with a steadfast eye.

Somebody, having occasion to testify to Juliu Caesar's clemency, said, 'He was mild in his vengeance: having forced the pirates to surrender, by whor he had before been taken prisoner and put to ranson nd since he had threatened them with the cross, he ondemned them to be crucified, but not until they ad been strangled. Philemon, his secretary, who had ttempted to poison him, he punished no more arshly than with simple death.' Without revealing the ame of that Latin author,[4] who dares to allege as an vidence of mercy the mere killing of those by whom e have been injured, it is easy to guess that he is ruck by the horrible and villainous examples of ruelty practised by the Roman tyrants.

For my part, even in justice, all that is over and bove a simple death appears to me pure cruelty, and specially with us[5] who ought to make it our duty to ismiss a soul in a state of grace; which cannot be hen it has been agitated and driven to despair by nsufferable tortures.[6]

In these latter days a soldier, having perceived, from tower in which he was imprisoned, carpenters busy work erecting a scaffold and people assembling in e marketplace, concluded that it was for himself; in is despair, finding nothing else to kill himself with, e seized upon an old rusty nail out of a cart which hance had thrown in his way, and therewith dealt imself two serious wounds about the throat; but eing this had no effect on his life, he soon after dealt imself a third in the belly and fell into a swoon. In is state he was found by the first of his jailers who ntered to see him. They brought him round and, to ke advantage of the time before he expired, they at

Suetonius, in his *Life of Julius Caesar*.

Who profess ourselves Christians.

When Montaigne was in Rome in 1581, he was urged by the Papal authorities to suppress the above passage, which however he did not do.

once read his sentence to him, which was that he wa to be decapitated, whereat he was greatly rejoicec and accepted the wine he had before refused; an after thanking the judges for the unexpected lenienc of their sentence, he said that his resolve to kill himse was due to his horror of a more cruel punishmen which the sight of the preparations had increasec The change in the mode of death appeared to him deliverance from it.

I should recommend that these examples (severity, whereby it is intended to keep the people i awe, be exercised on the dead bodies of criminals. Fc to see them deprived of burial, boiled and cut i pieces, would affect the populace almost as much a the torments that the living are made to suffe although in reality that amounts to little or nothing, a God says: *Be not afraid of them that kill the body, an after that have no more that they can do* (SAINT LUKE)

And the poets singularly dwell upon the horrors (this picture, as something worse than death:

Ah! that the remnant of a king, half-burnt,
The bones laid bare, with blood and
filth besmeared,
Should be thus foully dragged along the ground!

ENNIUS, *quoted by Cicer*

One day at Rome I happened to be on the spot a the moment when they were executing a notoriou brigand named Catena. He was strangled without th spectators exhibiting any emotion; but when the came to cut his body in pieces, the hangman dealt n blow that the people did not follow with pitiful crie and exclamations, as if everyone had lent his ow sense of feeling to that carrion.

Those inhuman excesses should be performed upon the shell, not upon the quick. Thus, in a somewhat similar case, Artaxerxes mitigated the harshness of the ancient laws of Persia by ordaining that those nobles who had failed in their charge, instead of being scourged, as was the custom, should be stripped and their garments flogged in their stead; and, instead of the customary tearing out of the hair, that they should only be stripped of their high tiaras.

The Egyptians, who are so devout, thought they sufficiently satisfied the divine justice by sacrificing effigies and pictures of pigs: a bold idea, to think to pay God, so essential a substance, with picture and shadow!

I live in a time when we abound in incredible examples of this sin, through the licence bred by our civil wars. And we can read of nothing in ancient histories more extreme than what we may witness any day. Yet that has in no wise reconciled me to it. I could hardly have believed, until I saw it with my own eyes, that there could have been found souls so unnatural that they could commit murder for the mere pleasure they took in it; that they could hack and mangle others' limbs, that they could sharpen their wits to invent unheard-of tortures and new kinds of death, without enmity, without profit, and to the sole end of enjoying the pleasing spectacle of the pitiful gestures and motions, the lamentable cries and groans, of a man dying in agony. For that is the utmost pitch to which cruelty can reach. *O that a man should kill a man without anger, without fear, only for pleasure in the sight!* (SENECA).

For my part I could not even witness without distress the pursuing and killing of a harmless and defenceless animal, that has done us no injury. And I have always been pained by the common sight of a stag, weak and panting, reduced to surrender and cast itself on the mercy of its pursuers, with tears in its eyes,

> Blood-stained, with piteous and imploring eyes,
>
> VIRGIL

which has always been to me a very unpleasant sight.

I seldom capture a live animal but I restore it to the fields. Pythagoras used to buy them of the fishermen and fowlers, to do the same:

> 'Twas slaughter of wild beasts, methinks, that made
> Man first with blood to stain his cruel blade.
>
> OVID

Men of bloodthirsty nature where animals are concerned display a natural propensity to cruelty.

At Rome, after the people had become accustomed to the spectacle of the slaughter of animals, they proceeded to that of men and gladiators. Nature herself has, I fear, fastened on man a certain instinc to inhumanity. No man finds his recreation in seeing animals playing together and fondling one another and none fails to take a delight in seeing them tearing each other limb from limb.

And, that no man may jeer at me for my sympathy with them, Theology herself enjoins us to show them some kindness; and, considering that one and the same master has lodged us in this palace for his service, and that they like ourselves are of his family she is right in commanding us to show them consideration and affection.

Pythagoras borrowed the theory of metempsychosis

of the Egyptians; but it was since accepted by several nations, and notably by our Druids:

> The spirit is immortal, cannot die;
> It only changes dwelling and survives
> In other dwelling, where anew it lives. OVID

In the religion of our ancient Gauls it was held that the soul, being eternal, never ceases to move and change from one body to another; which idea was also accompanied with some consideration of divine justice. For, according to the behaviour of the soul, whilst it had been in Alexander, they said that God assigned to it another body to inhabit, more or less painful and suitable to its condition:

> The silent chains of brutes he made them wear:
> Encased in bearish form were cruel souls,
> Robbers in wolves', the sly in foxes' hides;
> Where, after ending, through successive years
> And many thousand shapes, their sad careers,
> In Lethe's stream their souls were duly purged,
> And back to their primeval shape restored.
> CLAUDIAN

If it had been valiant they lodged it in the body of a lion; if voluptuous, in that of a pig; if timorous, in that of a stag or a hare; if cunning, in that of a fox; and so with the rest, until, purified by this chastening, it resumed the body of some other man.

> Well I remember I was Pantheus's son
> Euphorbus, in the fatal war of Troy.[7] OVID

7 These words are put into the mouth of Pythagoras.

As to that cousinship between the animals and ourselves, I do not take much account of it; nor of the fact that several nations, and especially some of the most ancient and most noble, have not only received animals into their society and companionship, but have ranked them much higher than themselves, sometimes regarding them as the familiars and favourites of their gods, and paying them a more than human respect and reverence. And others recognized no other god or divinity but them. *Beasts were made sacred by barbarians on account of the benefits they bestowed* (CICERO).

The crocodile is here adored, and there
The snake-gorged ibis fills all hearts with awe;
The long-tailed monkey here is graved in gold;
Here fish of Nile are reverenced, and there
The multitude falls down before a dog. JUVENAL

And even the very ingenious explanation which Plutarch gives of this error is to their honour. For he says that it was not the cat or the ox, for example, that the Egyptians worshipped, but that in these animals they worshipped some image of the divine attributes. In the latter, patience and usefulness; in the former, activity, or, like our neighbours the Burgundians, as well as all Germany, intolerance of being imprisoned, whereby they represented Freedom, which they loved and adored above any other divine attribute; and so with the others.

But when, among the most moderate opinions, meet with arguments which endeavour to demonstrate the close resemblance between us and the animals, and to show how large a share they have in our greatest privileges, and with how much reason they have been likened to us, truly I abate a great deal of our presumption, and willingly renounce that imaginary kingship which we are supposed to have over the other creatures.

But even though all this were an error, there is yet a certain consideration and a general duty of humanity which attaches us not only to those animals that have life and feeling, but even to trees and plants. To men we owe justice, and mercy and kindness to the other creatures that are capable of receiving it. There is a certain commerce and mutual obligation between them and ourselves. I am not afraid of confessing my natural tenderness, which is so childish that I cannot very well refuse my dog when he offers to frolic with me, or appeals to me to frolic with him, at an inopportune moment.

The Turks have almshouses and hospitals for animals. The Romans made the keeping of geese a public care, since by their vigilance the Capitol had been saved. The Athenians ordained that the mules and hinnies which had served them in building the temple which they called Hecatompedon, should be free and allowed to graze wherever they pleased without hindrance.

Among the inhabitants of Agrigentum it was the usual custom to give a serious interment to the animals they held dear, such as horses of rare merit, dogs and birds which had been of some use, or even had helped to amuse their children. And the magnificence they ordinarily showed in all other things was particularly apparent in the number and costliness of the monuments they raised to that end, and which remained in all their pomp many centuries after.

The Egyptians buried bears, wolves, crocodiles, dogs and cats in consecrated places, after embalming their bodies; and after their death they put on mourning.

Cimon gave an honourable burial to the mares with which he had three times won the prize for the race at the Olympian games. The ancient Xantippus buried his dog on a promontory on the sea-coast, which has since been called after it. And Plutarch tells us that it went against his conscience to sell and send to the slaughter-house, for a small gain, any ox that had long been in his service.

Of judging of another's death

When judging of another's assurance at the point of death, which is without doubt the moment in the life of a man that should be most carefully noted, we must take care to remember one thing, That it is difficult for a man to believe that he has reached that stage. Few people, when they are dying, have made up their minds that it is their last hour; and at no point of our lives are we more deluded by deceptive hope. She keeps dinning into their ears, 'Others have been in a much worse condition, and have not died. Your case is not as hopeless as they think; and, at the worst, God has worked greater miracles.'

And that comes of thinking too much of ourselves. We imagine that the universe will suffer some loss by our annihilation, and that it commiserates our condition. Our sight being disturbed, things appear to it equally disturbed, and we imagine that things are passing from us when we lose sight of them; as to those who travel by sea, the mountains, fields, cities, heaven and earth appear to be tossed about in the same way as they are:

> From harbour fare we; lands and cities fade.
>
> VIRGIL

Who ever knew an old man who did not praise the past and blame the present, laying his troubles and misery to the charge of the world and the conduct of men?

The aged ploughman shakes his head and sighs;
And when he puts the present by the past,
His father's fate he blesses, often prates
How those of old with piety were filled.

LUCRETIUS

We drag everything along with us. As a consequence we look upon our death as a great matter which does not come to pass lightly, nor without a solemn consultation of the stars; *so many gods making a stir over one head* (SENECA). And of this we are more convinced the more we prize ourselves: 'What, is so much learning to be wasted, to the great detriment of the world, without the Fates being specially concerned about it? Does it cost them no more to kill so rare and exemplary a mind than one that is common and of no use to the world? This life of ours, that shelters so many others, on which so many other lives depend, which employs such a world of people, that fills so many places, is it to be dismissed like one that holds by its one single thread?'

Not one of us lays it sufficiently to heart that he is but one.

Hence those words of Caesar to his pilot, more tumid than the sea which threatened him:

If thou to sail to Italy decline
Under the gods' protection, trust to mine;
The only cause thou justly hast to fear
Is that thou knowest not thy passenger;
But I being now aboard, slight Neptune's braves,
And fearlessly cut through the swelling waves.

LUCAN

And these:

But Caesar now
Thinking the peril worthy of his Fates:
'Are such the labours of the gods? exclaimed;
Bent on my downfall have they sought me thus,
Here in this puny skiff in such a sea?'

And that fantastic idea entertained by the people, that the sun for a whole year shrouded its face, in mourning for his death:

Yea, he it was that showed
At Caesar's death compassion upon Rome,
Veiling in umber haze his dazzling head.

VIRGIL

And a thousand such, by which the world is so easily gulled, imagining that our loss changes the face of the heavens, and that they, in their infinity, take a keen interest in our paltry distinctions. *We are not so intimate with heaven that the light of its stars should die at our death* (PLINY).

Now it is not reasonable to judge of the resolution and firmness of a man who, though he be in certain danger, is not yet convinced of it; and it is not enough that he dies in this frame of mind, unless he be really prepared for that event. In most cases they put on a brave face and utter brave words in order to acquire a reputation, which they still hope to live long enough to enjoy.

All those whose death I have observed were beholden to chance for their demeanour and not to their own design.

And even in the case of those who in ancient times took their own lives, we should carefully consider whether it was a sudden death, or a death that took time. That cruel Roman Emperor used to say of his prisoners that he wished to make them feel death; and if one made away with himself in prison, he would say, 'That fellow has escaped me.'[1] He would rather he had felt the torments of a lingering death.

> His every limb
> Maimed, hacked and riven; yet the fatal blow
> The murderers with savage purpose spared.
>
> LUCAN

It is not indeed so great a matter, in a man in perfect health and in his right mind, to resolve to kill himself; it is very easy to swagger before coming to grips. So we see the most effeminate man that the world has seen, Heliogabalus, amid all his vulgar debaucheries, making preparations for dying artistically, when occasion should force him to do so. And, that his death might not belie the rest of his life, he expressly built a sumptuous tower, the base and front of which was floored with boards enriched with gold and precious stones, from which to hurl himself. He also had cords made of gold and crimson silk threads to strangle himself; a sword forged in gold wherewith to run himself through; and kept poison in vessels of emerald and topaz to poison himself, according as the whim should seize him to choose between these different ways of dying:

> By a forced valour, resolute and brave.
>
> LUCAN

Yet in respect of this man, the luxuriousness of his

1 The first part of the sentence applies to Caligula, the second to Tiberius, whose cruelty a certain Carvilius escaped by suicide.

preparations makes it more likely that he would have bled at the nose,[2] had he been put to the test.

But even in the case of those men of stouter heart who have resolved to dispatch themselves, we must consider (I say), whether it was with a stroke which left them no time to feel the effect of it. For it may be questioned whether, on feeling life draining away little by little, the body's senses mingling with those of the soul, and with the means at hand of undoing his action, a man would still obstinately persist in so dangerous an intent.

During Caesar's civil wars, Lucius Domitius, who took poison after being made prisoner in the Abruzzi, afterwards repented. It has happened in our time that a man, having resolved to die, and not having struck deep enough at the first attempt, the itching of the flesh repelling his arm, afterwards dealt himself two or three very serious wounds, but could never screw up enough courage to thrust home.

Whilst Plantius Sylvanus was on his trial, Urgulania, his grandmother, sent him a poniard with which, having failed to kill himself outright, he made his slaves open his veins.

Albucilla, in the time of Tiberius, attempted to kill herself, but struck half-heartedly, and still gave her adversaries the opportunity to imprison her and put her to death in their own way. The same thing happened to Demosthenes the general, after being routed in Sicily. And C. Fimbria, having struck himself too feeble a blow, entreated his slave to finish him.

On the other hand, Ostorius, unable to use his own

2 His courage would have failed him; or, in the familiar phrase, he would have got 'cold feet'.

arm, and disdaining to employ that of his slave except to hold the poniard with firm and steady hand, hurled himself forward, thrust his throat against the point, and so ran himself through.

It is indeed a meat that must be swallowed without chewing by one whose throat is not lined with paving-stones; and so the Emperor Hadrian made his physician accurately mark and encircle the spot on his pap at which the man he had charged to kill him was to aim. For this reason it was that Caesar, when asked what death he thought the most desirable, replied, 'the least premeditated and the quickest'.

If Caesar had the courage to say so, it is no cowardice in me to believe it.

'A quick death, said Pliny, is the supreme good fortune in human life.' People are loath to acknowledge it. No man can say he is resolved on death who fears to reflect on it, and cannot bear to look on it with open eyes. They who, under sentence of death, in order to make a rapid end of it, urge and hasten on their execution, do so not because they are resolved, but because they would rather not have time to think it over. It is not death that troubles them, but very much the dying:

I fear not death, but dying gives me pause.

EPICHARMUS

That is a degree of firmness which I know by experience I could attain to, like those who plunge into danger, as into the sea, with eyes shut.

There is nothing, in my opinion, more illuminating in the life of Socrates, than that he had thirty whole days in which to ruminate over his death sentence, and that he digested it all that time in certain expectation of its being carried out, without dismay, without change, his train of words and actions rather depressed and languid than strained and exalted by the weight of such thoughts.

That Pomponius Atticus to whom Cicero wrote his letters, being ill, sent for Agrippa, his son-in-law, and two or three other friends, and said to them that, having found by experience that he gained nothing by trying to cure himself, and that all he did to prolong his life only prolonged and aggravated his pain, he was resolved to put an end to both, and begged them to approve of his determination, or, at the most, not to waste their labour in trying to dissuade him from it. Now, having chosen to die by abstaining from food, behold him accidentally cured of his disease! The remedy he had employed to do away with himself restored him to health. When the physicians and his friends came to celebrate this happy event and rejoice with him, they were greatly disappointed, for, in spite of their efforts, they could not make him change his mind; he said that some day he would in any case have to go through with it, and being now so far on his way, he would save himself the pains of beginning all over again on a future occasion.

This man, having made acquaintance with death at his full leisure, not only is not disheartened, but is eagerly bent on overtaking it; for, being satisfied with the reason which made him enter into the combat, he makes it a point of bravery to see it out. There is a great distance between not fearing death and being ready to taste it and relish it.

The story of the philosopher Cleanthes is very similar. His gums were swollen and decayed. The physicians advised him to be very abstemious. After fasting for two days he is so much better that they pronounce him cured, and permit him to return to his usual diet. He, on the other hand, having already tasted the sweets of faintness, resolved not to go back, and ended the journey on which he was so far advanced.

Tullius Marcellinus, a young Roman, wishing to anticipate the hour of his destiny, to be rid of a disease which tyrannized over him more than he was minded to endure, although the physicians promised him a certain if not a speedy cure, called his friends together to discuss his case. Some, says Seneca, gave him the advice they would themselves have taken through faintheartedness. Others, to gratify him, that which they thought would be most acceptable to him. But a Stoic spoke as follows: 'Do not let it worry you, Marcellinus, as if you were considering a weighty matter. It is no great thing to live; your slaves and animals live. But it is a great thing to die nobly, wisely and firmly. Think how long you have been doing the same things, eating, drinking, sleeping; drinking, sleeping, and eating. We are continually going the same daily round; not only evil and intolerable calamities, but the mere satiety of living, make a man wish to die.'

Marcellinus wanted no man to give him advice; he wanted a man to help him. His slaves feared to meddle, but this philosopher explained to them that domestic slaves fall under suspicion only when it is doubtful whether the death of their master is voluntary; that otherwise it would be as bad an example to prevent him as to kill him, seeing that

To save a man against his will
Is just the same as 'tis to kill.

HORACE

He then suggested to Marcellinus that, just as after a meal we give the dessert to the attendants, so when life is ended it would not be unbecoming to distribute something among those who have ministered to our needs. Now Marcellinus was of a free and generous disposition; he divided a certain sum among his slaves, and comforted them. For the rest he needed neither steel nor blood. He resolved to walk out of this life, not to run away from it; not to escape death, but to experience it. And, to give himself time to meditate over it, he gave up eating, and on the third day after, having had himself sprinkled with warm water, he became gradually weaker and weaker, and not, as he said, without a certain voluptuousness.

Indeed they who have experienced this failing of the heart due to weakness declare that they feel no pain, but rather a certain pleasure, as when passing into sleep and repose.

Those are studied and digested deaths.

But, in order that Cato alone might furnish an example of virtue in all respects, it would seem as if his kind destiny had injured the hand with which he dealt himself the blow, that he might have opportunity to meet death face to face, and hug him, fortifying his courage in the face of danger instead of abating it. And if it had been my lot to picture him in his most superb attitude, I should have represented him covered with blood and tearing out his bowels, rather than with sword in hand, as did the sculptors of his times. For this second murder was much more relentless than the first.

How our mind stands in its own way

It is an amusing idea, that of a man exactly balanced between two equally strong desires. For it is not to be doubted that he will never make up his mind, since choice and inclination would imply that things were unequally prized; and if we were placed between the bottle and the ham, with an equal desire to eat and drink, there would doubtless be no help for it, but we must die of thirst and hunger.

To provide against this dilemma, the Stoics, when asked how our mind comes to choose between two indifferent things, and why, from a large number of coins, we take one rather than another, when they are all alike, and there is no reason to incline us to any preference, reply that this movement of the soul is out of the common and irregular, coming to us by an outside, accidental, and fortuitous impulsion.

I think we might rather say that nothing meets our eyes which does not show some difference, however slight; and that, either to the sight or the touch, there is always something additional which attracts us, however imperceptibly. Similarly, if we could imagine a piece of string equally strong in every part, it is impossible by all impossibility that it should snap; for where would you have the break to begin? And it is not in Nature that it should break everywhere at the same time.

If we should add to this the geometrical propositions

which conclude, by certain proofs, that the contents are greater than the containing, and the centre as great as its circumference; and which discover two lines eternally approaching one another without ever meeting, and the philosopher's stone, and the squaring of the circle, where reason and experience are so opposed; we might perhaps find some argument to support this bold saying of Pliny: *There is nothing certain but uncertainty, and nothing more miserable and arrogant than man.*[1]

1 This is one of the sentences inscribed on the ceiling of Montaigne's library.

That difficulties increase our desires

There is no reason but has its opposite, says the wisest school of philosophers.[1] I was just ruminating over that fine saying which one of the ancients adduces as a reason for despising life, 'No good thing can bring us pleasure but that for whose loss we are prepared:' *Grief for a lost thing and the fear of losing it equally affect the mind* (SENECA); thinking to make clear thereby that we cannot truly enjoy life if we are in fear of losing it.

It might, however, be said, on the other hand, that we clasp and embrace this good thing the more closely and affectionately for seeing it to be less sure, and fearing to have it taken from us. For it is felt to be obvious that, as cold air helps to stir up a fire, our desire is also whetted by opposition:

> Ne'er had Danaë been by Jove embraced,
> Had she not been confined in brazen tower;
>
> OVID

and there is nothing that so naturally destroys an appetite as the satiety that comes of facility; nothing that so whets it as rarity and difficulty. *In all things pleasure gains a new attraction from the very danger which should deter us* (SENECA).

> Deny thy favours, Galla; love is cloyed
> When bliss is not with torment blent. MARTIAL

1 The Pyrrhonian.

To keep love in breath, Lycurgus decreed that married couples in Sparta should only meet by stealth, and that they should be as much ashamed at being discovered sleeping together as if they had been caught in adultery. The difficulty of assignations, the danger of surprise, the shame of the morrow,

Silence and listlessness and piteous sighs
Drawn from the inmost soul,

HORACE

these things it is that give piquancy to the sauce. How many most lasciviously pleasant sports are the result of the modest and shamefaced style of books on Love! Lust even seeks an additional zest in pain. The pleasure is sweeter when it smarts and scorches. The courtesan Flora[2] used to say that she had never lain with Pompey but she made him carry away the marks of her teeth:

The parts they sought for, those they
squeeze so tight,
And pain the body; implant their teeth upon
The lips, and crush the mouth with kisses, yet
Not unalloyed with joy; for there are stings
Which goad them on to hurt the very thing,
Whate'er it be, from whence arise for them
Those germs of frenzy.

LUCRETIUS

So it is in everything; difficulty gives value to things. The people of the March of Ancona prefer to pay

2 Dictes-moy où, n'en quel pays,
Est Flora la bele Romaine.
Villon, *Ballade des Dames du temps jadis.*

their devotions to Saint James, and the people of Galicia to Our Lady of Loreto.[3] At Liège they have a high opinion of the baths of Lucca, and in Tuscany they think as highly of those at Spa. You rarely see a Roman in the fencing-school at Rome, which is filled with Frenchmen.

The great Cato became as weary of his wife as any of us might do, as long as she was his wife, and desired her when she became another's.

I have turned an old horse into the stud, as he got quite out of hand when he scented a mare. Facility presently sated him towards his own; but at sight of the first stranger that passed along his paddock, he would neigh as impatiently, and become as hot and furious, as ever.

Our appetite despises and looks beyond what is at hand, and runs after what it does not possess:

He slights what's near at hand, and longs
For what's beyond his reach. HORACE

To forbid us a thing is to make us long for it:

If thou no better guard that girl of thine,
She'll soon begin to be no longer mine.
OVID

To give it wholly into our possession is to breed in us contempt for it. Want and abundance each have their disadvantages:

You of your superfluity complain,
And I of want. *adapted from* TERENCE

3 Saint James of Compostela in Galicia: the Italians go on pilgrimage to Spain, the Spaniards to Italy. Loreto is near Ancona.

Desire and enjoyment make us equally impatient. The severity of a mistress becomes a weariness, but an easy and yielding disposition becomes, to tell the truth, a greater; seeing that dissatisfaction and anger are the result of the value which we put on the desired object, sharpening and kindling love. But satiety breeds distaste; it is a blunt, dull, weary, and drowsy feeling.

If you would keep your lover at your side,
Treat him with scorn.

OVID

Treat your mistress with neglect;
If yesterday she said you nay,
She'll come to you another day.

PROPERTIUS

What was Poppaea's intention, when she hid her beauty behind a mask, but to enhance it in the eyes of her lovers? Why do they veil, even down to the heels, the beauties that every woman desires to show, and every man to see? Why do they cover with so many obstacles, one on top of another, the parts on which are chiefly concentrated our desires and their own? And what purpose is served by those great bastions which our ladies have recently adopted, to fortify their flanks, except to allure our appetites, and attract us to them by keeping us at a distance?

She hies her to the willows, hoping to be seen.

VIRGIL

Her tunic interposed would ofttimes rouse
my passion.

PROPERTIUS

What is the object of that maidenly modesty, that deliberate coolness, that severe expression, that profession of ignorance of things they know better than we who instruct them, but to increase in us the longing to overcome, bear down, and trample upon all those affected airs and those obstacles to our desire? For there is not only a pleasure, but a source of vainglory, in seducing that meek, mild and childlike bashfulness, in inflaming and goading it into madness, and in subduing to our ardour a cool and calculated sternness. It is a matter for boasting, they say, to triumph over rigour, modesty, chastity and temperance; and whoever dissuades the ladies from those attitudes, betrays both them and himself. We are to believe that their hearts shudder with fright, that the sound of our words offends the purity of their ears, that they hate us for them, and yield to our importunities by a forced constraint. Beauty, all-powerful as it is, has no power to make itself relished without that interposition.

Look at Italy, where there is most beauty on sale, and the most perfect of its kind, and how they are obliged to seek extraneous means and other arts to make it acceptable; and yet, to tell the truth, whatever they may do, being venal and public, it remains feeble and languid. Just as, even in the case of valour, when two deeds are alike, we hold that to be the nobler and more worthy, which offers the most difficulty and risk.

It is the work of divine Providence to suffer its holy Church to be disturbed, as we see it now, by so many troubles and storms, in order that pious souls may be roused up by this strife, and rescued from that drowsy lethargy in which they were plunged during a prolonged period of tranquillity. If we weigh the loss we have suffered by the many who have gone astray, against the gain that accrues to us through having recovered our breath, and resuscitated our zeal and our strength as the result of this strife, I know not whether the profit does not outweigh the loss.

We thought we had tied the knot of our marriages more firmly by removing all means of dissolving them; but the bond of hearts and affections has become more loose and slack as that of constraint has been drawn closer. And, on the other hand, what made marriages to be so long honoured and so secure in Rome was the liberty to break them off at will. They loved their wives the better as long as there was the chance of losing them, and, with full liberty of divorce, five hundred years and more passed by before any took advantage of it.

What's free we are disgusted at, and slight;
What is forbidden whets the appetite.

OVID

We might here mention the opinion of an ancient writer which is to the point, 'That punishments rather whet than dull the edge of sins; That, instead of making us careful to do good, which is the work of reason and discipline, they only make us careful not to be caught doing ill':

Though rooted out, the infection of the plague
Spreads more luxuriantly.

RUTILIUS

I do not know whether that be true; but I know this by experience, that never was a civil government reformed by that means. It needs some other power to make us orderly and regular in our morals.

Greek history makes mention of the Argippaeans, neighbours of the Scythians, who live without either rod or stick for striking; yet not only does no one attempt to attack them, but any man who wishes to take refuge among them is safe, by reason of their virtue and sanctity of life, and there is no one who is so daring as to touch him. People of other regions have recourse to them to settle their differences.

There is a country where gardens and fields are made safe by being enclosed by a cotton thread only, which is found to be more firm and secure than our hedges and moats. *Things sealed up invite the thief. The burglar passes by an open door* (SENECA).

The easy access to my house is perhaps a reason among others why it has escaped the violence of our civil wars. Defence allures the enterprising, and distrust provokes them. I have baffled the designs of the soldiery by depriving the exploit of all danger and all chance of military glory, which have usually provided them with an excuse and a pretext. Every courageous deed is an honourable deed in times when justice is dead. I have thus made the conquest of my house a cowardly action and a treachery. It is closed to nobody who knocks. It is provided with no other safeguard but a porter with old-fashioned ceremonious manners, whose office it is not to forbid my door, but rather to offer it with the more grace and decorum. I have no other sentinel nor watch but what the stars keep for me.

It is a mistake for a gentleman to make a show of defence, unless his defence be perfect. What is open on one side is open on all. Our fathers did not think of building frontier garrisons. The means of attacking, I mean without armies and artillery, and of falling upon our houses by surprise, every day grow greater than the means of guarding them. Men's wits generally are sharpened in that direction. Poor and rich alike are interested in invading, the rich alone in defending.

My house was strong for the time when it was built. I have added nothing to it in the way of strength, and should be afraid that its strength might be turned against me. Besides that a peaceful period would require it to be unfortified; and there is the risk of being unable to recover it. And it is difficult to make sure of being safe. For in the matter of intestine wars, your own footman may be on the side you fear. And where religion serves as a pretext even kinship becomes unreliable, under the cloak of justice. The public exchequer will not support our domestic garrisons; it would be drained thereby. We have not the means of doing so without ruin to ourselves, or, more unfitly and unjustly, without ruin to the people. My loss could hardly be greater.

Moreover, if you should ruin yourself, your friends will even go out of their way, rather than pity you, to accuse you of want of vigilance and caution, of ignorance and carelessness in the exercise of your profession.

The fact that so many strongly guarded houses have been destroyed, whilst mine endures, makes me suspect that they were destroyed because they were strongly guarded. That arouses the assailant's desire, and provides him with an excuse. All defence wears the aspect of war. If God wills it, let them attack me; but in any case I will not invite attack. It is my retreat and resting-place from wars. I try to keep this corner as a haven against the tempest outside, as I do another corner in my soul. Our war may well assume different forms, factions may vary and multiply; for my part, I do not budge. When so many houses were fortified in France, I alone of my rank, so far as I know, simply entrusted mine to the protection of heaven. And I never removed even a silver spoon or a title-deed. I will neither fear nor save myself by halves. If by full gratitude I can gain the divine favour, it will remain with me to the end; if not, I have still survived long enough to make my survival remarkable and fit to be recorded. How long? For quite thirty years.[4]

4 i.e., since the beginning of the civil wars, 1560 or 1562.

Of freedom of conscience

It is a common thing to see good intentions, unless guided by moderation, driving men to very mischievous acts. In this conflict which has now stirred up France to civil wars, the best and the soundest side is no doubt that which upholds both the old religion and the old government of the country. Yet amongst the honourable men who follow that side (for I do not mean those men who make a pretence of it, either to wreak their private vengeance, or to gratify their avarice, or to court the favour of princes; but those who follow it out of true zeal to their religion and a godly desire to maintain the peace and the present state of their country), among these, I say, we see many who are driven by passion beyond the bounds of reason, and sometimes adopting unjust, violent, and even foolhardy measures.

It is certain that in those early days when our religion first gained authority with the laws, many armed themselves with zeal against pagan books of every kind, in consequence of which men of letters have suffered an enormous loss. In my estimation this devastation has done more harm to letters than all the fires of the barbarians. A good witness to this is Cornelius Tacitus; for although the Emperor Tacitus, his kinsman, had, by express command, furnished all the libraries in the world with his works, not a single complete copy was able to escape the careful search of those who desired to destroy them, on account of five or six insignificant sentences adverse to our religion.

Another characteristic of theirs was their readiness to lend undeserved praise to all the Emperors who were on our side, and to condemn generally all the actions of those who were hostile to us; as we may plainly see in the case of the Emperor Julian, surnamed the Apostate.

He was indeed a very great and very uncommon man, with a mind deeply imbued with the teachings of philosophy, by which he professed to regulate all his actions. And indeed there is no kind of virtue of which he has not left behind some very notable examples. In respect of chastity (of which in the course of his life he gives very clear evidence), they tell of him a similar story to that related of Alexander and Scipio, that of a number of very beautiful captive girls he would not even look at one, although he was then in the prime of life, for he was killed by the Parthians at the early age of thirty-one.

As to his justice, he went to the trouble of personally hearing the parties to a suit; and, although out of curiosity he would inquire of what religion they were who appeared before him, yet the hostility he bore to ours never weighed down the scales. He himself made sundry good laws and cut down a great number of the subsidies and imposts which his predecessors had levied.

We have two good historians who were eye-witnesses of his actions. One of them, Marcellinus, strongly condemns, in several passages of his history, that edict of his which forbade all Christian rhetoricians and grammarians to keep school and teach;

and he adds that he could wish this action of his to be buried in silence. It is probable that, had Julian adopted any harsher measures against the Christians, Marcellinus would not have omitted to mention them, being very favourably inclined to our religion.

He was indeed a harsh, but not a cruel, enemy to us; for our own people tell this story of him: One day, as he was walking about the city of Chalcedon, Maris, the Bishop of the place, had the temerity to call him 'wicked traitor to Christ', to which he merely answered, 'Go, wretched man, and deplore the loss of your eyes.' To which the Bishop retorted, 'I thank Jesus Christ for having deprived me of sight, that I might not see your insolent face.' Wherein they say he affected a philosophic tolerance. It is at least true that this action cannot be reconciled with the cruelties he is reported to have exercised against the Christians. He was (says Eutropius, my other witness) an enemy to Christianity, but without touching blood.

And, to return to his justice, there is nothing to be brought up against him except the severity he exercised, in the beginning of his reign, against those who had sided with Constantius, his predecessor.

As to his sobriety, he always lived a soldier's life; and even in peace times he dieted himself like a man who is preparing and training for the hardships of war.

His vigilance was such that he divided the night into three or four parts, the least part of which was allotted to sleep; the rest of it was spent either in supervising in person the state of his army and his bodyguard, or in study; for, among other rare qualities of his, he was a very eminent scholar in all branches of literature.

They tell of Alexander the Great that, having gone to rest, lest sleep should divert him from his thoughts and studies, he had a basin placed at his bedside, and grasping a copper ball in one hand held it over the basin, in order that, should sleep overtake him and cause his fingers to relax their hold, the noise of the ball dropping into the basin might awaken him. Our man had his mind so bent on what he was about, and so little disturbed by the fumes of wine, by reason of his singular abstinence, that he was able to dispense with that artifice.

As to his eminence in military matters, he was wonderfully endowed with all the qualities appertaining to a great general, and no wonder, since he was nearly all his life continually engaged in warfare, for the most part with us in France, against the Germans and Franks. We have hardly any record of a man who looked on more dangers, or more often gave proof of his personal valour.

His death has something in common with that of Epaminondas; for he was pierced by an arrow and tried to pull it out, and would have done so but that, the arrow having a sharp edge, he cut and disabled his hand. He incessantly requested to be carried back, as he was, into the thick of the battle, to encourage his soldiers, who very bravely held their own without him, until night separated the armies.

To philosophy he was indebted for the singular contempt in which he held his life and things human. He had a firm belief in the eternity of the soul.

In the matter of religion he was wrong throughout. He was called the Apostate for having abandoned ours; yet there seems to be more likelihood in this explanation: That he never had Christianity at heart, but that, in obedience to the laws, he dissembled until he held the Empire in his own hands.

He was so superstitious in his own religion that even his co-religionists of the time ridiculed him; they said that if he had gained the victory over the Parthians, he would have drained the world of oxen to satisfy his sacrifices. He was also infatuated with the art of divination, and encouraged all kinds of prognostications.

He said at his death, among other things, that he was grateful to the gods, and thanked them, for having decreed that he should not be surprised by death, since they had long before apprised him of the time and place of his end, and that he should neither die a soft and ignominious death, more suitable to idle and effeminate persons, nor a prolonged, lingering, and painful death; that they had held him worthy of dying in this noble way, in the full tide of his victories and at the height of his fame. He had had a vision like Marcus Brutus, which first threatened him in Gaul and afterwards reappeared to him in Persia, at the point of his death.

These words that they have put into his mouth when he felt himself wounded, 'You have vanquished, Nazarene,' or, according to others, 'Be satisfied, Nazarene,' would not have been forgotten, if they had been believed, by my witnesses, who, being present in the army, observed his slightest movements and words at the end; any more than certain other miracles attached to his name.

And, to come back to the subject of my essay, he had, according to Marcellinus, long cherished paganism in his heart. But since his army was wholly composed of Christians, he did not dare to disclose it. In the end, when he found himself strong enough to venture to proclaim his change of mind, he caused the temples of the gods to be thrown open, and did his utmost to restore idolatry. To effect his purpose, having found the people at Constantinople at loggerheads, and the prelates of the Christian church divided among themselves, he summoned them to his palace, and earnestly admonished them to suppress their civil dissensions, promising that every man should, without fear or hindrance, follow his own religion. He was very careful to urge this point, in the hope that this liberty would strengthen the factions and the schisms which divided them, and would prevent the people from becoming reunited, and consequently fortifying themselves against him by unanimous concord and mutual understanding, having learned by experience, from the cruelty of some of the Christians, 'That there is no beast in the world so much to be feared by man, as man.'

Those are very nearly his words. Wherein this is worthy of consideration, that the Emperor Julian, to stir up civil troubles and dissensions, uses the same remedy of freedom of conscience that our Kings have lately employed to stifle them. It may be said, on the one side, that to give a loose rein to the factions to hold to their opinions, is to sow and scatter division, and almost to lend a hand to increase it, there being no barrier and restraint of the laws to check and impede its course. But, on the other side, it might also be said that to give the factions the reins to hold to their beliefs is to render them soft and lax through ease and facility, and to blunt the edge which is sharpened by rarity, novelty and difficulty. And so I think it is better, for the honour of the piety of our kings, that, not having been able to do what they would, they have made a show of willing what they could.

Of not malingering

There is an epigram of Martial, which is among his good ones (for they are of all sorts), and in which he tells in a humorous way the story of Caelius who, to avoid paying his court to several of the great men in Rome, assisting at their levee, following and attending upon them, pretended to have the gout; and, to make his excuse the more plausible, had his legs rubbed with ointment and swathed, and in all respects assumed the behaviour and looks of a gouty person. In the end Fortune gratified him by making him really so:

> What may not man with care and art obtain;
> He feigned the gout, and now has ceased to feign.
>
> MARTIAL

I have read, somewhere in Appian, I think, a similar story of one who, wishing to escape the proscriptions of the triumvirs at Rome, and to evade recognition by those who were in pursuit of him, disguised and hid himself, pretending in addition to be blind in one eye. When he came to recover a little more liberty, and removed the plaster he had so long worn over that eye, he found that under the disguise he had really lost the sight of it.

It may be that the action of sight had become dulled through having been so long without exercise, and that the visual power had wholly transferred itself to the other eye. For if we keep one eye covered we can very plainly feel it conveying some part of its virtue to its fellow, with the result that the eye which remains free dilates and grows bigger. So also idleness, combined with the heat of the bandages and medicaments, might very well have attracted some podagric humour to the gouty man of Martial's epigram.

Having read in Froissart of the vow taken by a band of young English noblemen to keep their left eye covered until they had crossed over into France and distinguished themselves in fighting against us, I have often been tickled by the idea that they might have been caught, like the abovementioned, and might have returned with only one good eye to the mistresses for whom they had taken this rash vow.

Mothers are right to scold their children when they mimic blindness, lameness, squinting, and other personal infirmities of the same kind. For besides that their body at that tender age might take on some evil ply, Fortune somehow seems to deride us and take us at our word. I have heard of many instances of people becoming ill after pretending to be so.

I have always been accustomed, when riding or walking, to burden my hand with a switch or stick, even affecting an air of elegance by using it as a support. Several have warned me that Fortune might one day turn this foppery into a necessity. I rely upon the fact that I should be the very first of my clan to have the gout.

But let us prolong this chapter and checker it with another story on the subject of blindness. Pliny tells of a man who, dreaming in his sleep that he was blind, next morning found himself really so, though he had not previously suffered any infirmity. The power of imagination may easily be a contributing cause, as I have explained elsewhere; and Pliny seems to be of that opinion. But it is more probable that the agitation which the body felt within (of which the physicians may, if they please, discover the cause), and which deprived him of his sight, occasioned the dream.

We will add one more story, akin to this subject, which Seneca relates in one of his letters: 'You know, he says, writing to Lucilius, that Harpaste, my wife's idiot, has been thrown upon my hands as a hereditary burden; for I have a natural aversion to these freaks; and if I have a mind to laugh at a fool, I have not far to go, for I can laugh at myself. This idiot has suddenly lost her sight. I am telling you something strange but true. She is not conscious of being blind, and keeps urging her keeper to take her out, because she says my house is dark.

'What we laugh at in her I pray you to believe happens to every one of us: no man knows that he is avaricious or covetous. The blind at least ask for a guide; we go astray of our own accord. I am not ambitious, we say; but at Rome a man cannot live otherwise. I am not a spendthrift, but the city requires a great outlay. It is not my fault if I am choleric, if I have not yet laid down a certain plan of life; it is the fault of youth.

'Let us not seek our evil outside of us; it is within us, it is rooted in our entrails. And the mere fact that we are not conscious of being sick makes the cure more difficult. If we do not begin in good time to look after ourselves, when shall we have time to attend to so many sores and maladies? And yet we have a very sweet medicine in philosophy; for of the others we do not feel the pleasure until after the cure. This one pleases and cures at the same time.'

Those are the words of Seneca, who has carried me away from my theme. But there is profit in change.

Of a young monstrosity

This tale shall be told quite simply; for I leave it to the doctors to discuss it. Two days ago I saw a boy that was being carried about by two men and a nurse, who said they were his father, his uncle and aunt, to make a few coppers by exhibiting him on account of his strangeness. In all other respects he was of ordinary shape; he could stand on his feet, walk and chatter much as other boys of the same age. He had not yet taken to any food except his nurse's milk, and when, in my presence, they tried to put something into his mouth, he chewed it a little and spat it out without swallowing it. There was certainly something unusual in his crying. He was just fourteen months old.

Below the paps he was fast stuck to another boy that had no head, the spinal canal being stopped up; the rest of the body was entire. One arm was indeed shorter than the other, but it had been broken by accident at birth. They were joined face to face, as if a smaller child were trying to embrace one a little bigger. The juncture and the space where they held together was only four fingers' breadth or thereabouts, so that if you turned up the imperfect child you could see below it the navel of the other; so the joining was between the paps and his navel. The navel of the smaller child could not be seen, but you could see all the rest of his belly. Thus the unattached parts of the imperfect child, as the arms, the rump, the thighs and legs, remained hanging and dangling from the other, and might reach half-way down his legs. The nurse told us besides that he urined from both places; also that the limbs of this other were nourished and living, and throve as well as his own, except that they were smaller and thinner.

This double body and its several limbs corresponding to a single head might indeed serve as a favourable augury to the King, that he will maintain those several parties and factions of our State under the union of his laws. But, lest the issue might belie the prophecy, it will be better to let it go on before; for there is no prophesying except in things already past. *So that, when things have come to pass, we may interpret them as prophecies* (CICERO). So they said of Epimenides that he prophesied backwards.

I have just seen a shepherd at Medoc, thirty years of age or thereabouts, who has no show of genital parts. He has three holes from which he continually drops his water. He is bearded, has desires, and readily seeks contact with women.

What we call monstrosities are not so to God, who sees in the immensity of his work the infinity of shapes which he has comprehended within it; and it may be believed that this figure which arouses our astonishment corresponds to and resembles some other figures of the same kind unknown to man. From his all-wisdom there proceeds nothing that is not good, usual and regular; but we do not see the relationship and the harmony. *What he often sees does not excite his wonder, even though he knows not the cause of it. But if a thing happen that he has not already seen, he regards it as a prodigy* (CICERO).

We call contrary to Nature what happens contrary

to what is customary; there is nothing whatsoever that is contrary to Nature. This universal and natural reason should dispel from our minds the errors and the wonder caused by what is new and strange.[1]

1 Nowhere perhaps does Montaigne more clearly show how far he is in advance of his age than in his attitude to deformities and monstrosities, which in his day and long after were usually regarded as a judgement of God.

Of three good wives

Good women are not found by the dozen, as everybody knows, and especially in the duties of marriage; for that is a bargain fraught with so many difficulties, that a woman's will is strained to keep to it entirely for long. The men, although they enter into it under somewhat better conditions, yet have enough to do to keep to it.

The touchstone of a good marriage, and its real proof, is the duration of the partnership, and whether it has been constantly pleasant, loyal, and smooth. In our days the women more commonly reserve the display of their good offices and the strength of their affection for their husbands until after they have lost them; then at least they seek to give evidence of their goodwill. A tardy and unseasonable testimony! They prove thereby rather that they only love them when dead.

Life is full of tumult; death, of love and courtesy. As fathers conceal their affection for their children, so the wives likewise are wont to conceal their affection for their husbands, in order to keep up a modest respect. That mystery is not to my liking. In vain do they tear their hair and lacerate their faces; I should go to the lady's maid or the secretary and whisper in their ear, 'How did they get on? How did they live together?'

I am always reminded of that wise saying: *They make most ostentation of sorrow who grieve the least.*[1]

1 Altered from Tacitus.

Their glum looks are offensive to the living and useless to the dead. We should willingly give them leave to smile after, if only they smile on us during life. Is it not enough to bring one back to life in vexation to find her who spat in his face when alive coming and rubbing his feet when he is hardly dead? If there is any honour in weeping over a husband, it is only for one who has smiled upon him; let those who have wept during his life smile at his death, outwardly as well as inwardly.

Therefore pay no heed to those tear-stained eyes and that pitiful voice; observe rather her bearing, her colour and the plumpness of her cheeks under those thick veils; it is by them that they speak plain French. There are few who do not improve in health, an infallible sign. That ceremonious demeanour looks not so much backward as forward; it means acquisition more than payment. When I was a boy, an honest and very fair lady, the widow of a Prince and still living, dressed a little more ornamentally than is permitted by our laws of widowhood; to those who reproved her for it, she replied, 'The meaning of it is that I am not on the look-out for a new lover, and have no desire to marry again.'

In order not to be quite out of harmony with our customs, I have here made choice of three women whose extreme tenderness and affection also centred around their husbands' death. Yet they are examples of a somewhat different kind, and of a love so convincing that they bravely threw life into the scale.

Pliny the Younger had a neighbour living near one of his houses in Italy who was grievously afflicted with ulcers on his private parts. His wife, seeing his prolonged anguish, entreated him to allow her to examine at leisure the condition of his malady, that she might tell him more frankly than any other what hopes he had. His permission being obtained, and having carefully considered his case, she found that a cure was impossible, and that all he could hope for was to drag out a painful and lingering life. Therefore she advised him, as the surest and most sovereign remedy, to kill himself; and finding him a little reluctant to adopt so heroic a measure, she said, 'Do not think, my friend, that the pain I see you suffering does not touch me as much as yourself, and that I am not willing to use, to rid myself of it, the same medicine I am prescribing for you. I will accompany you in the cure as I have done in the disease. Put away your fear, and believe me that we shall derive only pleasure from this passage which is to deliver us from such torments. We will depart happily together.'

Having said that, and warmed up her husband's courage, she resolved that they should leap into the lake[2] through a window of their house that overlooked it. And, to preserve to the last that loyal and vehement affection with which she had embraced him during life, she desired that he should die in her arms. But, lest they should fail her and the closeness of her embrace be relaxed in the fall through fear, she had herself fast bound to him by the waist; and so gave up her own life for the repose of her husband's.[3]

This was a woman of humble origin; and in this

2 Lake Larius, the modern Como.

3 Montaigne rather elaborates the story, which Pliny tells in a third as many words; introducing it with the remark: 'How much does the fame of human actions depend upon the station of those who perform them!'

class of people it is not so unusual to see occasional acts of uncommon goodness:

> When Justice fled this world of wickedness,
> 'Twas in their midst that last her steps were seen.
>
> VIRGIL

The other two are noble and rich, among whom examples of virtue are rarely found.

Arria, wife of Cecinna Paetus, a man of consular rank, was the mother of another Arria, the wife of Thrasea Paetus, so renowned for his virtue in Nero's time, and through this son-in-law, grandmother of Fannia; for the resemblance between the names and fortunes of these men and women has led many to confuse them. When Cecinna Paetus, her husband, was taken prisoner by the Emperor Claudius' soldiers, after the defeat of Scribonianus, whose party he had joined, this first Arria entreated those who were leading him captive to Rome, to take her into their ship, where she would be of much less expense and trouble to them than a number of persons they would need to wait upon her husband, since she alone would undertake the whole charge of his cabin, his cooking, and all other services. They refused her request. She embarked in a small fishing-vessel which she hired on the spot, and in this craft followed him from Sclavonia.

One day, when they were at Rome, in presence of the Emperor, Junia, the widow of Scribonianus, having familiarly accosted her on the strength of their similar fortunes, she repulsed her rudely with these words, 'I, speak to you, or listen to anything you say! you, in whose lap Scribonianus was killed, and you still alive!' These words, together with several other indications, made her relations suspect that, unable to endure her husband's fate, she was designing to do away with herself. And when Thrasea, her son-in-law, on hearing those words, entreated her not to throw her life away, saying, 'What! if I incurred the same fate as Cecinna, would you expect my wife, your daughter, to do the same?' 'Would I? she replied, most certainly I would, if she had lived as long and in such harmony with you as I have done with my husband.' These answers increased their solicitude about her, and made them watch her conduct more carefully.

One day she said to those who were keeping guard over her, 'You may do what you please, you may drive me to a much more painful death, but prevent me from dying you cannot;' and thereupon, rushing madly from the chair on which she was seated, she dashed her head with all her might against the nearest wall, so that sorely bruised she fell down in a swoon. After they had with great trouble brought her round, she said, 'I told you that if you refused me some easy way of dying, I would choose another, however painful it might be.'

The end of so admirable a virtue was this: When her husband Paetus was sentenced to death by the Emperor's cruelty, he had not sufficient courage of his own to take his life. One day, among others, after employing all the arguments and persuasions which she thought best calculated to prevail upon him to do her bidding, she snatched the dagger which her husband was wearing and, holding it naked in her hand, said, as a last exhortation, 'Do this, Paetus,' and at the same instant dealt herself a fatal stab in the heart. Then, tearing it out of the wound, she offered it to him, at the same time ending her life with these noble, generous, and immortal words, *Paete, non dolet.* She had only time to utter those three words of such beautiful meaning, 'See, Paetus, it does not hurt me.'

When from her breast chaste Arria snatched the sword,
And gave the fatal weapon to her lord,
'My wound, she said, believe me, does not smart;
'Tis thine alone, my Paetus, pains my heart.'

MARTIAL

The words are much more alive in the original, and richer in meaning; for both her husband's and her own wound and death were so small a matter to her, since it was she who advised and instigated them. But having taken this bold and heroic step solely for her husband's benefit, she had no thoughts except for him in the last gasp of her life, and for removing his fear of following her in death. Paetus immediately stabbed himself with the same blade; ashamed, as I think, of having needed so dear and precious a lesson.

Pompeia Paulina, a young and very noble Roman lady, had married Seneca in his extreme old age. Nero, his precious pupil, sent his satellites to announce to him his death decree, which was done in this wise: When the Roman Emperors of that time had sentenced any man of rank, they sent him word by their officers to choose what death he pleased, and to take his life within such and such a prescribed time, which was shorter or longer according to the temper of their choler; giving him leisure to arrange his affairs during that time, or sometimes making the interval so short that he was deprived of the opportunity of doing so. And, if the condemned resisted the order, they sent special men to execute it, either by cutting the veins of his arms and legs, or forcibly making him take poison. But a man of honour did not abide this necessity and employed his own physician and surgeon to that end.

Seneca heard their charge with calm and confident demeanour, and then asked for paper to make his will; which being refused by the centurion, he turned to his friends. 'Since I cannot, he said, leave you anything else in requital of what I owe you, I leave you at least the best thing I possess, which is the example of my life and character, which I pray you to cherish in your memory, that by doing so you may acquire the name of true and sincere friends.' At the same time, now with gentle words assuaging the bitterness of the grief he saw they were suffering, now hardening his voice to chide them, 'Where, he said, are those brave precepts of philosophy? What has become of the provisions that for so many years we have laid up against the accidents of Fortune? Was Nero's cruelty unknown to us? What could we expect of a man who has killed his mother and his brother, if not that he would also put to death the tutor who has fostered and brought him up?'

Having spoken these words to the company, he turned to his wife, and, closely embracing her, whose heart and strength were sinking under the weight of her grief, he entreated her for the love of him to bear this misfortune a little more patiently, and said to her that the hour was come when he had to show, no longer by words and arguments, but by deeds, the fruit he had gathered from his studies; and that he really embraced death, not only without pain, but cheerfully. 'Wherefore, my love, he added, do not dishonour it by your tears, that you may not seem to love yourself more than my reputation; moderate your grief, and comfort yourself with the knowledge you have had of me and my actions, and pass the remainder of your life in the honest occupations to which you are devoted.'

To this Paulina, having a little recovered her spirits and warmed her great heart by a very noble affection, replied, 'No, Seneca, I am not the woman to leave you without my company in such a need; I will not have you think that the virtuous examples you have set by your life have not also taught me how to die well; and how could I do so better and more honourably, or more to my own desire, than in your company? So be assured that I am departing with you.' Then Seneca, approving this noble and glorious resolution of his wife, and glad to be delivered of the fear of leaving her after his death at the mercy and cruelty of his enemies, said, 'I have advised you how to lead your life more happily; you prefer then the honour of death. Truly I will not begrudge it you; the fortitude and resolution in our common end may be alike, but the beauty and glory will be greater on your part.'

When he had said that, the veins of their arms were opened at the same time, but Seneca's being shrunk both through old age and abstinence, and the blood flowing too long and too sluggishly, he ordered them also to cut the veins of his thighs; and lest the anguish he was suffering might pierce his wife's heart, and to be delivered from the affliction he felt at seeing her in so pitiable a condition, after taking a very tender leave of her, he prayed her to allow herself to be carried into the adjoining room; which was done.

But all these incisions being still insufficient to

cause his death, he ordered his physician, Statius Annaeus, to give him a poisonous draught, which had scarcely more effect; for, by reason of the feebleness and chilliness of the limbs, it could not reach the heart. Therefore they prepared in addition a very hot bath; and then, feeling his end to be near, as long as he had any breath he continued to talk very excellently on the subject of his present condition, his secretaries taking down his words as long as they were able to hear his voice. And his last words were long after treasured and held in honour by men (it is a grievous loss to us that they have not been preserved to this day). As he felt the last pangs of death, with some of the bath-water mixed with blood he wetted his head,[4] saying, 'I make libation of this water to Jove the Deliverer.'

When Nero was informed of all this, fearing lest he might incur the blame of Paulina's death, who was a lady allied to some of the best families in Rome, and towards whom he felt no particular enmity, he sent in all haste to command her wounds to be bound up; which her people did without her knowledge, she being already half dead and unconscious. And, though she continued to live against her design, she lived very honourably and as befitted her virtue; her wan complexion testifying how much life had flowed from her wounds.

Those are my three very true stories, which I find as entertaining and as tragic as any of those that we make up out of our heads to please the public. And I wonder

4 According to Tacitus, who appears to be Montaigne's authority, he did not wet his head, but 'sprinkled' some of his slaves.

that it does not occur to those who are devoted to that kind of composition to choose rather one of ten thousand very fine stories which are found in books, which would give them less trouble and bring more pleasure and profit. And if any man should wish to build up a whole and connected body of them, he need provide nothing of his own but the link, like the solder of some other kind of metal; by this means he might accumulate a store of true incidents of all sorts, arranging and varying them as the beauty of the work may require, pretty much as Ovid sewed and pieced together, from that great number of different fables, his *Metamorphoses*.

In respect of the last couple, this is also worthy of consideration, that Paulina voluntarily offers to relinquish this life for love of her husband, and that her husband had once also relinquished death for the love of her. To us there is no great equivalence in this exchange, but, according to his Stoic way of thinking, it seems to me that he thought he had done as much for her in prolonging his life for her sake, as if he had died for her.

In one of the letters he wrote to Lucilius, after giving him to understand that, having caught a fever at Rome, he immediately took coach to retire to one of his country houses, against his wife's advice, who tried to make him stay; and that he had replied that his fever was not a fever of the body, but of the place, he continues as follows: 'She allowed me to go, strongly recommending me to look after my health. Now I, knowing that her life is involved in mine, begin to look after myself in order to look after her. I lose the privilege which my old age had given me of being more firm and resolute in many things, when I remember that in this old life there is a young life to which I am of some use. Since I cannot bring her to love me more courageously, she brings me to love myself more carefully; for we must allow something to honest affections. And at times, although occasions urge us to the contrary, we must call back our life, even though it be a torture. We must arrest the soul between our teeth, since with men of honour the law of living is determined not by their pleasure but by their duty.

'The man who does not value his wife or one of his friends sufficiently to prolong his life for them, and obstinately persists in dying, is too squeamish and lax in his love. The soul must command itself to do this, when it is requisite to serve our dear ones. We must sometimes lend ourselves to our friends, and, when we would rather die for our own sake, renounce our intention for theirs. It is evidence of a great heart to return to life out of consideration for others, as many eminent men have done. And it is a sign of a singular good nature to preserve old age (the greatest advantage of which is that it makes us less solicitous about prolonging it, and more courageous and disdainful in the conduct of life), if we feel we are doing some sweet, agreeable, and profitable service to one to whom we are very dear. And we reap a very pleasant reward; for what is sweeter than to be so dear to your wife that for her sake you become dearer to yourself? So my Paulina has charged me not only with her fear, but also with my own. It was not enough for me to consider with how much fortitude I might die, but I have also considered with how little fortitude she might bear my death. I have forced myself to live, and to live is sometimes the mark of a great soul.'

Those are his words, excellent as they always are.

BOOK THREE

Of the useful and the honest

No man is exempt from saying silly things; the mischief is to say them deliberately:

> With all his pains he says most foolish things.
>
> TERENCE

That does not touch me; mine slip from me as heedlessly as they deserve. All the better for them. I would part with them at once for the little they are worth. And I neither buy nor sell them except for what they weigh. I speak to my paper as I speak to the first person I meet. That this is true, observe what follows.

To whom should not treachery be detestable, when Tiberius refused it when it was so much to his interest? They sent him word from Germany that, if he approved, they could rid him of Arminius by poison. He was the most powerful enemy the Romans had, since he had treated them so villainously under Varus, and was the only obstacle to the expansion of their dominion in those parts. Tiberius replied, 'that the Roman people were accustomed to take revenge on their enemies by open means, with arms in their hands, not by fraud and stratagem.' He renounced the profitable for the honest.

He was (you will tell me) an impostor. I believe it; it is no great miracle in men of his profession. But the recognition of virtue carries no less weight in the mouth of one who hates it, since truth forcibly wrests it from him, and, if he will not receive it into his heart, he at least covers himself with it, as with an ornament.

Our structure, both public and private, is full of imperfection. But there is nothing useless in Nature; not even uselessness itself. Nothing has thrust itself into this universe that has not its fitting place. Our being is cemented with diseased qualities: ambition, jealousy, envy, vindictiveness, superstition, despair, quarter themselves upon us with so natural a possession, that we recognize the semblance of them even in animals. Nay, cruelty too, so unnatural a vice; for, with all our compassion, we feel within us a kind of bitter-sweet pricking of malicious pleasure in witnessing the sufferings of others; and the children feel it:

'Tis sweet when, down the mighty main, the winds
Roll up its waste of waters, from the land
To watch another's labouring anguish far.

LUCRETIUS

Whoever would root out the seeds of those qualities in man would destroy the fundamental conditions of our life. Similarly, in every government there are necessary offices which are not only base but wicked. Wickedness finds a place there, and is employed in sewing and binding us together; as poison is used for the preservation of our health. If it becomes pardonable, since we are in need of it and the common necessity blots out its real quality, we must allow that part to be played by the stoutest and least timorous citizens, who will sacrifice their honour and their conscience; as those others, in ancient times, sacrificed their lives for the good of their country. We others who are more feeble will assume easier and less dangerous parts. The public weal requires men to betray, to lie, and to massacre; let us resign that charge to men who are more obedient and more compliant.

It has often really angered me to see a judge, by deceit and false hopes of favour or pardon, alluring a criminal to betray his offence, using to that end a shameless trickery. It would be a good service to justice, and to Plato even who countenances that custom, to furnish me with other means more to my liking. It is a mischievous kind of justice, and is wronged, in my opinion, no less by itself than by others. Not long ago I answered that I could hardly betray my Prince for a private individual, since I should be very sorry to betray any private person for the Prince; and I hate not only to deceive, but I also hate that anyone should be deceived in me. I will not even provide matter and occasion thereto.

On the few occasions I have had to negotiate between our Princes, in these divisions and subdivisions by which we are today rent in pieces, I have carefully avoided that they should be mistaken in me, or deceived by my face. The men of the trade[1] are the least open; they profess and pretend to be as unbiassed and as near to you as they can. For my part I recommend myself by my readiest opinions and by a manner that is most my own. A mild negotiator and a novice, I would rather fail in the business than be

1 The diplomats.

untrue to myself. And yet I have followed that course to this day with so much luck (for indeed Fortune has the chief share in it) that few men have been bandied from one to another with less suspicion and with greater favour and familiarity.

I have an open and easily ingratiating manner that inspires confidence at the first acquaintance. Naturalness and the simple truth will always find their opportunity and pass current, in any age whatever. Besides, the freedom of speech of the man who acts without any self-interest attracts little suspicion and odium. He may truly make use of the answer of Hyperides to the Athenians who complained of the bluntness of his speech: 'Good sirs, do not consider whether I am free-spoken, but whether I am so without accepting anything and without thereby advancing my own affairs.' My candour has also readily cleared me from all suspicion of dissembling by its vigour (leaving nothing unsaid, however painful and bitter; I could not have said worse behind their backs), and by its evident show of simplicity and indifference. I expect no other result from acting than to act, and look to no far-reaching consequences or projects. Every action plays its own particular game; let it strike home if it can.

Moreover I am not swayed by any passion, either of love or hatred, towards the great; nor is my will strangled by offence or obligation for particular favours. I look upon our Kings simply with the loyal affection of a citizen, which is neither stimulated nor cooled by private interest; for which I think the better of myself. To the general and rightful cause I have only a moderate attachment, without any heat. I am not subject to those close and deep-seated pledges and engagements. Anger and hatred go beyond the duty of justice, and are feelings which are useful only to those who are not sufficiently kept to their duty by simple reason. *Let him employ his passion who can make no use of his reason* (CICERO). All fair and lawful intentions are of themselves equable and temperate; if not, they degenerate and become seditious and unlawful. This it is that makes me walk ever with head erect, with open face and heart.

Indeed, and I am not afraid of confessing it, I could readily, in case of need, follow the example of the old woman and offer a candle to St Michael and another to his serpent.[2] I will follow the good side as far as the fire, but exclusively, if I can.[3] Let Montaigne be engulfed in the general ruin, if need be; but, if there is no need, I shall be grateful to Fortune if it escapes, and I will make use of all the length of rope my duty allows me, to save it.

Was it not Atticus who, holding to the right side, which was the losing side, in that general shipwreck of the world, amid so many changes and divisions, saved himself by his moderation? It is easier for a private citizen, as he was; and I think one may be justified in not being ambitious to thrust oneself uninvited into that kind of business.

When one's country is disturbed and the people are

2 To propitiate both parties. St Michael, who was presumably Montaigne's patron saint, was usually represented on altar-pieces in the act of slaying a dragon.

3 Montaigne is not in the habit of striking heroic attitudes, and we must not take him too literally. The words *jusqu'au feu exclusivement* are playfully adopted from Rabelais, who uses them several times. In the next sentence Montaigne means the château of that name.

divided I think it neither handsome nor honourable to be a wobbler and a hybrid, to be unmoved in one's affections and to incline to neither side. *That is not to steer a middle course; it is to steer no course at all. It is to await events, in order to join the fortunate side* (LIVY).

That may be allowed in the case of affairs with neighbours. And so Gelo, tyrant of Syracuse, in the war between the barbarians and Greeks, so suspended his inclination, keeping an ambassador with presents at Delphi, to be on the watch and see to which side Fortune should turn, and seize the right opportunity to make up to the victors. It would be a kind of treachery to act in this manner in the home affairs of one's own country, in which a man must necessarily and designedly make up his mind to join one side or the other.

But for a man to hold aloof from affairs who is not in public service, or driven by express command, I hold to be more excusable (and yet I do not accept this excuse for my own part) than not to join in foreign wars, in which, however, by our laws, no one need be engaged against his will. Nevertheless, even those who are wholly engaged in them may conduct themselves with such order and moderation that the storm will pass over their heads without injury to themselves. Had we not reason to expect this in the case of the late Bishop of Orleans, the Sieur de Morvilliers? And among those who at this moment are valiantly labouring at it, I know some of such even and mild temper that they are likely to remain standing, however great the ruin and desolation that Heaven has in store for us.

I am of opinion that it properly belongs to kings alone to quarrel with kings, and can see the absurdity of those spirited persons who gaily stand up to so uneven a contest. For to march openly and bravely against a Prince in defence of our honour and at the call of duty is not to pick a private quarrel with him. If he does not love such a man, he does better, he esteems him. And especially the cause of the laws and of the defence of the old State has always this privilege, that even those who, for private ends, attack the same, excuse, if they do not honour, the defenders.

But we must not call by the name of duty, as we do every day, a bitterness and asperity of the soul that is born of private interest and passion; nor must we call a treacherous and malicious conduct by the name of courage. Their mischievous and violent propensities they call zeal. It is not the cause that excites them but their self-interest. They stir up war, not because it is just, but because it is war.

There is nothing to prevent a man acting in an accommodating manner between men who are enemies, without being disloyal. Bear yourself with an affection, if not altogether equal (for it may be of different degrees), at least moderate, and which will not so pledge you to one of them that he can require everything at your hands. Content yourself too with a moderate measure of their favours, and with swimming in troubled waters without trying to fish in them.

The other way, that of offering to do one's best for both parties, shows imprudence rather than want of conscience. Does not the man to whom you betray another, who receives you with equal favour, know that you will treat him in the same way, when his turn comes? He regards you as a scoundrel; meanwhile he will listen to you, he will draw what he can out of you and turn your disloyalty to his own account. For double-dealers are useful for what they bring; but you must take good care that they carry away as little as they can.

I say nothing to the one that I could not say to the other at the right moment, with only a little change of accent; and I report only things that are either indifferent, or known, or which are serviceable to both sides. For no useful end would I permit myself to lie to them. What is entrusted to my silence I religiously keep; but I receive as few secrets as I can. The secrets of princes are an awkward trust to one who has no use for them. I willingly offer them this bargain, that they trust me with little, but that they confidently trust me in what I bring them. I have always known more than I wished.

Open speaking opens the way to another's speaking, and draws it out, like wine and love.

Philippides replied wisely to King Lysimachus, who asked him, 'Which of my goods do you wish me to hand over to you?' 'Whatever you please, provided it is not one of your secrets.' I have observed that men generally grumble if you keep from them the gist of the business on which you employ them, and if you conceal something that lies at the back of it. For my part, I am satisfied if they tell me no more than what they wish me to do; and do not desire that my knowledge of the business should exceed or restrict what I have to say. If I am to serve as a tool of deceit let me at least salve my conscience. I would not be thought either so affectionate or so loyal a servant as to be judged fit to betray any man. He who is untrue to himself is excusably so to his master.

But the Princes I have in my mind will not accept men by halves, and scorn limited and conditional services. There is no way out of it; I tell them frankly how far I will go. For if I must be a slave I will be so to reason alone; and yet I can hardly compass even that. And they too are wrong to demand of a free man the same submission and obligation to their service, as they do of a man they have created and bought, or whose fortunes are particularly and expressly bound up with theirs.

The laws have saved me great pains; they have chosen a side for me and given me a master. All other authority and obligation should be relative to that of the laws, and restricted. That does not mean however that, if my affection should otherwise incline me, my hand would immediately obey it.[4] Will and desire make their own laws; actions have to submit to the law of public policy.

My method of negotiating as a whole, as here described, is a little out of harmony with that practised in our country. It would produce neither great nor lasting results. Innocence itself could not negotiate between our parties without dissimulation, nor strike a bargain without lying. And besides, public employments are not in my line; what my profession requires I perform in as private a manner as I can.

As a youth I was plunged up to the ears in public affairs, and that not without success; and yet I let go of them in good time. Since then I have often declined, seldom consented, and never volunteered to meddle with them; keeping my back turned upon ambition, but, if not like rowers who thus advance backwards, yet so that I owe it more to my good

4 That if my affections inclined to the Protestants I should act with them.

fortune than to my resolution that I am not wholly embarked in them. For there are ways less inimical to my taste, and more within my capacity, by which, if Fortune had at one time invited me to take public service and to seek advancement in the world's honours, I know that I should have stepped over my better judgement, and followed her.

Those who usually declare, in contradiction to what I profess, what I call frankness, simplicity, and ingenuousness in my conduct to be art and cunning, and discretion rather than goodness, cleverness than naturalness, good sense than good luck, do me more honour than they rob me of. But indeed they make my subtlety too subtle; and if anyone has closely followed and spied upon me, I will own myself beaten, if he does not confess that there is no rule in their school[5] that could, on such various and tortuous roads, produce this natural impulse, and keep up an appearance of freedom and independence so uniformly inflexible; and that all their ingenuity and watchfulness are unable to bring them to it.

The way of truth is one and simple; that of private gain and of advantage, in the conduct of affairs a man is charged with, is double, uneven, and accidental. I have often seen that counterfeit and artificial freedom in practice, but for the most part without success. It is often too suggestive of the ass in Aesop's fable who, in imitation of the little dog, quite happily planted his two hoofs on his master's shoulders; but, whilst the little dog received caresses in abundance, the poor ass was treated to twice as many bastinadoes. *That best becomes a man which is most natural to him* (CICERO).

5 The school of diplomacy.

I will not deprive deceit of its place; that would be to misunderstand the world. I know that it has often been of profitable service, and that it supports and feeds most of the avocations of men. There are lawful sins, just as there are many either good or pardonable actions which are unlawful.

True justice, which is natural and universal, is otherwise regulated, and more nobly, than that other special, national justice, which is restricted by the necessities of our governments. *Of true right and real justice we have no solid and positive model; we practise only the shadow and image of it* (CICERO). The sage Dandamis,[6] hearing tell of the lives of Socrates, Pythagoras, and Diogenes, judged them to be great men in every other respect except that they were too much enslaved to reverence of the laws, to justify and support which true virtue must abate much of its original vigour; and added that many wicked actions are done not only with their permission, but by their instigation. *There are crimes authorized by the decrees of the Senate and the popular vote* (SENECA). I follow the ordinary language which makes a distinction between things that are profitable and things that are honest; so that some natural actions, which are not only profitable but necessary, are called dishonest and unclean.

But let us continue our examples of treachery. Two pretenders to the kingdom of Thrace had started a quarrel about their rights. The Emperor[7] prevented their coming to blows; but one of them, under colour of

6 A Hindu sage who lived in the time of Alexander the Great.

7 Tiberius; the pretenders were Rhescuporis and Cotys, the brother and son of Rhemetalces, the last King of Thrace.

bringing things to a friendly issue by a conference having invited his competitor to an entertainment in his own house, had him imprisoned and killed. Justice required that the Romans should demand satisfaction for this crime. There was a difficulty in obtaining it by ordinary means. What they could not lawfully do without war and risk, they attempted to do by treachery. What they could not do honestly they did profitably. For this they found a fit and proper instrument in Pomponius Flaccus. This man, having drawn the other into his nets by feigned words and assurances, instead of the honours and favours he promised him, sent him bound hand and foot to Rome.

Here one traitor betrays another, contrary to the usual custom; for traitors are full of distrust, and it is difficult to catch them with their own wiles; witness the sad experience we have lately had.[8]

Let who will be a Pomponius Flaccus, and there are men enough who are willing. For my part, both my word and my good faith are, like the rest of me, parts of this common body.[9] The best they are capable of is at the public service; I take that as a matter of course. But just as, if I were commanded to take charge of the Palace of Justice and the lawsuits, I should answer, 'I know nothing about them'; or, if commissioned to be a leader of pioneers, I should say, 'I am called to play a worthier part'; so also, if any man proposed to employ me to lie, to betray, commit perjury, not to speak of assassinating and poisoning, for some important end, I should say, 'If I have stolen or robbed from any man

8 Montaigne here perhaps refers to the feigned reconciliation between Catherine de' Medici and Henry, Duke of Guise, in 1588.

9 The State.

end me rather to the galleys.' For a man of honour nay be allowed to say as did the Lacedemonians, vhen, after their defeat by Antipater, they were ırranging terms, 'You may put upon us as many heavy ınd ruinous burdens as you please, but if you :ommand us to do shameful and dishonourable hings, you will waste your time.'

Every man should take to himself the oath which the Kings of Egypt made their judges solemnly take, 'that hey would not deviate from their conscience, though hey themselves should command them to do so.'

In a command to act dishonestly there is an evident nark of ignominy and condemnation. The man who ;ives it you, accuses you; and he gives it to you, if you ınderstand him rightly, for a burden and a punishnent. In the same degree that public affairs are ›ettered by your action your own state has become vorse. The better you do in it, so much the worse do 'ou do for yourself. And it will be no new thing, nor ›erhaps without some colour of justice, if the very same nan who has set you to the work punishes you for it.

If perfidy can ever be excusable it is only so when it s employed to punish and betray perfidy.

There are examples enough not only of treachery ›eing disowned, but of its being punished by those on vhose behalf it was practised. Who does not know of Fabricius' denunciation of Pyrrhus' physician?[10]

o When Pyrrhus, King of Epirus, was at war with the Romans, his physician wrote to Fabricius, the Roman consul, offering to poison the King and so put an end to the war. Fabricius denounced him to Pyrrhus, 'lest your death, he wrote, should bring a disgrace upon us, and we should seem to have put an end to the war by treachery when we could not do it by valour.'

But this also we find, that some person has commanded an act of treachery, and has rigorously avenged the victim of it upon the man he had employed to carry it out; disclaiming such unbridled authority and power and refusing an obedience so abject, slavish, and unprincipled.

Jaropelc, Duke of Russia, suborned a Hungarian nobleman to betray Boleslaus, King of Poland, either by killing him or by putting the Russians in the way of doing him some notable injury. This man set to work with great cunning; he became more assiduous than ever in that King's service, contriving to become his counsellor and one of his most trusted servants. With these advantages, taking an opportune occasion of his master's absence, he betrayed Vislicza to the Russians, a great and rich city, which was completely sacked and burned by them, with total slaughter, not only of the inhabitants of whatever age or sex, but of a great number of the nobles of the neighbourhood, whom he had assembled to that end.

Jaropelc, his vengeance and anger being assuaged, for which he was, however, not without justification (for Boleslaus had done him great injury, and in the same way), sated with the fruit of this treachery, when he came to consider the foulness of it, naked and by itself, and to look upon it with sane vision no longer blinded by passion, was seized with so great remorse and disgust, that he commanded his agent to be blinded, and his tongue and privy parts to be cut off.

Antigonus persuaded the Argyraspides[11] to betray to him Eumenes, their commander-in-chief and his adversary; but no sooner had he put him to death after

11 A body of soldiers who carried silver shields.

they had delivered him into his hands, than he himself desired to be the agent of the divine justice, for the punishment of so detestable a crime. He handed them over to the governor of the province, with most express command to destroy them and bring them to an evil end in any manner whatsoever. So that not one of them, although so numerous a body, ever again saw the air of Macedonia. The better he had been served by them the more wickedly he judged it to be, and the more punishably.

The slave who betrayed the hiding-place of his master, P. Sulpicius, was given his freedom, in accordance with the promise of Sulla's proscription; but in accordance with the promise of public justice, freeman though he was, he was hurled from the Tarpeian rock. They hang them, so to say, with the purse of their payment around their necks. After carrying out their second and special promise, they satisfy their general and primary conscience.

Mahomet the Second, wishing to be rid of his brother, by reason of his jealousy as a ruler, so common in that race, employed for the purpose one of his officers, who choked him by pouring too suddenly a great quantity of water down his throat. That being done, to expiate the murder he delivered the murderer into the hands of the dead man's mother (for they were brothers only on the father's side). She, in his presence, opened the murderer's stomach, and, whilst still quite warm, with her own hands searched for his heart, tore it out and threw it to the dogs to eat.

And our King Clovis, instead of the golden arms he had promised the three slaves of Cannacre, hanged them after they had, at his own instigation, betrayed their master.

And even to the most abandoned person it is so pleasant a feeling, after profiting by a wicked deed, subsequently to be able to sew upon it, in all security, a stitch of goodness and justice, as by way of compensation and conscientious correction. To which may be added that they look upon the ministers of such horrible crimes as a living reproach, and seek by their death to smother the knowledge and testimony of such proceedings.

Now, if by chance you are rewarded for it, in order that the public necessity for such extreme and desperate remedies may not be frustrated, the man who rewards you cannot but regard you as an accursed and execrable fellow, unless he be so himself, and as more treacherous than does the man you have betrayed; for he tests the wickedness of your heart by your own hands, which act without disapproval and without object. But he employs you as they do hopelessly degraded men to be the executors of high justice, an office as necessary as it is dishonourable; not to speak of the vileness of such commissions, there is a prostitution of conscience.

Since the daughter of Sejanus could not, by a certain provision of the laws at Rome, be punished with death, because she was a virgin, in order to allow the law to take its course, she was violated by the hangman before being strangled. Not only his hand, but his soul, is a slave to public convenience.

When the first Amurath, to aggravate the punishment of his subjects who had given their support in the parricidal rebellion of his son against him, commanded their nearest relations to lend their assistance in the execution, I think it highly honourable in some of them to have rather chosen to be unjustly thought guilty of another's parricide than to serve justice by parricide of their own.

And when, after the storming of some wretched fortress in my time, I have seen a rascal consenting, in order to save his own life, to hang his friends and comrades, I thought him worse off than the hanged.

It is said that Witolde, Prince of the Lithuanians, once made it a law that the condemned criminal should with his own hand carry out his execution. He thought it strange that a third person, innocent of the fault, should be employed and laden with the guilt of homicide.

When, by urgent circumstances, or some sudden and unexpected event, a ruler is obliged, for reasons of state necessity, to shuffle out of his word and break his faith, or is otherwise forced out of the ordinary path of duty, he must regard this necessity as a stroke of the divine rod. A sin it is not, for he has abandoned his own reason to a more universal and powerful reason; but it is indeed a misfortune. So that to some one who asked me, 'What remedy?' 'No remedy, I replied; if he was really squeezed between those two extremes – *but let him beware of seeking a pretext for his faithlessness* (CICERO) – he was obliged to do it; but if he did it without regret, if it did not weigh upon his mind, it is a sign that his conscience is in a bad way.'

Even if there were any ruler of so tender a conscience as to think no cure worth so serious a remedy, I should not esteem him the less. He could not ruin himself more excusably and more becomingly. We cannot do everything. In any case we must often entrust the protection of our vessel to the simple guidance of Heaven, as to our last anchorage. For what more justifiable necessity does he reserve himself? What is less possible for him to do than what he can do only at the price of his good faith and honour, things which should perhaps be dearer to him than his own safety, nay, than the safety of his people? Though he should stand with folded arms and merely call God to his aid, may he not hope that the divine goodness will not refuse exceptional favours from its hand to a hand that is so clean and just?

Those are dangerous examples, rare and sickly exceptions to our natural laws. We must yield to them, but with great moderation and circumspection. No private interest is worth so great a strain upon our conscience; public interest certainly, when it is both very apparent and very important.

Timoleon fitly expiated his extraordinary deed by the tears he shed when he called to mind that it was with a brother's hand that he had killed the tyrant; and his conscience justly pricked him that he should have been put to the necessity of purchasing the public weal at so high a price as his honesty of character. Even the Senate, delivered from thraldom by his means, did not venture roundly to pass judgement upon a deed so sublime and split into two so important and contrary aspects. But the Syracusans having, very opportunely at that moment, sent to the Corinthians to solicit their protection by sending them a leader able to restore their city to its former dignity and cleanse Sicily of a number of petty tyrants by whom it was being oppressed, they deputed Timoleon, with this new-fangled quibble and declaration, 'That according as he bore himself well or ill in his charge, they would decide to pardon him as the liberator of his country, or disgrace him as his brother's murderer.' This fantastic decision is somewhat to be excused, by reason of the danger of the example and the seriousness of so singular a deed. And they did well to throw off the burden of passing sentence, and to make it depend on other and extraneous considerations.

Now the conduct of Timoleon on this mission soon made his cause more clear, so worthily and virtuously did he bear himself in every way. And the good fortune which attended him in the difficulties he had to overcome in this noble business seemed to have been sent to him by the gods conspiring in favour of his vindication.

This man's aim was excusable, if ever any could be. But the advantage of increasing the public revenue, which served the Roman Senate as a pretext for that unsavoury decision which I am about to tell of, is not great enough to warrant any such injustice.

Certain cities had by a money payment redeemed themselves and regained their freedom, by the order and permission of the Senate, from the hands of L. Sulla. The matter having come up again for decision, the Senate condemned them to be taxable as before, and decided that the money they had paid for their redemption should remain lost to them.

Civil wars often give rise to such villainous cases, as when we punish private individuals for following the advice we gave them when we were other than we are now, and the self-same judge lays the penalty for his own change of mind upon one who is innocent of it. The master whips his pupil for his docility, and the leader his blind charge. A horrible counterfeit of justice!

There are rules in philosophy which are both false and weak. The example that is proposed to us to make private advantage to prevail over a given promise, does not receive sufficient weight from the circumstance they mix up with it. Robbers have seized you; they have set you at liberty after extracting an oath from you to pay a certain sum. They are very wrong who say that a man of honour, once out of their power, will be quit of his word without paying. Nothing of the kind. What fear has once made me will I am bound still to will when the fear is past. And even though fear forced only my tongue without my will, I am still bound to pay to the last farthing what I have promised. For my part, when my tongue has sometimes heedlessly outstripped my thoughts, I have yet scrupled to disown it. Otherwise we shall, little by little, come to upset all the claims that a third person has upon us on the strength of our oaths and promises. *As though a man of courage could be wrought upon by force!* (CICERO)

In this case only does private interest justify us in failing to keep our promise: when we have promised a thing that is in itself wicked and iniquitous. For the right of virtue should prevail over the right of our obligation.

I erstwhile placed Epaminondas in the front rank of great men; and I do not retract it. To how high a pitch this man raised the consideration of his private duty, who never killed a man he had vanquished, who, for the inestimable blessing of restoring freedom to his country, scrupled to put a tyrant or his accomplices to death without the forms of justice, and who regarded him as a wicked man, however good a citizen he might be, who, among the enemy and in battle, did not spare his guest-friend! There we have a richly compounded soul! To the rudest and most violent human actions he wedded goodness and humanity, even the most delicate that may be found in the school of philosophy.

Was it nature or art that softened this heart, so big, so full, so obstinate against pain, death, and poverty, to such an extreme degree of sweetness and gentleness of disposition? A dreaded man of blood and iron, he goes breaking and shattering a people invincible against any but himself, and, in the midst of such a fray, turns aside to avoid an encounter with a guest-friend. Truly he was a fit and proper man to control war, who forced it to submit to the curb of loving-kindness in the very heat of battle, when, all inflamed, it foamed with fury and slaughter. It is wonderful to be able to mingle with such actions any semblance of justice; but only a man as strong as Epaminondas was able to mingle with them the most gentle and affable manners and pure innocence.

And whereas one said to the Mamertines that 'laws were powerless when opposed to armed men'; another, to the tribune of the People, 'that the time of justice and the time of war were two'; and a third, 'that the noise of arms drowned the voice of the laws':[12] this man was not deaf even to the voice of urbanity and pure courtesy. Had he not borrowed from his enemies the custom of sacrificing to the Muses when he went to war, to dilute its martial fury and fierceness with their sweetness and gaiety?

After so great a teacher let us not be afraid of concluding that there are things which should not be allowed even in fighting the enemy, and that the common interest should not require all things of all men, against their private interest: *the memory of private right continuing even in the midst of public dissensions* (LIVY);

12 Respectively Pompey, Caesar, and Marius.

No power on earth can sanction treachery
Against a friend;
OVID

and that not all things are permissible to a man of honour, in the service of his king, the general cause and the laws. *For duty to one's country does not override all other duties; she herself requires that we be dutiful towards our parents* (CICERO).

This teaching befits our times; we have no need to harden our hearts with these steel blades. It is enough that our shoulders are hardened by them. It is enough to dip our pens in ink, without dipping them in blood. If it is the sign of a great heart and the effect of a singular and rare virtue to despise friendship, private obligations, one's word and one's kinsmen, for the common good and obedience to authority, we are truly sufficiently excused from showing it by the consideration that it is a greatness that can have no place in the great heart of Epaminondas.

I abominate those crazy exhortations of this other unruly spirit:

When weapons flash, let no fond thoughts of love,
Friendship and piety compassion move;
But boldly strike the venerable face
Of your own fathers, if opposed in place.
LUCAN

Let us deprive wicked, bloodthirsty, and treacherous natures of this pretence of reason; let us thrust aside that atrocious and insane justice, and imitate more humane examples. How much cannot time and example bring to pass! In an encounter during the civil war against Cinna, one of Pompey's soldiers, having unwittingly killed his brother who was on the opposite side, immediately took his own life for shame and sorrow; and a few years later, in another civil war of the same nation, a soldier demanded a reward from his captains for having killed his brother.

To judge an action to be fine and honourable because it is useful is a poor argument; as also to hold that every man is obliged to perform such an action, and that it becomes him as long at it is useful:

All things are not alike for all men fit.

PROPERTIUS

Let us take that action which is most necessary and useful for human society; which will surely be marriage. And yet the council of the saints has concluded the contrary to be more honourable, and excludes from it the most venerable profession of men; as we destine for our studs the least valuable of our cattle.

On some lines of Virgil

An edifying thought is engrossing and burdensome in proportion to its fullness and substance. Sin, death, poverty, disease, are solemn and depressing subjects. Our minds should be taught the means to support and combat evils, and the rules of right living and right thinking, and should be often stirred up and exercised in that noble study. But by a mind of ordinary stamp it should be done intermittently and with moderation; if it is too continually strained it will become deranged.

In my younger days I needed self-exhortations and urgings to keep myself in moral trim; a cheerful and healthy nature does not go very well, so they say, with such wise and serious reflexions. I am now differently situated; the conditions attending old age are only too ready to give me warnings and preach me wisdom. From an excess of high spirits I have dropped into the more regrettable excess of seriousness.

For that reason I now purposely indulge myself a little in licence, and sometimes occupy my mind, to give it a rest, with youthful and wanton thoughts. I am at this age only too sober, too heavy and too mature. Every day my years read me lessons in coldness and temperance. This body flees irregularities and dreads them. It is taking its turn in guiding my mind towards reformation. In its turn it is beginning to domineer, and that more rudely and imperiously. It leaves me not an hour of respite, either sleeping or waking, from preaching to me about death, patience, and repentance. I am now on the defensive against temperance, as I was once against sensuality. It pulls me back too much, to the extent of making me insensible.

Now, I desire to master myself in every way. Wisdom has its excesses, and, no less than folly, needs to be moderated. So, lest I should dry up and wither, and be weighed down with prudence, in the intervals that my infirmities allow me,

> Lest mind be too intent upon my ills, OVID

I gently turn aside, and avert my eyes from that stormy and cloudy sky that faces me, which, thanks be to God, I can regard indeed without terror, but not without effort and study; and I divert my thoughts with recollections of my youthful follies:

> My soul would have again what she has lost,
> And revels but in memories of the past.
>
> PETRONIUS

Let childhood look ahead, and old age behind it; was that not the meaning of Janus' double face? Let years drag me along, if they will, but backward! As long as my eyes are able to distinguish that lovely expired season of life, I turn them off and on in that direction. If it escapes from my blood and my veins, I will not at least tear the picture of it out of my memory:

> The man lives twice who can the gift retain
> Of memory, to enjoy past life again.
>
> MARTIAL

Plato recommends old men to look on at the exercises, dances and games of youth, to enjoy in others the beauty and suppleness of body which they no longer possess, and recall to their mind the gracefulness and charm of their prime; and would have them award the honour of victory in those sports to the youth who has provided most recreation and amusement to the greatest number of people.

Formerly I used to mark the dull and cloudy days as extraordinary; these are now almost ordinary with me, and the extraordinary are the fine and bright days. I shall soon have come to such a pass that I shall leap for joy, and regard it as an unwonted favour, to be without pain. Though I tickle myself I cannot force a poor laugh out of this wretched body. I am merry only in fancy and in day-dreams, to divert by artifice the chagrin of old age. But, in faith, it would require another remedy than that of a dream. A feeble struggle of art against nature!

It shows great simplicity to prolong and anticipate human discomforts, as most men do. I would rather be old for a shorter time than be old before my time. I eagerly grasp even the slightest occasions for pleasure that I meet with.

I know indeed, from hearsay, several kinds of delights that are discreet, powerful, ostentatious; but I am not such a slave to public opinion as to wish to acquire an appetite for them. I prefer them not so much grand, brilliant and showy as luscious, easy and ready to hand. *We depart from nature; we follow the people, who are never a good guide* (SENECA).

My philosophy lies in action, in natural and present practice; little in imagination. O that I could take a pleasure in playing at cobnut or spinning a top!

For he regarded not the foolish prate
Of idle people – but his own good health.

ENNIUS *adapted*

Pleasure is an unambitious pursuit; it is rich enough in its own estimation without adding to it the reward of fame, and prefers to be in the shade. A young man who spends his time in acquiring a taste for choice wines and sauces deserves a thrashing. There is nothing I have known so little about and valued so little. I am now beginning to learn. I am greatly ashamed of it, but what can I do? I am still more ashamed and vexed at the occasions which drive me to it.

It is our part to dote and trifle; it is for the young to gain a reputation and climb the ladder. They are going into the world and the world's opinion; we are withdrawing from it. *Let them keep arms, horses, spears, clubs, tennis, swimming, and races. Of so many sports let them leave the dice-box to us old men* (CICERO). Even the laws send us home. I cannot do less, to gratify this wretched condition into which my age is forcing me, than to provide it with toys and playthings, as we do children; and after all it is a second childhood that we fall into. And wisdom and folly will have a hard task to prop and succour me with alternate services in this calamity of old age:

Mingle your wisdom with glimpses of folly;
'Tis delightful at times the fool to play.

HORACE

And I try to escape the lightest punctures; and those that once would not have left a scratch now pierce me through and through. My habit of body begins to be so easily susceptible to pain. *To a frail body every shock is intolerable* (CICERO):

> A sickly mind can suffer nought that's hard.
>
> OVID

I have always been delicately sensitive and susceptible to injuries: I am now still more tender and exposed to them on all sides:

> It needs no force to break a dish that's cracked
>
> OVID

My judgement certainly keeps me from kicking and murmuring against the discomforts that nature commands me to suffer; but it cannot keep me from feeling them. I, who have no other aim but to live and be merry, would travel from one end of the world to the other in search of one good year of agreeable and cheerful tranquillity. A dull and melancholy tranquillity may suffice me, but it benumbs and stupefies me; and that is not to my liking. If there is any person, any good company, in country or town, in France or elsewhere, whether stay-at-home or travellers, who like my humours, whose humours I like, they have but to whistle in their palms, and I will come and provide them with Essays in flesh and bone.

Seeing that it is the privilege of the mind to escape from old age, I advise mine to do so to the best of its power; let it bud, let it flower meanwhile, if it can, like the mistletoe on a dead tree!

But I fear my mind is a traitor; he has formed so close a tie with the body that he forsakes me at every turn, and leaves me to follow him in his need. I take him aside to coax him, I make up to him, but to no purpose. In vain do I try to wean him from this intimacy, and offer him Seneca and Catullus, the ladies and royal dances; if his comrade has the colic he seems to have it too. Even the activities which are peculiarly and essentially his own cannot then be stirred; they so evidently smack of a cold in the head. In his productions there is no joy if it is not shared by the body.

Our masters are wrong in this: when seeking the causes of the extraordinary soarings of our soul, besides those they attribute to a divine rapture, to love, to martial fierceness, to poetry, to wine, they have not given its due share to health; a full, lusty, exuberant, lazy health, such as once the verdure of youth and the feeling of security provided me with in increasing measure. That fire of good humour kindles in the mind bright and vivid flashes beyond our natural capacity, and some of the most joyous, not to say extravagant, enthusiasms.

It is no wonder then if a contrary state depresses my spirits, nails them down, and produces a contrary effect:

When body flags 'twill rise to no achievement.

PSEUDO-GALLUS

And yet my mind expects me to be grateful to it because, as it tells me, it acquiesces much less in this languor than is usual with most men. Let us at least, while we are under truce, drive away the evils and difficulties of our partnership:

While yet we may,
We'll drive old age with clouded brow away.

HORACE

'Tis good to sweeten black cares with pleasantries

(SIDONIUS APOLLINARIS). I love a gay and sociable wisdom, and steer clear of all sour and austere morality; I suspect a forbidding mien,

> The arrogant gloom of a scowling face.
>
> BUCHANAN
>
> Austerity hides many a debauchee. MARTIAL

I heartily agree with Plato when he says that an easy or difficult humour contributes much towards making a soul either good or wicked. Socrates had a settled expression, but serene and smiling; not settled like that of the elder Crassus, who was never seen to laugh.

Virtue is a pleasant and cheerful quality.

I know well that very few people will frown at the looseness of my writings who will not have more reason to frown at the looseness of their own thoughts. My sentiments agree with theirs, but I offend their eyes.

It shows a nice habit of mind indeed to cavil at Plato's writings, and glide over his supposed relations with Phaedo, Dion, Stella,[1] Archeanassa! *Let us not be ashamed to say what we are not ashamed to think*. I hate a gloomy and dismal person who allows the pleasures of life to pass him by, and fastens and browses on its miseries. Like flies that cannot fasten on a very smooth and polished surface, but fix and rest on rough and uneven places; or like leeches that suck and crave only for bad blood.

For the rest I have made it a rule to dare to say all that I dare to do; and I dislike even unpublishable thoughts. The worst of my actions and qualities does

1 i.e., Aster, of which Stella is the Latin equivalent.

not appear to me so ugly at it appears ugly and base not to dare to own it.

Every man is discreet in confession; we should be the same in action.

Boldness to sin is somewhat compensated and curbed by the boldness to confess it. If a man forced himself to tell everything, he would force himself not to do anything that he is obliged to conceal.

God grant that my extreme outspokenness should induce our men to be more free, and to be above those timorous and affected virtues, born of our imperfections; that at the cost of my immodesty I may lead them on to the point of good sense!

A man must see and study his faults before he can criticize them. They who conceal them from others usually conceal them from themselves. And they do not think them sufficiently hidden if they can see them; they disguise them and withdraw them from their own consciousness.

Why does no man confess his faults? Because he is still a slave to them. We must be awake to tell our dreams (SENECA).

The diseases of the body become more distinct as they increase. What we thought was a cold or a sprain turns out to be gout. The diseases of the mind become more obscure as they increase; the most sick are least sensible of them. Therefore we must often, with pitiless hand, bring them to the light of day, lay them bare, and tear them out of the hollow of our bosom.

As in the case of good deeds, so also in the case of evil deeds, the mere confession is sometimes a reparation. Is any sin so ugly that one can be excused the duty of confessing it?

It is so painful to me to conceal anything that I shun being trusted with another's secrets, not having the assurance to deny what I know. I am able to keep it to myself; but deny it I cannot without effort and great reluctance. To be really secretive, one must be so by nature, and not by obligation. In the service of a prince it is of little use to be secretive if one is not also a liar.

If the man who asked Thales of Miletus whether he should solemnly deny having committed adultery had referred to me I should have told him not to do so. For lying appears to me still worse than adultery. Thales advised him quite otherwise, that he should swear in order to shield the greater by the lesser sin.[2] Yet he advised him not so much a choice as a multiplication of sins.

Whereupon let us say this by the way, that we make it easy to a conscientious man when we offer him some difficulty to counterbalance a sin; but when we hem him in between two sins, we put him to a rude choice, as in the case of Origen. He was given the alternative of either practising idolatry or suffering himself to be carnally enjoyed by a big ruffian of an Ethiopian who was brought before him. He submitted to the former condition; and sinfully, according to one writer. On this assumption, those ladies would not be in the wrong, according to their erroneous views, who *protest* to us in these days that they would rather charge their conscience with ten men than one mass.[3]

2 Either Montaigne's memory here played him false, or he was misled, as has been suggested, by the absence of an interrogation mark in his Greek text of Diogenes Laertius. His answer was, 'Is not perjury worse than adultery?'

3 Montaigne enjoys his joke, but he felt neither ill-will nor

If it is an indiscretion thus to publish abroad one's errors, there is no great danger that it will become a precedent and custom; for Aristo said that the winds that people fear most are those which uncover them. We must tuck up this silly rag that covers our manners. They send their conscience to the brothel and preserve a starched countenance. Even traitors and murderers observe the laws of decorum, and make it a matter of duty. Yet neither can injustice complain of incivility[4] nor knavery of indiscretion. It is a pity that a wicked man is not at the same time a fool, and that outward decency should palliate his sin. Such a rough-cast is only suitable to a good and sound wall, that deserves to be preserved or whitewashed.

In common with the Huguenots, who condemn our auricular and private confession, I confess in public, simply and scrupulously. St Augustine, Origen, and Hippocrates published the errors of their belief; I, besides, those of my morals. I am hungering to make myself known; and I care not to how many, provided I do so truly; or, to speak more correctly, I hunger for nothing, but I have a deadly fear of being thought other than I am by those who come to know me by name.

What does that man who will do anything for honour and glory think to gain by showing himself to the world with a mask, hiding his real nature from public knowledge? Praise a hunchback for his handsome figure, and he must take it for an insult. If

intolerance towards the Protestants.

4 i.e., a man who violates the laws is not entitled to rebuke a man for rude behaviour.

you are a coward and someone compliments you on being a man of valour, is it you he is speaking of? He takes you for another. I should as soon commend him who was pleased with the bonnetings that somebody bestowed upon him, thinking he was master of the company, when he was the meanest of the retinue.

As Archelaus, King of Macedon, was passing along the street, someone poured water upon him; his attendants said he ought to be punished. 'Yes, but, said he, it was not me he poured the water upon, but the man he took me for.'

Socrates said to one who informed him that people were speaking ill of him, 'Not of me; there is nothing in me of what they say.'

For my part, if any man commended me for a good pilot, or as very modest, or as very chaste, I should owe him no thanks. And, on the other hand, if one called me a traitor, a thief, a drunkard, I should just as little take offence. Those who misknow themselves may feed on undeserved approbation. Not I, who can see myself, who can search my very heart, and know very well what is due to me. I am content to be less commended, provided I be better known. I might be thought wise in such a sort of wisdom as I take to be folly.

It annoys me that the ladies use my Essays merely as a common piece of furniture, furniture for the reception-room. This chapter will make me suitable for the boudoir. I love their society when it is a little private; in public it is without favour or savour.

In taking farewell we warm up, more than ordinarily, our affection for the things we are leaving. I am taking my last leave of the sports of the world. These are our last embraces. But let us come to my theme.

What harm has the genital act, so natural, so

necessary, and so lawful, done to humanity, that we dare not speak of it without shame, and exclude it from serious and orderly conversation? We boldly utter the words, *kill*, *rob*, *betray*; and the other we only dare to utter under our breath. Does this mean that the less of it we breathe in words, the more are we at liberty to swell our thoughts with it? For it is amusing that the words which are least used, least written, and most hushed up, should be the best known and the most generally understood. There is no person of any age or morals but knows them as well as he knows the word *bread*. They are impressed upon each of us, without being expressed, without voice and without form. And the sex that does it most is charged to hush it up.

It is also amusing that it is an action we have placed in the sanctuary of silence, from which to tear it by force is a crime, even for the purpose of accusing it and bringing it to justice. And we do not dare to scourge it but in roundabout and figurative terms. A great favour indeed for a criminal to be so execrable that justice thinks it wrong to touch and see him; free and saved by the favour of the severity of his sentence! Is it not the same as with books, that sell better and become more public for being suppressed? For my part I will take Aristotle's word for it, who says, 'To be shamefaced is an ornament of youth, but a reproach to old age.'

These lines are preached in the old school, a school with which I hold much more than with the modern; its virtues appear to me greater, its vices less:

Who strives too much to shun fair Venus' wiles
Sins equally with him who is too keen
In her pursuit. AMYOT *after* PLUTARCH

Thou, Goddess,
Dost rule the world alone, and without thee
Naught rises to the shining shores of light,
Nor aught of joyful or of lovely is born.

LUCRETIUS

I know not who could have set Pallas and the Muses at variance with Venus, and made them cool towards Cupid; but I know of no deities that agree so well together, and are more indebted to one another. Take from the Muses their amorous fancies and you will rob them of the best entertainment they have, and of the noblest matter of their work. And if you deprive Cupid of the society and service of poetry you will blunt his best weapons. In this way you charge the god of sweet intimacy and amity, and the patron goddesses of humanity and justice, with the sin of ingratitude and forgetfulness.

I have not been so long cashiered from the staff and retinue of this god but that I still retain a memory of his power and worth:

Too plain
I know the traces of the long-quenched flame.

VIRGIL

There is still some remnant of heat and emotion after the fever:

In wintry age let not this love grow cool!

JOHANNES SECUNDUS

Withered and drooping though I be, I still feel a few tepid remains of that past ardour:

As the deep Aegean, when no more blow the winds,

That rolled its tumbling waves with
troublous blasts,
Doth yet of tempests passed some show retain,
And here and there its swelling billows casts.

TASSO

But, if I understand the matter, the power and importance of this god, as portrayed in poetry, are much greater and more alive than they are in reality:

And Poetry has fingers too
To titillate and please.

adapted from JUVENAL

Her pictures are somehow more amorous than Amor himself. Venus is not so beautiful, quite naked and alive and panting, as she is in these lines of Virgil:

The Goddess ceased, and with the soft embrace
Of snowy arms about his body wound
Fondled him as he faltered. Quick he caught
The wonted fire; the old heat pierced his heart,
Ran through his melting frame: as oftentimes
A fiery rift, burst by the thunder-clap,
Runs quivering down the cloud, with flash of light.
. . . So saying, he gave
The embrace she longed for, on her bosom sank,
And wooed calm slumber to o'erglide his limbs.

VIRGIL

What strikes me is that he depicts her a little too passionate for a married Venus. In this sober contract the desires are not generally so wanton; they are dull and more blunted. Love hates to be held by any tie but himself, and goes feebly to work in intimacies formed and continued under a different name, such as marriage. Family and fortune are there rightly accounted as important, or more so, than charm and beauty. We do not marry for ourselves, whatever they may say; we marry as much, or more, for posterity, for the family. The custom and interest of marriage concern our stock, long after we are dead.

For this reason I approve of its being arranged by a third hand rather than by our own, by others' good sense rather than our own. How totally different is all this to a love compact! Besides, it is a kind of incest in this sacred and time-honoured alliance to employ the extravagant actions of amorous licence, as I think I have said elsewhere. We should, says Aristotle, approach our wives discreetly and soberly, lest the pleasure of being touched too lasciviously should transport them beyond the bounds of reason. What he says upon the account of conscience the physicians say upon the account of health, 'that an over-heated, voluptuous and assiduous pleasure corrupts the seed and hinders conception.' They say, on the other hand, 'that in a languid intercourse, as this is by its nature, the man should offer himself rarely and at considerable intervals, in order that a proper and fertile heat may be stored up':

To eagerly absorb
Their fill of love, and deeply entertain. VIRGIL

I know of no marriages that are so soon troubled and that so soon come to grief as those which are contracted on account of beauty and amorous desires. It needs more solid and permanent foundations, and we should proceed circumspectly; such an exuberant vivacity serves no purpose.

They who think to do honour to marriage by the

addition of love are in the same case, it seems to me, as those who, thinking to honour virtue, maintain that virtue and nobility are the same thing. They are qualities which have some affinity, but there is a great difference between them. There is no need to confuse their names and titles, whereby both of them are wronged. Nobility is a fine quality and introduced with good reason; but as it is a quality dependent on others, and may fall to the share of any vicious or worthless person, in estimation it falls far short of virtue. If it can be called a virtue, it is an artificial and visible virtue, depending on time and fortune, varying in its nature according to country, of this life and mortal, with no more source than the river Nile, genealogical and common to many, a thing of succession and resemblance, derived by inference, and a very weak inference.

Knowledge, strength, goodness, beauty, wealth, all other qualities, have their value in intercourse and commerce; this is self-centred, and of no use in the service of others.

One of our kings was offered the choice of two competitors for the same office, one of whom was a nobleman, and the other not. He ordered them to elect the man of greatest merit, without regard to that kind of quality; but in case of their being of exactly equal merit, that they should take nobility into consideration. This was to give it its proper place.

Antigonus said to a young man who was a stranger to him, and who entreated him to be allowed to succeed to his father's command, a man of valour, lately dead, 'My friend, in such preferments I regard not so much the noble birth of my soldiers as their prowess.'

In truth it should not be as with the functionaries of the Kings of Sparta, trumpeters, musicians, cooks, who were succeeded in their office by their sons, however incompetent they might be, in preference to the most experienced in the profession.

The people of Calicut look upon their nobles as a superhuman species. They are forbidden to marry, or adopt any profession except war. Of concubines they may have their fill, and the women as many gallants, without any mutual jealousy. But it is a capital and unpardonable crime to mate with a person of different rank to their own. They think themselves contaminated if they have been merely touched by them in passing, and, as their nobility is damaged and injured thereby to a remarkable degree, they will kill any who have only come a little too near them. So the ignoble are obliged to shout as they walk, like the gondoliers at Venice, at the street-corners, for fear of collisions; and the nobles order them, as they choose, to step to one side or the other. By this means the one avoids what they regard as a perpetual disgrace, and the other a certain death. No length of time, no princely favour, no office, no virtue, no wealth, can ever make a noble of a plebeian. To which the custom contributes that marriages between different trades are forbidden. A girl of shoemaker stock may not marry a carpenter; and the parents are rigorously obliged to train a son to his father's calling, and to no other, by which means the distinction and continuity of their fortunes is preserved.

A good marriage, if there is such a thing, rejects the company and conditions of love. It tries to imitate those of friendship. It is a sweet partnership for life, full of constancy, trust, and an endless number of useful and substantial services and mutual obligations. No woman who relishes the taste of it,

> On whom the nuptial torch has shed a welcome light,
>
> CATULLUS

would like to hold the position of her husband's mistress or leman. If she is lodged in his affections as a wife she is much more honourably and securely lodged. Even if he is paying ardent attentions to another, let any one ask him 'on which of the two, his wife or his mistress, he would rather a disgrace should fall? whose misfortune would grieve him most? for whom he would desire the greatest honour?' These questions would admit of no doubt in a sound marriage.

It is a sign of the value and excellence of marriage that we see so few good ones. If rightly established and properly understood, there is no better institution in modern society. We cannot dispense with it, and we continue to dishonour it. It may be compared to a cage; the birds outside are desperately anxious to get in, and those that are in it are equally anxious to get out.

Socrates, when asked whether it was better to take a wife than not, replied, 'Whichever you do, you will repent it.' It is a compact to which the saying fitly applies, 'Man is to man either a god or a wolf.' It needs the conjunction of many qualities to build it up. In these days it is better adapted for simple souls, those of the people, who are not so much disturbed by pleasures, curiosity and idleness. Men of loose morals, like myself, who hate any kind of tie or obligation, are not so well fitted for it:

> To me 'tis sweeter far to live with neck unyoked.
>
> PSEUDO-GALLUS

If I had followed my own bent, I would have shunned wedlock with Wisdom herself, if she would have had me. But, say what we please, custom and the uses of everyday life carry us along. Most of my actions are guided by example, not by choice. In any case it was not properly at my own prompting that I married. I was led and brought to it by outside occasions. For not only inconvenient things, but anything, however offensive, wicked and repulsive, may be rendered acceptable by some condition or circumstance; so unsteady are we on our feet!

And I certainly was drawn into it at the time more ill-prepared and more reluctantly than I should be at present, after having made trial of it. And, however loose I may be thought, I have in truth observed the laws of wedlock more strictly than I either promised or expected. It is too late to kick when once we have been hobbled. We must manage our freedom wisely; but, having once submitted to bondage, we must keep within the laws of common duty, or at least make an effort to do so.

Those men who enter into this bond with the intention of behaving with hatred and contempt act wrongly and improperly; and this pretty rule which passes from hand to hand among the ladies, like a sacred oracle,

Serve your husband as a master;
Trust him not, for he betrays you,

which is as much as to say, 'Bear yourself towards him with a constrained, hostile and distrustful reverence,' as if it were a war-cry and a challenge, is equally hard and unjust. I am too mild to harbour such repellent intentions. To tell the truth, I have not yet arrived at such perfection of cleverness and refinement of wit as to confound reason with injustice, and make a mockery of all rule and order that does not fall in with my desires. Though I may hate superstition I do not forthwith take refuge in irreligion. If we do not always do our duty, we should at least always love and acknowledge it. To marry without being wedded is treachery. Let us proceed.

Our poet depicts a marriage in which there is perfect harmony and propriety, in which there is, however, not much loyalty. Did he mean to imply that it is not impossible to yield to the power of love, and yet reserve some duty towards marriage; and that it may be bruised without being altogether broken? Many a serving man shoes his master's mule[5] without necessarily hating him. Beauty, opportunity, fate (for Fate also has a hand in it),

> There is a Fate that rules our hidden parts;
> For if the stars be not propitious,
> Virility will not avail thee aught,
>
> JUVENAL

have attached her to a stranger; not so wholly perhaps but that there remains some tie by which she is still held to her husband. It is like two plans, with distinct routes, not to be confounded with one another. A woman may surrender to a certain man whom she would in no case have married; I do not mean on account of the state of his fortune, but for his personal qualities. Few men have married their mistresses without repenting it.

And even in the other world, what a poor match

5 Pilfers from him.

Jupiter made of it with the wife whom he had first seduced and enjoyed in love's dalliance! That is, as the proverb puts it, 'to cack in the basket, and then put it on your head.'

I have seen in my time, in a good family, love shamefully and indecently cured by marriage; the considerations are too different. We love, without pledging ourselves, two different and contradictory things.

Isocrates said that the city of Athens pleased after the manner of the ladies we serve for love. Every man loved to go there, to saunter and pass the time; but no one loved it so well as to marry it, that is to say, to reside and settle there.

I have been annoyed to see husbands hate their wives merely because they themselves have wronged them. We should at all events not love them less for our own faults; pity and repentance should at least make them more dear to us.

They are different ends, he says,[6] and yet in some sort compatible. Marriage has, for its share, usefulness, justice, honour and constancy; a stale but more durable pleasure. Love is grounded on pleasure alone, and it is indeed more gratifying to the senses, keener and more acute; a pleasure stirred and kept alive by difficulties. There must be a sting and a smart in it. It ceases to be love if it have no shafts and no fire. The liberality of the ladies is too profuse in marriage, and blunts the edge of affection and desire. Observe what pains Lycurgus and Plato take, in their Laws, to avoid that disadvantage.

Women are not by any means to blame when they

6 Isocrates.

reject the rules of life which have been introduced into the world, seeing that it is the men who made them without their consent. Intrigues and wranglings between them and ourselves are only natural; the closest agreement we enjoy with them is still attended with tumults and storms.

In the opinion of our author we treat them without consideration in this respect: After knowing that they are incomparably more capable and ardent in the sexual act than we, of which that priest of antiquity was a witness, who was first a man and then a woman:

Tiresias must decide
The difference, who both delights has tried;

OVID

after hearing moreover from their own lips the proof that was given, in different centuries, by an Emperor and an Empress of Rome,[7] both famous master-workers in the art – he indeed deflowered in one night ten Sarmatian virgins, his captives, but she actually suffered in one night twenty-five assaults, changing her company according to need and liking:

Still burning with unconquerable lust,
Weary she gave up, but still unsatisfied;

JUVENAL

– and after the dispute which took place in Catalonia, when a woman complaining of her husband's too unremitting attentions, not so much, I take it, because she was inconvenienced by them (for I believe in no miracles, except in matters of faith), as, under this pretext, to restrict and curb, in this the most

7 Proculus and Messalina.

fundamental act of marriage, the authority of husbands over their wives, and to show that their perverseness and ill-will extend beyond the nuptial couch and tread under foot even the sweets and delights of Venus; and the husband, certainly an unnatural brute, replying that even on fast-days he could not do with less than ten, the Queen of Aragon interposed with that notable sentence, by which, after mature deliberation with her Council, that good Queen, to establish for all times a rule and example of the moderation and modesty required in a rightful marriage, prescribed as a lawful and necessary limit the number of six per diem; thus renouncing and surrendering a great part of her sex's needs and desires, to set up, as she said, 'an easy and consequently permanent and immutable formula'; against which the doctors exclaim, 'what must be the appetite and lust of women, when their reason, their amendment and virtue are taxed at such a rate!'

Considering these varying estimates of our sexual needs, and seeing that Solon, head of the school of lawgivers, assesses this conjugal intercourse, if we are not to be found wanting, at no more than three times a month; after believing and preaching all this, we have gone and allotted them continence for their particular portion, at the risk of the last and extreme penalties.

There is no passion more exacting than this, which we expect them alone to resist, as being not simply an ordinary vice, but an abominable and accursed thing and worse than irreligion and parricide; whilst we men at the same time yield to it without blame or reproach. Even those of us who have tried to master it have often enough had to admit how difficult, or rather how impossible it was, by the use of material remedies, to deaden, to weaken and cool the body.

On the other hand, we expect them to be healthy, robust, plump, well nourished and chaste at the same time; that is to say, both hot and cold. For marriage, whose function we say it is to keep them from burning, brings them but little relief, as we live nowadays. If they take a husband who is still exuberant with the vigour of youth, he will make a boast of expending it on others:

> If you don't mend your ways, we'll go to law.
> Your vigour, bought with many thousand crowns,
> No longer's yours, my Bassus; you have sold it.
>
> MARTIAL

The philosopher Polemon was rightly haled before justice by his wife, for sowing in a barren field the fruit that was meant for the genital field.

If on the other hand, they take one of the worn-out kind, behold them in full wedlock worse off than virgins and widows! We think they are well provided for because they have a man at their side. By the same reasoning the Romans held Clodia Laeta, a Vestal virgin, to have been violated, because Caligula had approached her, although it was averred that he had no more than approached her. Their need is, on the contrary, thereby redoubled, since the contact and company of any male whatever excites their heat, which in solitude would remain more dormant.

And, in order, in all probability, to render their chastity the more meritorious by this circumstance and consideration, Boleslas and Kinge, his wife, King and Queen of Poland, by mutual agreement consecrated it by a vow, while lying together on their very wedding-night, and kept it in the teeth of conjugal opportunities.

We train them from childhood in the service of love; their charm, their dressing up, their knowledge, their language, all their instruction, have only this end in view. Their governesses keep suggesting amorous ideas to them, though always with the intention of exciting their disgust. My daughter (who is the only child I have) is at an age when the most precocious of them are allowed by the laws to marry; she is constitutionally backward, thin and delicate, and has accordingly been brought up by her mother in a retired and particular manner, so that she is only now beginning to put off her childish naïveté.

She was reading a French book when I was present, and came across the word *fouteau*, the name of a well-known tree (beech). The woman to whose care she was entrusted rather rudely stopped her short and made her pass over the danger spot. I let her have her way in order not to disturb their rules, for I never meddle with that government; feminine policy has a mysterious procedure, and we must leave it to them. But, if I am not mistaken, the conversation of twenty lackeys could not, in six months, have implanted in her imagination, the meaning and use and all the consequences of the sound of those criminating syllables, as this good old lady did by her reprimand and interdict.

The ripening virgin joys to learn
In the Ionic dance to turn
  And bend with plastic limb;
Still but a child, with evil gleams
Incestuous love's unhallowed dreams
  Before her fancy swim. HORACE

Let them but drop their formal modesty a little, give them occasion to talk freely; compared with them we are but children in that science. Only hear them describing our pursuits and our conversation; they will very soon let you know that we can bring them nothing they have not known and digested without our help. Can it be, as Plato says, that they have once been dissolute boys?

My ear once happened to be in a place where it was able, without being suspected, to snatch a little of their talk. Why cannot I repeat it? By our Lady, said I, what need is there to study the phrases of Amadis and the books of Boccaccio and Aretino, and think ourselves so knowing? It is a mere waste of time. There is no word, no example, no proceeding, that they know not better than our books; it is an instruction that is born in the veins,

> By Venus herself inspired of old, VIRGIL

which those good schoolmasters, Nature, Youth and Health, continually breathe into their souls. They have no need to learn it; they breed it:

> Not more delighted is the snow-white dove,
> Or if there be a thing more prone to love,
> Still to be billing with her male than is
> Woman with every man she meets to kiss.
>
> CATULLUS

If the natural violence of their desire were not held a little in check by the fear and honour with which they have been provided, we should be shamed. The whole movement of the world resolves itself into and leads to this pairing; it is a matter infused throughout; it is a centre to which all things are directed. We may still see some of the laws of old and wise Rome, drawn up for the service of Love; and Socrates' precepts for the instruction of courtesans:

On silken cushions they love to lie,
Those little books the Stoics write.

HORACE

Zeno, amongst his laws, gives rules for the spreading and the attack in deflowering. What was the drift of the philosopher Strato's book, Of Carnal Conjunction? Of what did Theophrastus treat in those he called, one The Lover, the other Of Love? Of what Aristippus, in his work Of Ancient Delights? What was the aim of Plato's so lengthy and lively descriptions of the boldest amours of his time? And of the book Of the Lover, by Demetrius of Phalera? And Clinias, or the Ravished Lover, of Heraclides of Pontus? And Antisthenes' Of Begetting Children, or Of Weddings, or his other, Of the Master or the Lover? And Aristo's Of Amorous Exercises? Those of Cleanthes, one Of Love, the other Of the Art of Loving? The Amorous Dialogues of Sphaerus? And the Fable of Jupiter and Juno, by Chrysippus, which is shameless beyond all bearing, and of his fifty so lascivious Epistles? For I must omit the writings of the philosophers who followed the Epicurean school, the protectors of sensuality.

In ancient times fifty deities were subservient to this business. And there were countries where, to assuage the lust of those who came to pay their devotions, they kept girls and boys in the churches for enjoyment, and it was a ceremonious act to use them before going to service. *Doubtless incontinence is necessary for continence, as a fire is extinguished by fire.*

In most parts of the world that part of the body was deified. In one and the same province some flayed off the skin to offer and consecrate a piece of it, and others offered and consecrated their semen. In another province the young men publicly pierced and opened it in several places between the flesh and skin, and through the openings thrust skewers, as long and thick as they could bear them; and of these skewers they afterwards made a fire, as an offering to the gods. They were reputed weak and unchaste if they were dismayed by the force of this cruel pain. In another place the most sacred magistrate was revered and known by that member; and in some ceremonies an effigy of it was carried about in state, to the honour of various divinities.

At the festival of the Bacchanals the Egyptian ladies carried about their necks a wooden effigy of it, exquisitely carved, big and heavy according to their capacity; besides which the statue of their god exhibited one which exceeded in size the rest of the body.[8]

In my neighbourhood the married women twist their kerchief over their forehead into the shape of one, to boast of the enjoyment they have out of it; and when they become widows they turn it behind them and hide it under their coif.

The most sedate of Roman matrons thought it an honour to offer flowers and garlands to the god Priapus; and the virgins at the time of their nuptials were made to sit upon his least seemly parts. And I know not but that I have seen something of the like devotion in my time.

More correctly, according to Herodotus, 'nearly as large as the rest of the body'.

What was the meaning of that ridiculous part of the hose our fathers wore, and which is still seen on our Swiss?[9] What is the idea of the show we still make of our pieces, in effigy under our breeches; and, what is worse, often, by falsehood and imposture, above their natural size?

I am inclined to think that a dress of this kind was invented in the best and most conscientious ages in order not to deceive the world, and that every man might, publicly and boldly, render an account of his capacity. The most simple nations still have it, nearly corresponding to the real thing. In those days the workman was taught the art, as it is practised in taking the measure of an arm or a foot.

That good man who, when I was young, castrated so many beautiful and antique statues in his great city that the eye might not be offended, following the advice of that other ancient worthy:

> The censure of this shame to those is due
> Who naked bodies first exposed to view,
>
> ENNIUS, *quoted by* CICERO

should have considered that, as in the mysteries of the Good Goddess[10] all male semblance was precluded nothing would be gained unless he also had horse and asses, and in short nature, castrated:

> All things terrestrial, whether man or brute,
> The ocean tribes, tame beasts, gay-feathered birds
> Rush on to passion's pyre.
>
> VIRGI

9 Probably the Swiss mercenaries quartered in the neigh bourhood.

10 The *Bona Dea*, worshipped by the women of Rome a

The gods, says Plato, have furnished us with a disobedient and tyrannical member, which, like an animal in its fury, attempts, in the violence of its desire, to subdue everything to its power. So also to the women they have given a greedy and voracious animal which, if denied its food in due season, goes mad in its impatience of delay; and, breathing its rage into their bodies, stops up the conduits, arrests breathing, and causes a thousand kinds of ills, till, having imbibed the fruit of the common thirst, it has copiously bedewed and sown the ground of their matrix.

Now my legislator[11] should also have considered that it is perhaps a more chaste and salutary practice to let them know betimes the living reality, than to leave them to guess it according to the licence and heat of their imagination. In place of the real parts their desire and hope substitute others triply magnified. And a certain man of my acquaintance ruined his chances by openly disclosing his in a place where he was not yet enabled to put them to their proper and more serious use.

What mischief is not done by these pictures of enormous size that the boys scatter all over the galleries and staircases of the royal houses! From them they derive a cruel contempt for our natural capacity.

How do we know that Plato had not an eye to this

---

the goddess of chastity and fidelity, whose temple no man was permitted to enter. In later times it became the resort of unchaste women, and the scene of licence.

11 The 'good man' who treated the statues at Rome in the aforementioned manner, supposed to have been Pope Paul III.

when he ordained, following other well-established republics, that men and women, young and old, should appear naked in view of one another in his gymnasiums?

The Indian women, who see their men undressed, have at least cooled their sense of sight. And, although the women of that great kingdom of Pegu, who have nothing to cover them below the waist but a cloth slit in front, and so skimp that, however much modesty they may try to observe, they reveal themselves at every step they take, may tell us that is a device for attracting the men to their sides and wean them from intercourse with their own sex, a practice to which that nation is universally addicted, we might reply that they lose thereby more than they gain, and that a complete hunger is sharper than one that has been satisfied at least by the eyes.

Besides, Livia said 'that to an honest woman a naked man is no more than a statue'.

The Lacedemonian women, more virginal as wives than our maidens are, every day saw the young men of their city stripped for their exercises, and were not very particular themselves to cover their thighs as they walked, esteeming themselves, as Plato says, sufficiently covered by their virtue without a farthingale.[12]

But those men, mentioned by Saint Augustine, who raised a doubt whether the women, at the

12 *Assez couvertes de leur vertu sans vertugade.* This pun perhaps suggested the ingenious derivation *vertugarde*, 'virtue-guard'. The farthingale (actually a corruption of *vertugade*, which is of Spanish origin) was certainly well contrived to keep men at a distance.

universal judgement, will rise again in their own sex, and not rather in ours, lest they should tempt us in that holy state, have ascribed a wonderful power of temptation to nudity.

In short we lure and flesh them by every means; we incessantly heat and excite their imagination, and then we shout when we are hurt. Let us confess the truth: there is hardly one of us who does not fear the disgrace his wife's misdeeds may bring upon him more than his own; who does not look more tenderly after his good spouse's conscience than his own (wonderful charity!); who would not rather be a thief and guilty of sacrilege, and that his wife were a heretic and murderess, than that she should be less chaste than her husband.

And they would willingly offer to seek a livelihood in the law-courts, or a reputation in war, rather than be obliged, in the midst of pleasures and idleness, to keep so difficult a guard. Do you think they do not see that there is not a tradesman, or an attorney, or a soldier, who will not leave his business to run after this other; nor even a street-porter or cobbler, weary and jaded as they are with labour and hunger?

For all that did Achaemenes possess,
Or wealth Mygdonian of rich Phrygia,
Or Arab treasure-house, would'st give one tress
Of thy Licymnia,

While to thy burning kiss her neck she bends,
Or with feigned cruelty that kiss denies
Which ravished then the thief she more commends,
Sometimes to ravish tries?

HORACE

What an iniquitous balancing of sins! Both we and they are capable of a thousand more mischievous and unnatural depravities than lasciviousness. But we create and weigh sins not according to nature, but according to our interest; wherefore they assume such unequal shapes. The harshness of our decrees makes the addiction of the women to that sin more serious and sinful than its nature admits of, and involves it in consequences which are worse than their cause.

I doubt if the achievements of an Alexander or a Caesar surpass in difficulty the steadfastness of a handsome young woman, brought up after our fashion, in the open view and in contact with the world, assailed by so many contrary examples, keeping herself entire in the midst of a thousand powerful and persistent solicitations. There is no activity more abounding in thorny difficulties, nor more active, than this inactivity. I should think it easier to wear a suit of armour all one's life than a virginity. And the vow of chastity is the most noble of all vows, as being the hardest. *The power of the Devil is in the loins*, says Saint Jerome.

Certainly the most arduous and rigorous of human duties is that we have resigned to the ladies, and we leave them the glory of it. That should serve them as a particular spur to persist in it; it offers them a fine occasion to challenge us, and to tread under foot that vain pre-eminence in courage and valour that we claim over them. They will find, if they take notice, that they will be not only very highly esteemed for it, but also better loved.

A gallant man does not give up his pursuit for a refusal, provided it be a refusal of chastity, not of choice. Though we swear and threaten and complain ever so much, we lie; we love them the better for it. There is no greater allurement than a chastity that is not hard and forbidding. It is stupid and vulgar to persist obstinately in the face of hatred and contempt; but to do so against a virtuous and constant resolution, accompanied by a grateful disposition, is the action of a noble and generous spirit. They may gratefully accept our services to a certain degree, and with due modesty make us feel that they do not disdain us.

For it is indeed a cruel law, if only for its difficulty, which commands them to abhor us because we adore them, and hate us because we love them. Why should they not listen to our offers and requests, so long as they keep within the bounds of modesty? Why should they try to detect the note of some more licentious meaning under our words? A Queen of our time wittily said that 'to repel these approaches was a testimony of weakness, and an accusation of her own facility; and that a lady who had not been tempted could not vaunt her chastity.'

The bounds of honour are not by any means cut so closely; it is quite able, without transgressing, to relax its severity, and give itself a freer rein. Beyond its frontier there is some expanse of land, free, indifferent and neuter. He who has hunted and forcibly run it home, even into its corner and stronghold, is wanting in tact if he is not satisfied with his fortune. The prize of victory is estimated by its difficulty.

Would you know what impression your assiduity and your merit have made on her heart? Judge of it by her character. Many a woman may give more without giving so much. The obligation of a benefit is entirely in proportion to the will of him who gives. Other circumstances which accompany the conferring of a benefit are dumb, dead and fortuitous. This little may cost her dearer to give than it may cost her companion to give her all. If ever rarity was a sign of esteem it must be so in this case; do not consider how little it is, but how few have it. The value of a coin changes according to the stamp and the place where it is minted.

Whatever the spite and indiscretion of some men, at the height of their discontent, may drive them to say, virtue and truth always recover their ground. I have known women, whose reputation had long been unjustly compromised, to recover their good name in the eyes of the world by their constancy alone, without any effort or cunning. All did penance and took back what they had once believed. From being a little under suspicion as girls they have risen to the first rank among good and honourable ladies.

Somebody said to Plato, 'All the world is maligning you.' 'Let them say, he said, I will live in such a way that they shall change their tone.'

Besides the fear of God and the reward of so rare a fame, which should incite them to keep themselves unspotted, the corruption of the world we live in compels them to do so; and if I were in their place, there is nothing I would not rather do than entrust my reputation in such dangerous hands.

In my time the pleasure of telling (a pleasure which in sweetness falls little short of that of doing) was only permitted to those who had some trusty and unique friend. Nowadays, when men come together at table or elsewhere, their ordinary talk consists of boasts of favours received and the secret liberality of the ladies. Truly it shows too mean and vulgar a spirit to allow those tender charms to be so cruelly followed up, pounded and tumbled about by ungrateful, indiscreet, and empty-headed fops.

This our intemperate and unjustifiable exasperation against that sin is born of the most futile and turbulent disease that afflicts the mind of man, which is Jealousy.

Who'd shrink from torch to take a light?
Whate'er they give, they nothing lose.

OVID *and another*

She and her sister Envy appear to me the most foolish of the tribe. Of the latter I can say little; though described as a strong and powerful passion, she has had the good grace never to come my way. As to the other, I know her, at least by sight. The animals have a sense of it: the shepherd Crastis having become enamoured of a goat, her ram, in a fit of jealousy, came and butted his head as he was asleep, and crushed it.

We have exceeded in this passion, after the example of some barbarian nations; the best disciplined have not escaped, which is reasonable, but they have not been driven to extremes by it:

Ne'er did adulterer, by sword of husband slain,
The purple blood of Stygian waters stain.

JOHANNES SECUNDUS

Lucullus, Caesar, Pompey, Antony, Cato, and other brave men were cuckolds and knew it without making a fuss about it. In those times there was only a fool of a Lepidus who died of grief for that reason:

Ah, wretch! if you are taken in the act,
They'll drag you feet first through the open door,
And make you food for turnips and red mullets.

CATULLUS

And the god of our poet, when he surprised one of his fellow-gods with his wife, was satisfied with putting them to shame;

> And one of the gods, not of the most austere,
> Wished he could share the shame;
>
> OVID

yet none the less is he warmed by the sweet caresses she offers him, and complains that for such a trifle she should distrust his affection:

> Why, Goddess mine, invent
> Such far-fetched pleas? Dost thou thy faith remove,
> And cease to trust in Vulcan?
>
> VIRGIL

Nay, she asks a favour of him for a bastard of hers,

> Thine arms I ask, a mother for her son;

which is generously granted by him; and Vulcan speaks honourably of Aeneas:

> Arms for a hero must the forge prepare.

Truly a superhuman humanity! And I am willing to leave this excess of kindness to the gods:

> Nor is it meet to equal men with gods.
>
> CATULLUS

With respect to the confusion of children, besides that the most thoughtful legislators consider it desirable and ordain it in their republics, it does not trouble the women, in whom, however, that feeling is, for some reason or other, still more justified:

Even the stately Juno, Queen of heaven,
Was maddened by the oft-repeated faults
Of her poor erring spouse. CATULLUS

When jealousy seizes those poor weak and unresisting souls, it is pitiful to see how cruelly it catches them in its toils and masters them. It worms itself into them under the cloak of affection, but when it once possesses them, the same causes which served as the foundation of kindness, serve as the foundation of a deadly hatred. Of all mental diseases it is the most easily fed and the most difficult to cure. The virtue, the health, the merit, the reputation of the husband are the firebrands of their fury and malevolence:

No hate implacable except the hate of love.
PROPERTIUS

This feverish passion disfigures and corrupts all that is otherwise good and beautiful in them; and there is no act of a jealous woman, however chaste and however good a housewife she may be, that does not reveal a bitter and nagging spirit. It is a furious perturbation of mind, which will drive them to an extreme the very opposite to its cause.

This was absurdly exemplified by one Octavius in Rome: Having lain with Pontia Posthumia, his affection was so much increased by enjoyment, that he pestered her with entreaties to marry him. Being unable to persuade her, his excessive love hurled him to the opposite extreme of the most cruel and deadly hatred, and he killed her.

In like manner the ordinary symptoms of that other love-malady are intestine hatreds, plots, and conspiracies:

We know what frantic woman scorned can do,

VIRGIL

and a rage which eats into itself the more it is obliged to shield itself under the cloak of kindness.

Now the duty of chastity is far-reaching. Is it their will that we would have them curb? That is a very supple and active thing. It is too nimble to be stayed. What if dreams sometimes carry them so far that they cannot deny them? It is not in them, nor perhaps in Chastity herself, since she is a female, to guard against lust and desire. If their will alone had the power of injuring us, where should we be? Imagine the great scramble, supposing any man had the privilege of being borne, fully equipped, without eyes to see or tongue to tell, to everyone who had the opportunity to receive him!

The Scythian women put out the eyes of all their slaves and prisoners of war, to make use of them more freely and more secretly.

O what a tremendous advantage is opportunity! Should anyone ask me what is the first advantage in love, I should reply that it is to be able to make one's opportunity; likewise the second, and the third as well. There you have the key to everything.

I have often wanted luck, but sometimes I have also wanted enterprise; God shield him from harm who can laugh at this! It needs greater temerity in these days, which our young men excuse under the name of ardour; but if the ladies looked closely into it, they would find that it rather proceeds from contempt. I used to be scrupulously afraid of giving offence, and am inclined to respect where I love. Besides, in this traffic, if you leave out the esteem, you will destroy the glamour. I like the lover to be something of a boy, timid, and a slave. If not quite in this, I have in other situations something of the foolish bashfulness that Plutarch speaks of, and which at various times in the course of my life has been to me a blemish and a source of harm. It is a quality that is not in keeping with my nature as a whole.

But what are we if not a bundle of rebellions and discrepancies? My eyes are as sensitive to suffer a refusal as they are to refuse; and it troubles me so much to be troublesome to others, that, on occasions where duty compels me to ask a favour of another when the granting of it is doubtful and would put him to any cost, I do so sparingly and reluctantly. But if it is for my own particular benefit (although Homer truly says, 'that in a poor man bashfulness is a foolish virtue') I usually commission a third person to blush for me. And if another requests a favour of me, I find it equally difficult to show him the door; so that I have sometimes had the inclination, but not the strength of will, to deny.

It is folly therefore to try to curb in women a desire that is so acute and so natural to them. And when I hear them boast of having so cold and virginal a disposition, I laugh at them; I tell them they are too backward. If she is a toothless and decrepit old woman, or, if young, sapless and consumptive, though it is not altogether credible, there may at least be a semblance of truth in it. But those who still move and breathe only make the matter worse, seeing that he who excuses himself incautiously accuses himself. Like a gentleman of my neighbourhood who was suspected of impotence,

> Whose dagger, hanging limp as well-cooked beet,
> Could never rise to middle height. CATULLUS

Three or four days after his wedding, to vindicate his reputation, he went about boldly declaring that he had ridden twenty stages the night before. His own words were afterwards used to convict him of pure ignorance, and to unmarry him.

Besides, when the women make the aforesaid boast they prove nothing; for there can be neither continence nor virtue where there is no temptation to resist. 'That is true, they should say, but I am not one to make an easy surrender.' Even the saints say the same. I am speaking of those who boast in good earnest of their coldness and insensibility, and expect to be believed with a serious countenance. For when they say it with an affected air, when their eyes belie their words, when they talk the cant of the profession, which must be taken against the grain, I find it amusing. I am a great admirer of naturalness and plainness of speech; but there is no hope for them. If it is not wholly simple and childish, it is improper for ladies, and out of place in that kind of intercourse; it very soon inclines to effrontery.

Only fools are taken in by their masks and faces. Lying is there in the seat of honour; it is a roundabout way, and leads to the truth by the postern-gate. If we cannot curb their imagination, what do we expect of them? Deeds? There are enough of these that avoid all outside communication, by which chastity may be corrupted:

> That's often done that's done without a witness.
>
> MARTIAL

And the people we fear least are perhaps the most to be feared; their silent sins are the worst:

I confess,
A simple prostitute offends me less.

MARTIAL

There are acts which, without immodesty on their part, may cost them their virginity, and, what is more, without their intention. *Sometimes a midwife, on pretence of examining a virgin's integrity, by evil-mindedness, unskilfulness or accident, has destroyed it* (ST AUGUSTINE). Many a one, in seeking her maidenhead, has lost it; many a one has killed it in sport.

We cannot precisely circumscribe the actions we would forbid them. Our rules must be worded in general and ambiguous terms. The very idea we create of their chastity is ridiculous; for, among the extreme patterns I have are Fatua, wife of Faunus, who never allowed any man to see her after her wedding, and the wife of Hiero, who did not realize the fact that her husband had a stinking breath, thinking it was a characteristic of all men. To satisfy us, they must become invisible and devoid of senses.

Now we must confess that our difficulty in estimating this duty lies chiefly in the disposition. There have been husbands who have suffered that mishap, not only without blaming their wives or feeling injured by them, but under a sense of singular obligation and acknowledgement of their virtue. Many a woman there has been who, though she loved honour more than life, has prostituted herself to the furious appetite of a deadly enemy, to save her husband's life; doing for him what she would never have done for herself. This is not the place to enlarge upon these examples: they are too sublime and too precious to be set off by this foil; let us reserve them for a nobler setting.

But for examples of more commonplace distinction, are there not women amongst us who every day lend themselves out for their husbands' sole benefit, and by their express command and mediation? And, in ancient times, Phaulius of Argos offered his wife to King Philip out of ambition. The same was done out of civility by that Galbus, who, entertaining Maecenas to supper, and seeing his wife and him beginning to conspire together by signs and oglings, sank down upon his couch, pretending to be overcome with sleep, in order to help on their understanding. And he very graciously gave himself away; for when, at this point, one of his slaves made bold to lay hands on the plate which was on the table, he called out, 'Don't you see, you rascal, that I am only asleep for Maecenas?'

This woman may be of loose conduct, and yet of a more moral disposition than that other whose behaviour appears more correct. As we hear some lamenting the fact that they had made a vow of chastity before the age of discretion, I have also heard others truly complain of having been given over to a dissolute life before the age of discretion. This may be due to the sin of the parents, or to the force of necessity, who is a rude counsellor. In the East Indies, although chastity was there held in singular esteem, yet custom permitted a married woman to abandon herself to any man who presented her with an elephant; and it reflected a certain glory to have been valued at so high a price.

Phaedo the philosopher, a man of good family, after the capture of his country Elis, made it his trade to prostitute his youthful beauty, as long as it endured, to any man who would pay the price, and thereby gained a livelihood.

And Solon is said to have been the first in Greece who by his laws gave women the liberty, at the cost of their chastity, to provide for the necessities of life; a custom which Herodotus asserts to have been usual, before his time, in several states.

And then, what do we gain by this painful anxiety? For, however justified this feeling may be, it still remains to be considered whether it carries us very far. Does any man think he can confine them, with all his ingenuity?

> Hang bolts and bars; keep her in close confinement.
> But who will watch the guards? The crafty wife
> Begins with them. JUVENAL

Will they ever lack opportunities in so knowing an age?

Curiosity is mischievous in all things; but here it is fatal. It is madness to seek enlightenment on a disease for which there is no physic that does not aggravate it and make it worse, the disgrace of which grows greater and becomes public chiefly through jealousy; revenge for which wounds our children more than it heals us. You will pine away and die whilst searching in the dark for proofs.

How pitifully they have fared who in my time have succeeded in this quest! If the informer does not offer a remedy and relief together with the information, he will only make mischief, and deserves the poniard more than if he kept back the truth. The man who is at pains to prevent it is laughed at no less than the man who is in ignorance. The mark of cuckoldry is indelible; the man who is once stamped with it will always carry it; the punishment makes it more visible than the guilt. It is a fine thing to see our private misfortunes dragged out of doubt and obscurity, to be trumpeted on the tragic boards; and especially misfortunes that only pinch us by being told. For we say 'Good wife' and 'Happy marriage' not of those that are so, but of those no man speaks of.

We must exercise our ingenuity to prevent that awkward and useless knowledge from reaching us. It was customary with the Romans, when returning from a journey, to send a messenger before them to the house, to give their wives notice of their coming, in order not to surprise them. And for the same reason a certain nation arranged that the priest should 'open the ball' with the bride on the wedding night, to relieve the bridegroom of doubt and curiosity, on his first trial, as to whether she comes to him a virgin, or bruised by another's love.

But the world will be talking. I know a hundred respectable men who are cuckolded, respectably and not discreditably. A gentleman is pitied for it, but not held in less esteem. See to it that your worth drowns your misfortune, that good men curse the occasion; and that he who wrongs you trembles at the mere thought of it. And besides, does anyone escape being talked of in that sense, from the little man to the greatest?

Many a man who mighty empires ruled,
And was by far a better man than you
In many things, you miserable wretch!

LUCRETIUS

When you hear so many decent men involved in this reproach in your presence, remember that neither will you be spared in other quarters. But even the ladies will laugh at it; and what are they more ready to laugh at in these days than a tranquil and well-settled married life?

There is not a man of you[13] who has not made someone a cuckold; now, Nature runs quite on parallel lines, in compensation, and turn for turn.

The frequency of this mishap must by this time have tempered the bitterness of it; it will soon have become the rule.

A miserable passion! which has this also, that it is incommunicable:

> And spiteful Fortune too denies
> An ear to our laments. CATULLUS

For where will you find a friend to whom you dare confide your doleful complaints, who, if he does not laugh at them, may not use them as a stepping-stone and an instruction to take his share in the quarry? Both the bitter and the sweet of marriage the wise man keeps to himself. And among its other awkward conditions one of the chief, to a communicative man like myself, is this, that custom makes it improper and prejudicial to confide to anybody all we know and feel about it.

To give the women the same advice, in order to disgust them with jealousy, would be a waste of time; their nature is so steeped in suspicion, vanity, and curiosity, that to cure them by legitimate means is not to be expected. They often recover from this infirmity by a form of health much more to be feared than the malady itself. For, as there are spells which cannot remove a disease except by laying it upon another, so

13 Montaigne originally wrote on the margin of the 1588 edition, 'There is not one of us', but he deleted 'us', and substituted 'you'.

they are apt, when they lose this fever, to transfer it to their husbands.

Yet I know not, to tell the truth, that a man can suffer worse at their hands than jealousy; it is the most dangerous of their conditions, as the head is of their members. Pittacus said, 'that every man had his trouble, and that his was his wife's jealous temper, but for which he would be perfectly happy.' It must be very hard to bear, when a man so just, so wise, so valiant, felt his whole life poisoned by it; what are we other little fellows to do?

The Senate of Marseilles was right to grant the request of the man who asked permission to kill himself, that he might be delivered from his wife's tempestuous temper; for it is a disease which is only removed by removing the whole piece, and has no effectual remedy but flight or suffering, both, however, very difficult.

That man, I think, knew something about it who said 'that a happy marriage might be arranged between a blind wife and a deaf husband.'

We must also see to it that that great and violent strictness of obligation we lay upon them does not produce two results that may run counter to our purpose; to wit, that it may spur on the followers, and make the women more ready to surrender. For, as to the first point, by enhancing the value of the fortress, we enhance the value and desire of conquest. Might not Venus herself have thus cunningly raised the price of her wares by making the laws her brokers; knowing how insipid a pastime it would be, if not heightened by the imagination and by its dearness? In short, it is all swine's flesh, varied by sauces, as Flaminius' host said. Cupid is a rogue of a god, who makes it his sport to wrestle with religion and justice; it is his glory that his power battles with every other power, and that all other laws give way to his:

> He ever seeks out victims for his guilt.
>
> OVID

And with regard to the second point: Should we not be less often cuckolded if we were less afraid of it, considering the nature of woman? For prohibition incites and invites them:

> You will, they won't; you will not, they insist.
>
> TERENCE

> They think it shame to go where we permit.
>
> LUCAN

How could we better interpret Messalina's behaviour? At first she conceals her amours from her husband, as they commonly do; but finding that, by reason of his dullness, she could carry on her intrigues too easily, she soon disdained that customary way. Behold her then making love openly, owning her admirers, entertaining and favouring them in the sight of all. She wished to make him resent it. When that animal was not to be roused by all this; when her pleasure was rendered flat and tasteless by his weak and easy-going nature, which appeared to authorize and legalize her conduct, what did she do? Wife of an Emperor still living and in good health, and at Rome, the theatre of the world, at full noon, with public pomp and ceremony, and to Silius, whom she had already long enjoyed, she is married on a day when her husband was outside the city.

Does it not appear as if she were on the way to

becoming chaste through her husband's nonchalance, or as if she were seeking another husband who might whet her appetite with his jealousy and rouse her by opposition? But the first difficulty she encountered was also the last. The beast woke up with a start. We often drive the worst bargain with those who appear to be deaf or asleep. I have found by experience that this extreme long-suffering, when once dissolved, will vent itself in the most cruel acts of revenge; for anger and fury, being heaped up in a mass and suddenly taking fire, discharge all their energy at the first attack:

> And so let loose the reins of wrath.
>
> VIRGIL

He put her to death, together with a large number of those who were intimate with her; even some who had been guilty against their will, having been invited to her bed with scourges.

What Virgil says of Venus and Vulcan, Lucretius more fitly said of a stolen enjoyment between her and Mars:

> Thou on whose breast, consumed with eager love,
> Mars throws himself, who rules with powerful sway
> O'er war's wild works, and then with gaze upturned
> All open-mouthed, with shapely neck flung back,
> Feeds his love-greedy eyes on thy dear face,
> While all his soul hangs quivering on thy lips.
> Oh, while he lies within thy fond embrace,
> With all thy godlike charms around him shed,
> Pour low sweet words from thy sweet lips.

When I reflect upon those words *rejicit* (throws), *pascit* (feeds), *inhians* (open-mouthed), *molli* (soft), *fovet* (fondles), *medullas* (marrow), *labefacta* (melting), *pendet* (hangs), *percurrit* (runs through), and that noble *circumfusa* (shed around), mother of the pretty *infusus* (infused), I despise those little conceits and verbal triflings, which have since cropped up. Those simple poets had no need of that clever and ingenious playing upon words; their language is quite full-bodied, and big with a natural and constant vigour. They are all epigram; not only the tail, but the head, stomach, and feet. There is nothing far-fetched, nothing that drags; it all proceeds at an even pace. *It is a texture of manly beauties; they are not concerned about flowers of rhetoric* (SENECA).

It is not merely a tame eloquence, where nothing offends. It is nervous and substantial, and does not so much please the palate, as it fills the mind with rapture, and especially the greatest minds. When I see those bold forms of expression, so vivid, so deep, I do not say 'This is well said', but 'This is well thought'. It is the healthy freshness of the imagination that elevates and swells the words. *It is the heart which makes one eloquent* (QUINTILIAN). We moderns confound language with judgement, and fine words with full conceptions.

This painting is not so much the result of manual dexterity as of having the object more vividly imprinted on the soul. Gallus[14] speaks simply because he conceives simply. Horace is not content with a superficial expression; it would betray him. He sees more clearly and more deeply into the matter. His mind unlocks and ransacks the whole storehouse of words and figures wherewith to express itself; and he

14 Cornelius Gallus or the Pseudo-Gallus, an elegiac poet, a friend of Virgil and Propertius.

needs them beyond the commonplace, because his conceptions are beyond the commonplace.

Plutarch said that he saw the Latin language through things.[15] It is the same here; the sense illuminates and brings forth the words, which are not mere wind, but flesh and bone. They mean more than they say. Even the feeble-minded show some reflection of this; for when I was in Italy I could say what I pleased in ordinary talk, but in serious conversation I should not have dared to trust myself with an idiom that I could not wind and turn out of its ordinary course. I like to be able to introduce something of my own.

It is the use and the handling of language by men of genius that sets it off; not so much by innovations as by putting it to more vigorous and varied services, by stretching and bending it. They do not contribute words to it, but they enrich their own, giving more weight and depth to their meaning and their use, teaching them unaccustomed movements, but discreetly and skilfully.

And how little that is given to all may be seen in the numerous French writers of our time. They are so bold and disdainful that they will not follow the common high-road; but want of inventiveness and of judgement is their ruin. We see in them only a miserable affectation of singularity, of frigid and absurd disguises which, instead of elevating, lower the matter. As long as they can strut about in new things,

15 'In the reading of Latin books, singular as it may appear, I did not find that the words assisted me to discover the meaning, but rather that my knowledge of the history enabled me to find out the meaning of the words.' – PLUTARCH, *Life of Demosthenes*.

they care little about the effect; if they can grasp at a new word, they will drop the usual one, which is often more forcible and energetic.

In our language I find plenty of stuff, but rather a want of style. For there is nothing that might not be done with our jargon of the chase and our military terms, which are a fruitful soil to borrow from. And forms of speech, like plants, improve and grow stronger by being transplanted. I find it sufficiently abundant, but not sufficiently pliable and vigorous. It usually succumbs under a powerful conception. If you try to strain it you will often feel it drooping and bending under you; and when it fails you, Latin comes to your aid, as Greek does to others.

Of some of those words I have picked out we find it harder to realize the energy, because the frequent use of them has somewhat debased and vulgarized their beauty for us; as in our vernacular we meet with excellent phrases and metaphors whose charm has withered with age, and whose colour is tarnished by too general handling. But that does not take away from their flavour for one who has a good nose, nor does it lessen the glory of those old authors who in all probability brought these words to their present prominence.

The scholars treat of things too subtly, in too artificial a manner, differing from the common and natural. My page makes love, and understands it. Read to him Leo Hebreus and Ficino; they speak of him, his thoughts and actions, and yet he will not understand a word of it. I do not recognize in Aristotle most of my ordinary motions; they have been covered and clothed in another gown, for the use of the school. God grant that they be right! If I were of the trade, I should naturalize art as much as they artialize nature. Let us leave Bembo and Equicola[16] alone.

When I write I can dispense very well with the company and remembrance of books, lest they should interfere with my style. Also because, in truth, the good authors humble me too much, and dishearten me. I would gladly do like the painter who, having made a wretchedly bad picture of some cocks, gave his boys strict injunctions to allow no natural cock into his shop. And to set myself off a little, I should rather have to adopt the idea of Antigenidas the musician, who, when he had to perform, took care that, before or after him, his audience was drenched by some other poor singers.

But I can more hardly do without Plutarch. He is so universal and so full, that on all occasions, and however extravagant the subject you have taken in hand, he will thrust himself into your business, and hold out to you a liberal, an inexhaustible handful of treasures and ornaments. I feel vexed that he should be so exposed to plunder by those who resort to him. I can hardly come near him without purloining a leg or a wing.

And it suits my present purpose to write at home, in these uncivilized parts, where I have nobody to assist or correct me; while I associate with no man who understands the Latin of his Paternoster, and who does not know even less French. I might have done it better elsewhere, but the work would have been less

16 Cardinal Pietro Bembo (1470–1547), a celebrated Italian scholar who wrote among other things *Gli Asolani*, supposed to be a licentious dialogue on Platonic love. Equicola, a theologian and philosopher of the sixteenth century, wrote a book *Della Natura d' Amore*.

my own; and its chief aim and perfection is to be precisely my own. I might indeed correct an incidental error, and these abound with me whenever I run on carelessly; but the imperfections which are common and constant with me it would be a treachery to remove.

When another tells me, or I say to myself, 'You are too thick in metaphors; here is a word of Gascon growth; there is a risky expression' (I avoid none that are used in the streets of France; those who would oppose grammar to usage are queer people); 'this is ignorant reasoning; that is paradoxical reasoning; this is too foolish; you often jest; people will think you are serious when you are pretending.' 'Yes, I reply, but I correct the faults of inadvertence, not those which are customary with me. Do I not speak like that throughout? Do I not portray myself to the life? Enough. I have done what I intended; all the world will recognize me in my book, and my book in me.'

Now it is in my nature to ape and copy. When I presumed to write verse (and I never wrote any except in Latin), they openly betrayed the poet I had last been reading; and some of my first Essays smell rather exotic. At Paris I speak a language somewhat differing from that I speak at Montaigne. If I look upon anyone attentively I easily take some impression of him. What I consider I usurp: a foolish deportment, a disagreeable grimace, a ridiculous way of speaking. Still more vices; as soon as they prick me they stick, and will not let go without shaking. I have more often been heard to swear by imitation than naturally.

It is a murderous imitation, like that of those terribly big and strong apes that King Alexander came across in a certain region of the Indies, and which he would have found it difficult to master if they had not afforded him the means by that propensity of theirs to copy everything they saw done. For this gave the hunters the idea of putting on shoes when they were looking, and tying them with many laces and knots, of wrapping their heads in some contrivance provided with running nooses, and pretending to anoint their eyes with bird-lime. So these poor beasts incautiously followed their ape-nature to their own ruin: they glued up their own eyes, hobbled their own feet and strangled themselves.

That other accomplishment of cleverly and purposely mimicking the words and actions of another, which often affords amusement and is much admired, I have no more than a log.

When I swear in my own way, it is only *Perdy*, which is the most straightforward of all oaths. They say that Socrates swore by a dog, that Zeno used the same interjection now used by Italians, *Cappari*, and that Pythagoras swore by water and air.

I am so apt unthinkingly to take those superficial impressions that if I have had the words 'Sire' or 'Your Highness' on my lips for three days in succession, they will slip from me for a week after instead of 'Your Excellency' or 'Your Lordship'. And if I begin to say a thing in sport or jest, I am likely to say it next day in earnest. Wherefore in writing I am more loath to choose a thrashed-out subject, lest I should treat of it at another's expense.

Every theme is equally pregnant for me. A fly will serve my purpose; and God grant that this I have now in hand has not been taken up at the bidding of too flighty a disposition! I need only begin with a subject that I fancy, for all subjects are linked to one another.

But I am dissatisfied with my mind in that it usually

brings forth its profoundest ideas, as well as its maddest and those I like best, unexpectedly, and when I least look for them, for they will instantly vanish if I have no means at hand for fixing them; on horseback, at table, in bed, but mostly on horseback, where my thoughts wander most widely.

When speaking I am rather sensitively jealous of attention and silence, if I am speaking forcibly; whoever interrupts me, stops me. When travelling, the necessities incidental to the road will cut conversation short; besides that I most frequently travel without company fit for connected discourse. Wherefore I take every opportunity to commune with my own thoughts.

It is the same with my dreams; when dreaming I recommend them to my memory (for I am apt to dream that I am dreaming); but next morning I can indeed call to mind what colour they were of, whether gay, or sad, or strange, but as to what they were besides, the more I labour to recover them, the more deeply do I plunge them into oblivion. So of those ideas that come accidentally into my mind I retain only a vague outline; only enough to make me worry and fret in pursuit of them, and all to no purpose.

Well then, setting books aside and speaking more materially and simply, I find after all that love is nothing else but the thirst for enjoying the desired object, and that Venus is but the pleasure of discharging one's vessels, like the pleasure Nature gives us in discharging other parts, which becomes vicious by immoderation or indiscretion. For Socrates love is the appetite for generation, by the mediation of beauty.

And when I think, as I have done many a time, of the ridiculous titillation of this pleasure, the absurd, giddy, crack-brained emotions which it stirs up in

Zeno and Cratippus, of that unreasonable rage, that countenance inflamed with fury and cruelty at the most delightful moment of love, and then that solemn, stern, ecstatic mien in so extravagant an action; when I consider besides that our joys and excrements are lodged together pell-mell, and that sensual pleasure at its height is attended, like pain, with faintness and moaning, I believe it is true what Plato says, that man is the plaything of the gods:

> Truly a cruel way to sport with us!
>
> CLAUDIAN

and that Nature was in a mocking mood when she left us that most common and most disturbing of our actions to make us all alike and put us on the same level, wise men and fools, men and beasts. The most contemplative and wisest of men, when I picture him in that attitude, appears to me a humbug with his wise and contemplative airs; it is the peacock's feet that humble his pride:

> Why may not truth in laughing guise be dressed?
>
> HORACE

Those who refuse to discuss serious matters playfully act, as somebody says, like the man who fears to worship the statue of a saint unless it has an apron.

We eat indeed, and drink like the animals; but these are not actions that hinder the workings of the mind. In these we maintain an advantage over them; the other brings every other thought under its yoke, brutifies and bestializes, by its imperious authority, all the theology and philosophy that is in Plato; and yet he does not lament it. In all other things you may observe some decorum. All other operations may be subjected to the rules of decency; this one cannot even be imagined other than vicious and ridiculous. Try to find, if you can, some modest and sober way of doing it.

Alexander said that he knew himself to be mortal chiefly by this action, and by sleeping. Sleep stifles and suppresses the faculties of our mind. The sexual act similarly absorbs and dissipates them. Truly it is a mark, not only of our original corruption, but also of our inanity and deformity.

On the one hand Nature pushes us on to it, having connected with this desire the noblest, most useful, and pleasant of all her operations; and on the other hand she allows us to condemn and fly from it as from a shameless and immodest action, to blush at it and recommend abstinence.

Are we not indeed brutes to call brutish the operation that makes us?

The nations, in their religions, have met together in a number of conventions, as sacrifices, candles, incense, fasts, offerings and, among other things, in their condemnation of this action. All opinions tend that way, as well as to the widespread custom of cutting off the foreskin, which is a punishment of it.

We are perhaps right in blaming ourselves for producing so foolish a thing as man; in calling the action shameful, and shameful the parts that serve that purpose. (At present mine are really shameful and shamefaced.)

The Essenians, of whom Pliny speaks, kept up their numbers for several centuries without nurses or baby-clothes, through the influx of foreigners who, following that pretty humour, continually joined them: a whole nation risking extermination rather than become entangled in a woman's embrace, and breaking the continuity of men rather than create one.

It is said that Zeno never had to do with a woman but once in his life, and then only out of civility, that he might not seem too obstinately to disdain the sex.

Everyone avoids seeing a man born; everyone runs to see him die. For his destruction they seek out a spacious field, in the full light of day; for his construction they creep into some dark little corner. It is a duty to hide and blush when making him; and it is a glory, and the source of many virtues, to be able to unmake him. The one is offence, the other is grace; for Aristotle says that in a certain phrase of his country, to benefit someone is to kill him. The Athenians, to equalize the disgrace of these two actions, having to purify the island of Delos and justify themselves to Apollo, forbade at once all burials and births within its territory. *We are ashamed of ourselves* (TERENCE); we regard our being as a sin.

There are countries where they cover themselves when they eat. I know a lady, and one of the greatest, who holds the same view, that a woman masticating is an unpleasant sight, as it takes away much of her charm and beauty; and she does not care to appear in public with an appetite. And I know a man who cannot bear to see another, or to be seen, eating, and is more shy of company when filling than when emptying himself.

In the empire of the Turk there are many who, to show their superiority over others, are never seen at their meals, and only take one a week; who cut and disfigure their face and limbs; who never speak to any man: all of them fanatic people who think they honour their nature by denaturalizing themselves, who prize themselves for their misprision, and think they become better by becoming worse. What an unnatural animal to be a horror to himself, to grieve at his pleasures, to regard himself as a misfortune!

There are some who conceal their lives,

> And change the sweets of home
> For exile kingdoms 'neath an alien sky;
>
> VIRGIL

and withdraw from the sight of other men; who shun health and cheerfulness as if they were hurtful enemies. There are not only many sects, but many nations, that curse their birth and bless their death. There are countries where the sun is abominated and the darkness worshipped.

We show no skill except in ill-treating ourselves; that is the true quarry for our powerful intellect: a dangerous tool when misapplied!

> O wretched men, whose pleasures are a crime!
>
> PSEUDO-GALLUS

Alas, poor human! you have sufficient necessary evils, without adding to them by your own invention; you are miserable enough by nature without being so by art. You have real and essential deformities in abundance without forging imaginary ones. Do you think you are too well off unless you find the half of your well-being an affliction? Do you think you have fulfilled all the necessary duties to which Nature binds you, and that she is wanting and idle in you, if you do not force yourself to create fresh duties? You are not afraid of sinning against her universal and unquestionable laws, and spur yourself to obey your own, which are partial and fanciful; and the more partial, uncertain and questionable they are the more do you persist in obeying them. You are possessed and bound by the positive orders of your own invention and the rules of your parish; those of God and the world leave you unconcerned. Consider for a moment the examples of this kind; all your life is reflected in them.

The lines of these two poets, treating lasciviousness as they do with so much reserve and discretion, appear to me to disclose it more fully and cast a strong light upon it. The ladies cover their bosoms with open-work lace, the priests keep many sacred things hidden, painters put shadows into their work to set off the light, and they say that the sun's rays and the wind are harder to bear when reflected than direct. The Egyptian who was asked, 'What are you hiding under your cloak?' answered discreetly, 'I am hiding it under my cloak that you may not know what it is.' But there are certain other things that are hidden to be shown. Listen to this man, who is more unreserved:

> And pressed her naked body unto mine.
>
> OVID

I feel as if he were caponizing me. Let Martial gather up Venus's skirts as high as he pleases, he will not succeed in making her appear so entire. He who says all sates and disgusts us. He who fears to be explicit leads us on to thinking more than is meant. There is treachery in this kind of modesty, and especially when they half open, as these do, so fair a path to imagination. And the action and the painting should smack of theft.

I like the Spanish and Italian methods of making love, which are more respectful, more timid, more affected and discreet. Somebody in ancient times, I forget who, wished for a gullet as long as a crane's neck, that he might the longer relish what he was gulping down. This wish is more appropriate to this quick and hasty pleasure, especially in a nature like mine, whose failing it is to be too sudden. To arrest its flight and lengthen out the preliminaries, everything serves as a favour and recompense between them: a look, a nod, a word, a sign. If we could dine off the steam of a roast joint, what an expense we could save!

It is a passion in which very little solid reality is mingled with much more unreality and feverish imagination; it should be paid and served accordingly. Let us teach the ladies to make the most of themselves, to observe self-respect, to keep us in suspense and fool us. We begin with the final attack, and always show our French impetuosity. When they spin out their favours and spread them out in small portions, each of us, even miserable old age, will find a little to glean, according to his substance and merit.

He who finds no enjoyment except in enjoyment, who wins nothing unless he sweeps the stakes, who loves the chase only for the sake of the quarry, has no business to intrude into our school. The more steps and degrees there are, so much higher is the uppermost seat, and so much more honourable it is to reach it. We should take a pleasure in being led to it, as into a magnificent palace, through divers porticoes and passages, long and pleasant galleries and many turnings. This dispensation would turn to our advantage; we should dwell there the longer, and love the longer. Without hope and without desire we can make no progress worth a rap.

They should infinitely dread our mastery and entire

possession of them. As soon as they have wholly surrendered to the mercy of our fidelity and constancy, their position is a little too risky; for those virtues are rare and hard to find. No sooner are they ours than we are no more theirs.

The lust of greedy soul once satisfied,
Nor oaths nor promises they reck.

CATULLUS

And Thrasonides, a young Greek, was so much in love with his love that, having won his mistress's heart, he refused to enjoy her, that he might not thereby deaden, sate, and weaken that restless ardour on which he fed and so prided himself.

Dearness gives relish to the meat. See how the form of salutation, which is peculiar to our nation, spoils by its cheapness the charms of the kiss which, as Socrates says, is so powerful and dangerous a stealer of hearts. It is a disagreeable and offensive custom for a lady to have to lend her lips to any man, however disgusting, who has three lackeys at his heels:

As from his snout, so like a dog's,
Hangs the rime of frozen fogs,
And the beard it fairly clogs
Around his throat . . .
A hundred times I'd rather kiss his —.

MARTIAL

And we ourselves do not gain much by it; for the world is so divided that for three pretty women we must kiss fifty plain ones. And for a tender stomach, such as we have at my age, a bad kiss is too high a price to pay for a good one.

In Italy they act the part of the languishing suitor

even with the ladies who are for sale, and defend this practice as follows: 'that there are degrees in enjoyment, and that by paying them homage we try to procure for ourselves the most complete. For these ladies sell only their bodies; their good will cannot be on sale, it is too free and too much at its own disposal.' Hence they say that it is the will they lay siege to; and they are right. It is the will we must serve and win by our attentions. To me it is a horrible idea that a body void of affection should belong to me. It can only be compared to the mania of that youth who defiled by his love the beautiful statue of Venus that Praxiteles made; or of that raving Egyptian whose lust was kindled by a dead body he was embalming and shrouding, which was the occasion of the law since made in Egypt, which ordained that the bodies of beautiful young women and those of good family should be kept for three days before being delivered into the hands of the undertakers. Periander acted still more unnaturally by carrying his conjugal affection (although more regular and lawful) to the point of enjoying his wife Melissa after she was dead.

Does it not appear a lunatic humour in Luna, when she could not otherwise enjoy her darling Endymion, to put him to sleep for several months, and browse in the enjoyment of a youth who stirred only in his dreams?

So I say that we love a body without a soul, or without feeling, when we love a body without its consent and desire. All enjoyments are not alike; some are hectic and some languid. A thousand other causes besides goodwill may win us this favour of the ladies; it is not a sufficient evidence of affection. Treachery may lurk there, as elsewhere; sometimes they respond with only one buttock:

As cool as at a sacrifice, you'd think
Her marble, or in quite another place. MARTIAL

I know some who would rather lend that than their coach, and who have nothing else to communicate. You must observe whether she enjoys your company on any other account, or on that alone, as if you were some burly stable-boy; in what degree of favour or esteem you are housed:

Whether she gives herself to thee alone,
And marks thy day out with the whiter stone.
CATULLUS

What if she eats your bread with the sauce of a more pleasing imagination:

She holds you in her arms,
But sighs for other loves. TIBULLUS

What! Have we not heard of someone, in our time, who turned this action to a horrible revenge, to poison and kill, as he did, an honest woman? They who know Italy will never think it strange if, in this connexion, I do not go elsewhere for examples. For that nation may be said to be the schoolmaster of the world in this practice.

Handsome women are more commonly met with in that nation, and fewer plain ones than here; but in rare and surpassing beauties I think we are on a par. And I judge the same of their intellects; of commonplace minds they have many more. A brutish stupidity, as may be plainly seen, is with them incomparably more rare. In exceptional minds and those of the highest degree we can hold our own with them.

If I were to carry this comparison further, I think I

may say, on the other hand, that, as compared with them, valour is common and natural with us; but sometimes we may see it on their side in so full and powerful a degree, that it exceeds all the boldest examples we can produce.

The marriages in that country are lame in this respect: their custom commonly imposes so rude and slavish a law upon the wife, that the most distant acquaintance with a stranger is for her as capital an offence as the most intimate. The result of this law is that every approach is necessarily of a substantial nature; and, since all comes to the same with them, they have a very easy choice. And, once they have broken through this partition, you may imagine that they catch fire. *Lust, like a wild beast, angered by its chains, breaks loose* (LIVY).

We must give them a little more rein:

Of late I saw, with firm bit held, a colt
Rush headlong like a mighty thunderbolt.

OVID

The desire for company is assuaged by giving it a little liberty.

We are pretty much in the same case; they go too far in restraint, we in licence. It is a pleasing custom we have in this country that our sons are received into good families to be brought up and trained as pages, as in a school of nobility; and it is regarded as a piece of discourtesy and an affront to refuse one of gentle birth.

I have perceived (for so many houses, so many different styles and methods) that those ladies who have tried to lay down the strictest rules for the maids of their retinue have not had the best luck. It needs moderation, and we must leave a good part of their conduct to their own discretion; for, taking all in all, there is no discipline that will curb them at every point. But it is most true that one who has come safe, with bag and baggage, out of a free schooling, inspires much more confidence than one who comes safely out of a school in which she has been kept a strict prisoner.

Our fathers trained their daughters to look bashful and timid (hearts and desires were the same); we train ours to put on an air of assurance. We understand nothing of the matter. That is all very well for the Sarmatian women, who are not allowed to lie with a man until they have with their own hands killed another in war.

For me, who have no authority over them except through the ears, it is enough if they retain me for their counsel, in accordance with the privilege of my age. So I counsel them, as well as ourselves, abstinence; but, if this generation is too hostile to it, at least discretion and modesty. For, as Aristippus, according to the tale, said to some young men who blushed to see him enter the house of a courtesan, 'The sin is not in entering, but in not coming out again.' If she has no care for her conscience, let her have some regard to her good name. Though the substance be not worth much, let the appearance hold good.

I commend gradation and delay in the dispensation of their favours. Plato points out that in every kind of love an easy and prompt surrender is forbidden in those who hold the fort. It is a sign of gluttony, which they should conceal with all their cunning, to surrender so heedlessly and impetuously all they have. By observing order and measure in granting their favours, they fool our desire the better, and conceal their own. Let them ever flee before us. I mean even if they wish to be caught. They will conquer us the better in flight, like the Scythians. Indeed, according to the law that Nature has given them, it is not properly their part to will and desire; their part is to suffer, obey, and consent. That is why Nature has given them a perpetual capacity; to us a rare and uncertain one. They always have their hour, that they may always be ready for ours; *born to be passive* (SENECA). And, whilst she has decreed that our appetites should show and declare themselves prominently, she has arranged for theirs to be hidden away and inward, and has provided them with parts fitted simply for the defensive, and not for show.

They must leave pranks like the following to Amazonian licence: when Alexander was marching through Hyrcania, Thalestris, Queen of the Amazons, came to see him with three hundred troopers of her own sex, well mounted and well armed, having left the remainder of a large army that was following her beyond the neighbouring mountains, and said to him aloud and publicly, 'that the reports of his victories and his valour had brought her thither to see him and offer her power and resources to help him in his enterprise; and that, seeing he was so handsome, young and strong, she, who was perfect in all his qualities, proposed to him that they should cohabit, that there might be born, of the most valiant woman in the world and the most valiant man then living, something great and rare for the time to come.' Alexander thanked her for the rest; but to gain time for the accomplishment of her last request, he stayed thirteen days at that place, which he spent in feasting and jollity to the best of his powers, to welcome so courageous a princess.

We are, in almost all things, unjust judges of their actions, as they are of ours. I confess the truth when it tells against me as when it is on my side. It is an infamous and badly ordered state of things that so often drives them to change, and prevents them from fixing their affections on any object whatever; as we see in that goddess to whom we attribute so much fickleness and so many lovers. Yet it is true that it is contrary to the nature of love not to be violent, and contrary to the nature of violence to be constant. And they who wonder at it, who exclaim against it and look for the causes of this frailty in them, as if it were unnatural and incredible, why can they not see how often they themselves share it, without being amazed and crying 'miracle'? It would perhaps be more strange to see them attached to one object. It is not a merely bodily passion. If there is no end to avarice and ambition, neither is there to lechery. It still lives after satiety; and neither constant satisfaction nor limit can be set to it; it ever outlives possession.

And besides, inconstancy is perhaps rather more pardonable in them than in us. They may plead, as we do, the inclination to variety and novelty common to both sexes; and secondly they may plead, as we do not, that they buy a cat in a poke.

Joan, Queen of Naples, had her first husband Andreasso hanged at the bars of her window with a cord of silk and gold thread twisted with her own hands, because in the matrimonial fatigue-duties she found that neither his parts nor his performances answered the expectations she had formed of him when she saw his stature, his beauty, his youth and activity, by which she had been caught and deceived.

They may plead that the active part needs more

effort than the passive, so that on their part the effort is always equal to the occasion, whilst on our part it may fall out otherwise. For this reason it was that Plato wisely made a law that, in order to decide upon the expediency of a marriage, the judges should see the youths who contemplated it stark naked, and the girls nude only down to the girdle.

When they come to try us they do not perhaps find us worthy of their choice:

All efforts vain to excite his vigour dead,
The married virgin flies the unjoyous bed.

MARTIAL

It is not enough that the will should drive straight. Weakness and incapacity lawfully dissolve a marriage:

A lover much more vigorous she needs
To undo her virgin zone. CATULLUS

Why not? and, according to her standard, a more licentious and more active capacity for love:

Lest to his pleasing toil he prove unequal. VIRGIL

But is it not a great impudence to bring our imperfections and weaknesses where we desire to please and leave a good opinion and recommendation of ourselves? For the little that I now need,

– For one encounter only am I fit, – HORACE

I would not trouble a person I have to respect and fear:

Let me not suspicion rouse
Who now, alas, have passed my fiftieth year.

HORACE

Nature should be satisfied with making this age miserable, without also making it ridiculous. I should hate to see it, for one inch of pitiful vigour that inflames it three times a week, strutting and swaggering as fiercely as if it had some big and lawful day's work in its belly: a regular straw-fire. What wonder if, after leaping up into a sudden and crackling flame, it dies down in a moment and becomes cold and lifeless!

That desire should only be found in the prime of youth and beauty. Trust your age, if you would be convinced, to back up that indefatigable, full, constant and courageous ardour you feel in yourself; it will leave you nicely in the lurch. Better to boldly hand on your experience to some nerveless, wide-eyed, ignorant boy, who still trembles under the rod, and will blush at it:

A crimson blush her glowing face o'erspread,
As Indian ivory, when stained with red,
Or lilies mixed with roses in a bed.

VIRGIL

He who can await, in the morning, without dying of shame, the contempt of those beautiful eyes that have witnessed his slackness and impertinence,

And truly eloquent with dumb reproof,

OVID

has never felt the satisfaction and pride of wearying them and setting dark rims around them by the vigorous exercise of an active and busy night.

When I have seen one dissatisfied with me, I did not at once accuse her of fickleness; I began to wonder whether I should not rather blame Nature, who has certainly treated me unfairly and unkindly:

He is not very tall, and not very stout.

PRIAPEA

The very matrons look with much disfavour
Upon a man with little parts; IBID.

and done me a most enormous hurt. Every part of me makes me what I am, as much as any other. And no other makes me more properly a man than this.

I owe it to the public to give them my full-length portrait. The wisdom I have learned lies wholly in truth, freedom of speech, reality. It disdains to include in the catalogue of its real duties those petty, invented, customary provincial rules. It is entirely natural, constant, universal. Its daughters, but bastard daughters, are civility and conventionality.

We shall easily get the better of the sins of appearance when we have conquered those of reality. When we have done with the latter, we may run full tilt at the others, if we find it necessary to run at them. For there is danger of our setting up new duties in our imagination, to excuse our neglect of our natural duties, and to obscure them. As a proof of this we may see that in places where faults are crimes, crimes are no more than faults; that with the nations where the laws of propriety are more uncommon and more laxly kept, the primitive and common laws are better observed; since the innumerable crowd of so many duties stifles, deadens, and scatters our attention. Our application to little things withdraws us from more urgent ones.

O what an easy and pleasant path do those superficial men take, in comparison with ours! They are shadowy things wherewith we plaster our conscience and pay one another's debts. But we do not pay, but rather pile up, our debts to that great judge, who pulls up our rags and tatters around our shameful parts, and does not pretend not to see through us, even to our inmost and most secret impurities. Our virginal modesty would be usefully covered if it could keep this discovery from him.

In short, whoever could sharpen the wits of man and rid him of these over-nice verbal superstitions would do the world no great harm. Our life is part folly, part wisdom. He who only treats of it reverently and canonically will leave more than half unsaid. I do not indulge in self-excuses, and if I did, I should rather excuse myself for my excuses than for any other fault. I excuse myself to those of a certain way of thinking, whom I hold to be more numerous than those on my side. For their consideration I will say this besides – for I wish to please everyone; though it is a difficult thing *for a single man to conform to that great variety of manners, discourses and wills* (Q. CICERO) – that they ought not strictly to blame me for the things I quote from authorities accepted and approved by many centuries; and that there is no reason why, because I do not write in verse, they should deny me the freedom that is enjoyed, in our days, even by church dignitaries, and those of our nation and the most tufted. Here are two specimens:

Rimula, dispeream, ni monogramma tua est.[17]

Un vit d'ami la contente et bien traite.

17 The line is by Theodore de Bèze, one of the most influential of the Genevese reformers, who in his youth wrote witty but indecent poetry. The second line is by Mellin de Saint-Gelais, who was chaplain to the Dauphin.

And what about so many others? I love modesty, and it is not judgement that prompts me to choose this scandalous way of speaking. It is Nature who has chosen for me. I do not commend it any more than I do all methods that are contrary to accepted custom; but I excuse it, and, by particular and general circumstances, lighten the accusation.

But to proceed. Whence too comes that sovereign authority you usurp over one who grants you favours at her own cost,

> Who in the dead of night has given you
> Many a little present;
>
> CATULLUS

and whom you immediately treat with the self-interest, coolness, and authority of a husband? It is a free compact; why do you not keep it as you would hold her by it? There is no law to bind voluntary actions.

It is contrary to custom, but it is true none the less that in my time I have carried out this bargain, as far as the nature of it would permit, as conscientiously as any other bargain, and with some appearance of justice; that I never pretended more affection than I felt; and that I gave simple expression to its decline, its vigour and birth, its outbursts and slack periods. One does not always go at the same pace. I was so sparing of promises that I think I did more than I promised or owed. They found me faithful to the point of serving their interest when they were inconstant to me, I mean awowedly and sometimes repeatedly inconstant. I never broke with them as long as I was attached to them even by a thread; and whatever cause they may have given me I never broke with them so far as to hate and despise them. For those intimacies, even when gained on the most shameful terms, still oblige me to have some kindly feeling for them.

At times I have given way to anger and somewhat unwise impatience on detecting their tricks and shifts, and in our quarrels; for I am naturally liable to sudden fits of temper which, though fleeting and soon over, are often prejudicial to my interest. If they were minded to test the freedom of my judgement, I did not shirk giving them some sharp paternal advice, and pinching them where they smarted. If I gave them any cause for complaint, it was rather because they found me too foolishly conscientious in my love, compared with modern ways. I have kept my word when I might easily have been excused from doing so; they would then sometimes surrender with credit to themselves, and on conditions which they would readily have allowed the victor to break.

More than once I have made the pleasure at its highest point to yield to the interest of their honour. And when urged by reason I have armed them against myself, so that they acted more securely and decorously by my rules, when they freely submitted to them, than they would have done by their own.

As often as I could I took upon myself all the risks of our rendezvous, to relieve them of responsibility; and always contrived our meetings at the most difficult and unexpected times and places, because they arouse less suspicion and are besides, I think, more accessible. A place is chiefly open at a spot which is supposed to be of itself covered. The less we fear a thing the less are we on the defensive and on the watch for it. You may more easily dare a thing that nobody thinks you will dare, so that it becomes easy through its difficulty.

No man ever acted with more regard to consequences. This way of loving is more correct; but who knows better than I how ridiculous it appears nowadays, and how little it is practised? Yet I shall not repent of it; I have nothing more to lose there:

My votive tablet, in the temple set,
Proclaims that I to Ocean's god have hung
The garments from my latest shipwreck wet.

HORACE

I can now speak openly about it. But, just as I might perhaps say to another, 'My friend, you are dreaming; love, these days, has little to do with faith and honesty':

Now if you try to make unstable counsel
Stable by reason's rules, you only add
To madness, and are reasonably mad;

TERENCE

so, on the contrary, if I had to begin anew I should certainly pursue the same path and the same course of proceeding, however fruitless it might be to me.

Incapacity and folly are praiseworthy in an unpraiseworthy action. The further I depart from their point of view in this, the nearer I keep to my own.

For the rest, in this traffic, I did not let myself go entirely; I took pleasure, but I did not forget myself, in it; I kept entire the little sense and judgement that nature has given me, for their sake as well as for my own; a little excitement, but no delirium. My conscience was also involved to the point of making me licentious and dissolute; but ungrateful, treacherous, malicious or cruel, never. I was not reckless in pursuing the pleasure of this vice, but bought it for what it cost and nothing more. *There is no vice that is self-contained* (SENECA).

I hate a stagnant and sleepy idleness almost as much as a toilsome and thorny activity; the latter pinches me, the other makes me drowsy. I like a wound as well as a bruise, a cut as well as a dry blow. I found in this traffic, when I was fitter for it, a right moderation between those two extremes. Love is an excitement, wideawake, lively and gay; it did not disturb or afflict me, but it made me warm and thirsty for more. One should stop there; it is hurtful only to fools.

A young man asked the philosopher Panaetius whether it was becoming in a wise man to be in love. 'Let us leave the wise man out of the question, he replied; but you and I, who are far from being wise, must not become entangled in so violent and exciting a business, which enslaves us to another and makes us contemptible to ourselves.' He spoke truth, that a soul is not to be trusted that has not the strength to withstand the attack of a thing that comes so suddenly, and that is not able practically to disprove the saying of Agesilaus 'that wisdom and love cannot go abreast'.

True, it is a vain pastime, unbecoming, shameful and unlawful; but, conducted in this fashion, I regard it as salubrious, proper to enliven a dull body and soul. And, as a physician I would prescribe it for a man of my temperament and condition as readily as any other remedy, to stir him up and keep him robust till well on in years, and to ward off the attacks of senility. Whilst we are yet but in the suburbs and the pulse still beats;

Whilst hair is yet but grey, and age still
stands upright,
While yet remain some threads for Lachesis to spin,
While on my feet I walk and need no staff to help,

JUVENAL

we need to be solicited and tickled by some such biting excitation as this. See what youth, vigour and sprightliness it put into the wise Anacreon. And Socrates, when older than I now am, said, speaking of a girl he fell in love with, 'With her shoulder touching mine, and my head near to hers, as we were looking together into a book, I suddenly felt a pricking in the shoulder, if you will believe me, like the bite of an insect; and for more than five days it tingled, and through my heart ran a continual itching pain.' What! a touch, and that an accidental one, and of a shoulder, disturb and kindle a soul cooled and weakened by age, and of all human souls the most chastened! Why not, in heaven's name? Socrates was a man, and desired neither to be nor seem anything else.

Philosophy does not strive against natural pleasures, as long as due measure be observed; she preaches moderation, not flight. Her power of resistance is used against exotic and bastard pleasures. She says that bodily desires must not be heightened by the mind, and wittily warns us not to try to excite hunger by surfeiting, not to stuff instead of merely filling the belly; to avoid all enjoyment that may bring us to want, and all food and drink that makes us thirsty and hungry.

So in the service of love she bids us to choose an object that simply satisfies the body's need, that does not stir the soul, which must not look to its own satisfaction, but should simply follow and assist the body.

But am I not right in thinking that these precepts, which by the way are in my opinion a little too rigorous, concern a body that is equal to its functions; and that when a body is in a low condition, like a disordered stomach, it is excusable to warm and sustain it artificially, and by means of the imagination to restore the appetite and cheerfulness which it loses when left to itself?

May we not say that there is nothing in us, during this earthly imprisonment, that is purely either corporeal or spiritual; that we wrongfully tear a living man to pieces, and that it seems but reasonable that we should look upon pleasure with at least the same favour as upon pain? The latter (for example) was violent to the point of perfection in the souls of the Saints, by means of penitence; the body naturally, by virtue of their alliance, shared the pain, and yet could have little share in the cause. And still they were not satisfied that it should simply follow and assist the ill-used soul; they tormented the body itself with atrocious and appropriate tortures, in order that soul and body might vie together in plunging man into anguish, the more cruel, the more salutary.

So in the case of bodily pleasures, is it not wrong to cool the soul with regard to them, and to say that she must be dragged to them as to some enforced and slavish obligation and necessity? It is her part rather to cherish and promote them, to offer and invite herself to share them, since it is her office to rule. As it is also, I think, her part, in respect of her own pleasures, to breathe and instil into the body all the feeling they are capable of arousing, and study to make them sweet and wholesome. For it is reasonable, as they say, that the body should not follow its appetites to the prejudice of the mind.

But why is it not also right that the mind should not follow hers to the prejudice of the body?

I have no other passion to keep me in breath. What avarice, ambition, quarrels, lawsuits, do for other men who, like myself, have no fixed occupation, love would do more beneficially. It would wake me up again, make me more sober, pleasing and careful of my person; it would recompose my countenance and prevent the grimaces of old age, those ugly and pitiful grimaces, from spoiling it; it would bring me back to wise and healthy studies, whereby I might become better loved and esteemed, driving from my mind its hopelessness in itself and its employment, and restoring it to itself; it would divert me from a thousand troublesome thoughts, a thousand melancholy humours, which idleness and the poor state of our health impose upon us at this age; would warm up, at least in dreams, this blood that Nature forsakes, would raise the chin and stretch out a little the nerves and the vigour and the gaiety in the soul of this poor man who is moving full speed towards disintegration.

But I know well that it is a blessing very hard to recover. Through failing strength and long experience our taste has become more delicate and fastidious. We demand more when we can bring less; we are more anxious to choose when we least deserve to be accepted. Knowing ourselves for what we are, we are less confident and more distrustful of our powers; nothing can make us sure of being loved, knowing our condition and theirs.

I am ashamed of being found in the midst of these green and exuberant young people,

> In whom undaunted vigour stands more firm
> Than sapling on the mountain-side. HORACE

Why should we go and intrude our misery into that gay throng,

> That fervid youngsters may behold,
> With laughter loud and long,
> The burnt-out torch into the ashes flung?
> HORACE

They have strength and reason on their side; let us give place to them; we can only look on.

And that germ of budding beauty will not be touched by such stiff old hands, nor won by mere material means. For, as the old philosopher replied to the man who jeered at him for being unable to win the good graces of a tender lass he was pursuing, 'My friend, the hook will not bite in such fresh cheese.'

Now, it is an intercourse that needs reciprocity and mutual exchange. The other pleasures we receive may be acknowledged by returns of a different nature; but this can only be paid for in the same kind of coin. Indeed in this pastime the pleasure I give tickles my imagination more agreeably than that which I feel. Now there is no generosity in the man who can receive pleasure where he confers none; it is a mean soul that would be beholden for everything, and is content to keep up relations with a person to whom he is a charge. There is no beauty, favour or intimacy so exquisite that a gentleman should desire it at that price. If they can be kind to us only out of pity, I would much rather not live, than live on alms. I would like to have the right to ask it of them in the way in which I heard them beg in Italy: *Fate ben per voi*;[18] or after the manner of Cyrus exhorting his troops: 'Who loves himself, follow me!'

You may tell me to consort with persons in my own state, who, sharing the same fortune, will be more easy of access. O foolish and insipid compromise!

I will not pluck the beard of lion dead.

MARTIAL

Xenophon makes it the ground of his objection and accusation against Menon, that in his amours he set to work on faded flowers.

I find more sensual pleasure in merely witnessing, or even in only imagining, the sweet and honest pairing of two fair young people, than in myself making a second in a pitiful and imperfect conjunction. I leave that fantastic appetite to the Emperor Galba, who preferred his meat when it was old and tough; and to this poor wretch:

O that the gods would grant me yet to see
And kiss thy own dear self with changed locks,
And clasp thy withered body to my arms!'[19]

And among the chief disfigurements I count a forced and artificial beauty. Emonez, a young boy of Chios, thinking by pretty ornaments to acquire the beauty that Nature had denied him, appeared before the philosopher Archesilaus and asked him whether a wise man might fall in love. 'Yes, by heaven, he replied, as long as it is not with a dressed up and

18 Charity, for the good of your soul.
19 Ovid, writing in exile to his wife at Rome.

sophisticated beauty like yours.' The confessed ugliness of old age is less old and less ugly, to my mind, than when it is painted and polished.

Shall I say it? Provided you do not seize me by the throat. Love, in my opinion, is not properly and naturally in season except in the age next to childhood:

Him should you, with dishevelled hair
And that ambiguous face bring in
Among a troop of pretty girls,
He would deceive the subtlest there,
So smooth, so rosy is his skin. HORACE

Nor beauty either. For while Homer extends it until the chin begins to be shaded, Plato himself remarked that that was rare. And the reason is notorious why the sophist Bion so wittily called the downy hairs of adolescence Aristogeitons and Harmodians.[20] In manhood I think it already out of date; not to speak of old age.

Ruthless is Love, for past the withered oak
He flies. HORACE

And Margaret, Queen of Navarre, being a woman, greatly extends the privileges of her sex, ordaining that thirty is the season for them to exchange the name of 'beautiful' for that of 'good'.

The shorter the possession we grant Cupid over our lives, the better we are for it. Look at his bearing, and his boyish chin! Who knows not how, in his school, all

20 As Harmodius and Aristogeiton delivered their country from the tyrant, so the first signs of virility delivered the Greek youth from a persecution of a different kind.

goes backward, against all rule? Study, exercise, use, are the ways that lead to inefficiency; there the novices are the teachers. *Love knows no order* (ST JEROME). Truly his conduct is much more charming when blended with heedlessness and irregularities; mistakes and checks give point and grace to it. Provided it be eager and hungry, it matters little whether it be prudent. See how he goes reeling, tripping and wantoning; you put him in the stocks when you guide him by art and discretion, and he is restrained in his divine freedom when put under those hirsute and callous hands.

For the rest, I have often heard the ladies describing this intercourse as entirely spiritual, and disdaining to consider the part the senses play in it. Everything serves, and I may say that I have often observed that we pardon their intellectual shortcomings in consideration of their bodily charms; but I have not yet observed any of them to be willing to favour intellectual beauty in us, however wise and mature, when joined to a body that shows the least signs of decay. Why does not one of them feel a desire to make that noble Socratic exchange of body for soul, purchasing a spiritual and philosophical generation and intelligence at the price of her thighs, the highest rate at which she can value them?

Plato, in his *Laws*, ordains that one who has performed a signal and useful exploit in war shall, as long as it is being waged, not be denied, however old or ill-favoured he may be, a kiss or any other amorous favour from any woman he may choose. Can that which he thinks so fair in consideration of military worth not also be fair in consideration of some other kind of worth? And why does not one of them seek to forestall her sisters and win the glory of so chaste a love? I may well say chaste:

A horse grown old,
Slow kindling unto love, in vain prolongs
The fruitless task, and, to the encounter come,
As fire in stubble blusters without strength,
He rages idly.

VIRGIL

The vices that are confined to thought are not the worst.

To conclude this remarkable commentary, which has slipped from me in a torrent of babble, a torrent sometimes impetuous and hurtful:

Like the red apple, her lover's secret gift,
In the chaste bosom of the maiden fair,
Where hidden it lies in tunic soft forgot;
Soon as she hears her mother's step she starts;
Away it rolls, and conscious of her crime
Her cheeks are steeped in red.

CATULLUS

I say that male and female are cast in the same mould; saving education and habits, the difference is not great. Plato, in his *Republic*, invites all indiscriminately to share all studies, exercises, charges and occupations, in peace and war; and the philosopher Antisthenes rejected all distinction between their virtue and ours. It is much easier to accuse one sex than to excuse the other; it is, in the words of the proverb, 'the poker calling the shovel black'.

Of the disadvantage of greatness

Since we cannot reach it, let us avenge ourselves by disparaging it. Yet to find defects in a thing is not absolutely to disparage it; there are defects in all things, however beautiful and desirable.

Greatness has as a rule this evident advantage, that it can descend from its height when it pleases, and can well-nigh choose between either condition. For one does not fall from every height; there are more from which one can descend without falling.

It really seems to me that we think too highly of it, and that we also think too highly of the resolution of those men who, in our own experience or from hearsay, have despised it and laid it down of their own accord. Its advantages are not so essentially manifest that one may not refuse it without performing a miracle.

I should think it needs great strength to bear adversity; but in being content with a mediocre degree of fortune and avoiding greatness I can see nothing to make a stir about. That is a virtue to which I think I myself, who am but a noddy, could attain without a great effort. What effort can it need in those who also consider the glory attending such a refusal, wherein there may lurk more ambition even than in the desire for and enjoyment of greatness; since ambition never better follows its own bent than along out-of-the-way and unused paths?

I urge on my heart to patience; I rein it in to desire.

I have as much to wish for as another, and allow my wishes as much freedom and indiscretion; and yet it has never occurred to me to wish for empire or royalty, nor for the eminence of those high and commanding fortunes. My aim lies not in that direction; I love myself too well. When my thoughts are bent on growth, it is a humble growth, a restricted and mean-spirited growth, of a more personal nature, towards firmness, wisdom, health, beauty, and even wealth. But such renown, such mighty authority, crushes my imagination. And, quite contrary to that other, I would perhaps rather see myself the second or third at Périgueux than the first in Paris; at least, without feigning, rather the third than the first in authority in Paris. I would neither wrangle, a wretched nobody, with a door-keeper, nor have a crowd of worshippers make room for me. I am accustomed, both by lot and by inclination, to a middle station. And I have shown, in the conduct of my life and my undertakings, that I have rather avoided, than not, climbing beyond the degree of fortune at which God placed me at my birth.

Everything that is constituted according to nature is equally right and easy.

My soul is so indolent that I do not measure good fortune by its height; I measure it by its facility.

But if my heart is not big enough, it is proportionably open, and commands me boldly to publish its defects. Should anyone ask me to compare the life of L. Thorius Balbus, a gentleman, handsome, learned, healthy, intelligent, with a superfluity of all kinds of pleasures and opportunities, leading a peaceful existence quite at his own disposal, his mind fully armed against death, superstition, grief, and other obstacles to human needs, ending his life in battle with sword in hand, in the defence of his country, on the one hand; and on the other, the life of M. Regulus, so great and eminent that it is known to all men, and his admirable end: the one without a name and without honours, the other so exemplary and famous as to excite wonder, I should certainly speak of them as Cicero does, if I could speak as well as he.[1]

But if I had to measure them by my standard, I should also say that the first is as much within my reach, and according to my desire, which agrees with my reach, as the second is far beyond it; that to the latter I can only attain by veneration; the former I could easily attain in practice.

Let us return to our temporal greatness, from which we started.

I have a dislike for mastery, either active or passive. Otanez, one of the seven who had a claim to the throne of Persia, took a step which I could easily have taken: he renounced to his competitors his possible right to come to it by election or by lot, provided that he and his family might live in that empire free from all subjection and mastery, saving that of the ancient laws, and could enjoy every freedom that was not prejudicial to these; averse either to commanding or being commanded.

The hardest and most difficult trade in the world is, to my mind, to play the part of a king worthily. I can excuse more of their faults than people usually do, in

1 'You call this man happy? As for me, I will not venture to name the man I prefer to him. Virtue herself shall speak for me, and she will not hesitate to rank Marcus Regulus before this happy man of yours.' – CICERO, *De Fin.* ii. 20.

consideration of the terrible weight of their burden, which confounds my reason. It is difficult to observe measure in a power so unmeasured.

And yet, even in men of a less excellent nature, it is a singular incitement to virtue to be seated in a place where you can do no good action that is not recorded and placed to your account; where the smallest good action affects so many people, and where your excellence, like that of a preacher, chiefly appeals to the people, no very exacting judges, easy to deceive and easily satisfied.

There are few things on which we can pass a sincere judgement, because there are few things in which we have not, in one way or another, a particular interest.

Superiors and inferiors, masters and subjects, are bound to be naturally envious of and hostile to one another; they must be perpetually robbing one another. I trust neither, when the rights of the other party are in question. Let us leave the decision to Reason, who is inflexible and impassive when we can get at her.

Less than a month ago I was perusing two books written by Scotchmen, who were debating this subject. The democrat makes the king out to be in a worse plight than a carter; the monarchist lodges him a few fathoms above God in power and sovereignty.

Now the disadvantage of greatness, which I have been led to discuss here by an event that has lately put me in mind of it, lies in this: There is perhaps nothing more pleasing in human intercourse than those trials of strength we make against one another, in rivalry of honour and worth, whether in exercises of the body or those of the mind, in which those in supreme power can have no true share. Indeed it has often seemed to me that through over-much respect princes are in this regard treated contemptuously and insultingly. For what used to offend me mightily as a boy, namely that those who competed with me in bodily exercises refused to take me seriously, because they thought I was not worth their exerting themselves for, is what we see every day happening to princes, since every one thinks himself unworthy to use his best efforts against them. If they are observed to have the least desire to gain the victory, there is no man who will not do his best to let them have it, and who will not rather betray his own honour than offend theirs; he only exerts his strength so far as is necessary to save his reputation.

What share can they have in the fray in which every one fights on their side? They remind me of those Paladins of olden times who entered the tournaments and battles with enchanted bodies and weapons.

Brisson, running a race against Alexander, only pretended and hung back; Alexander scolded him for it, but he should have had him flogged.

In this connexion Carneades used to say 'that the sons of kings learn nothing well except the management of horses; since in every other exercise every man gives way to them and yields them the victory. But a horse, who is neither a courtier nor a flatterer, will throw the son of a king as soon as the son of a porter.'

Homer was constrained to consent to Venus, so sweet a saint and so frail, being wounded at the battle of Troy, to show her courage and daring, virtues which never fall to the share of those who are immune against danger. The gods are made to show anger, to fear and run away, to give way to jealousy, grief, and passion, in order to honour them with the virtues which, in human beings, are built up on these imperfections.

He who does not share in the danger and difficulty can claim no interest in the honour and pleasure which attend dangerous actions.

It is a pity when a man is so powerful that everything gives way to him. His fortune removes him too far from the society and company of his fellow men; it plants him too far out of the way. That ease and facility, that needs no effort, in making everything bow to you is an enemy to every kind of pleasure. It is to slide, not to walk; to sleep, not to live. Imagine a man accompanied by omnipotence, you engulf him; he must entreat of you, as an alms, impediments and opposition; his being and substance lie in indigence.

Their good qualities are dead and wasted; for these are only felt by comparison, and they are disqualified from competing. They can little know true praise, being deafened with such perpetual and uniform approval. If they have to deal with the most stupid of their subjects, they have no means of gaining an advantage over him. If he says 'it is because he is my king', he thinks he has given a sufficient reason for lending a helping hand to his own defeat. That royal quality stifles and consumes the other real and essential qualities; they are drowned in royalty. And it leaves them nothing to recommend themselves by but those actions which directly concern and interest it, the duties of their charge.

It is so much to be a king, that he only exists as such. That external light that surrounds him hides and steals him from us; our sight is broken and dissipated by it, being filled and arrested by this strong glare.

The Senate allotted the prize of eloquence to Tiberius; he refused it, judging that he could derive no honour from so unfree an award, even if it had been just.

As we yield to them every advantage of honour, so we encourage and authorize their vices and defects, not only by approval, but even by imitation. Every one of Alexander's followers carried his head on one side, as he did; and the flatterers of Dionysius used to collide with one another in his presence, and kick and upset things at their feet, to make believe that they were as shortsighted as he. Even a rupture of the bowels has at times served as a recommendation to favour. I have known deafness to be affected. And Plutarch saw courtiers who repudiated their wives, although they loved them, because the master hated his.

What is more, we have known lechery to be in fashion for that reason, and every kind of dissoluteness, as well as disloyalty, blasphemy, cruelty, nay heresy, superstition, irreligion, cowardice, and worse, if worse there can be. Their example was even more dangerous than that of the flatterers of Mithridates who, when their master was most anxious to be reputed a good physician, brought him their limbs to be slashed and cauterized; for the others allowed their souls to be cauterized, a nobler and more delicate part.

But to end where I began. When the Emperor Hadrian was disputing with the philosopher Favorinus about the interpretation of some word, the latter soon yielded him the victory; and to his friends who expostulated with him, he said, 'You cannot be serious; would you not have a man be more learned than I who can command thirty legions?'

Augustus wrote some lines against Asinius Pollio. 'And I, said Pollio, will hold my tongue; it is not wisdom to enter the links as a scribe with one who has the power to proscribe.' And they were right; for Dionysius, because he was no match for Philoxenus in poetry and Plato in prose, condemned the one to the quarries, and sent the other to be sold for a slave in the island of Aegina.

Of the art of conversing

It is a custom of our justice to condemn some as a warning to others.

To condemn them because they have done wrong would be stupidity, as Plato says. For what is done cannot be undone. But they are condemned that they may not go wrong again in the same way, or that others may avoid following their example.

We do not correct the man we hang; we correct others through him. I do the same. My errors are sometimes natural and incorrigible; but whereas honest men benefit the public by setting an example, I may perhaps benefit them by making them avoid my example:

> Look, boy, he'd say, at Albius' son,
>   Observe his sorry plight;
> And Barrus, that poor beggar there!
>   Say, are they not a sight
> To warn a man from squandering his
>   patrimonial means?
>
> HORACE

If I disclose and publish my imperfections, some will learn to fear them. The qualities I most value in myself derive more honour from my self-accusation than from my self-commendation. That is why I so often fall back and dwell upon them. But when all is summed up, a man never speaks of himself without losing thereby.

His self-accusations are always believed; his self-praise disbelieved.

There may be some who are constituted like me, who learn more by avoiding the faults of others than by imitating their example; by flight than by following. That was the kind of teaching that the elder Cato had in mind when he said that the wise have more to learn of fools, than fools of the wise; and that ancient player on the lyre, of whom Pausanias tells us, that he used to make his pupils go to hear a bad performer who lived over the way, where they might learn to hate his discords and faulty phrasings.

The horror of cruelty impels me more to clemency than any model of clemency could draw me on. A good rider does not improve my seat as well as an attorney or a Venetian on horseback; and a bad style of speaking improves mine more than does a good one.

Every day the foolish demeanour of another warns and admonishes me. That which irritates will affect and arouse us more than that which pleases. These times are only good for reforming us backwards; more by disagreement than by agreement; more by difference than by similarity. Since I learn little by good examples, I make use of the bad, which give me daily lessons. I have tried to make myself as agreeable as I see others disagreeable; as energetic as I see others feeble; as mild as I see others fierce; as good as I see others wicked. But I set up unattainable standards.

In my opinion the most profitable and most natural exercise of our mind is conversation. To me it is a more agreeable occupation than any other in life; and for that reason, if I were at this moment obliged to choose, I would sooner consent, I think, to lose my sight than my hearing or speech. The Athenians, and still more the Romans, held this practice in great honour in their Academies. To this day the Italians preserve some traces of it, and greatly to their benefit, as may be seen if we compare ourselves with them in intelligence.

The study of books is a feeble and languid action which does not warm us, whilst conversation instructs and exercises us at the same time. If I converse with a man of strong mind and a stiff jouster, he will press on my flanks, prick me to right and left; his ideas will give an impetus to mine. Rivalry, vainglory, strife, stimulate me and lift me above myself. And agreement is an altogether tiresome element in conversation.

As our mind is strengthened by communication with vigorous and well regulated minds, it is not to be imagined how much it loses and deteriorates by continual intercourse and association with vulgar and feeble-minded people. There is no infection which spreads like that. I know well enough by experience how much a yard it costs.

I love to discuss and dispute, but in a small company of men, and in private. For to exhibit oneself before great people, and to parade one's wit and cackle in rivalry with others, is to my mind a trade very unbecoming a gentleman.

Foolishness is an unfortunate quality; but to be unable to endure it, to be vexed at and worry over it, which is my case, is another kind of infirmity that is not much less tiresome than foolishness. And it is this that I am about to condemn in myself.

I can enter into a conversation and debate with great freedom and ease, since opinions find in me a soil very hard to penetrate and strike deep roots. No propositions astonish me, no belief offends me, however much opposed to my own. No idea is so frivolous or so extravagant but it appears to me naturally produced by human wit. We others,[1] who deny our judgement the right of deciding, look indulgently upon opinions differing from our own; and if we do not lend credence, we readily lend an ear to them.

When one scale of the balance is entirely empty, I let the other waver under the weight of some old woman's superstitious fancies. And it appears to me excusable if I accept an odd rather than an even number; if I prefer a Thursday to a Friday; if I would rather make a twelfth or a fourteenth than the thirteenth at table; if, when I am travelling, I am more pleased to see a hare skirting than crossing my path; and rather offer my left than my right foot to be booted first.

All such idle fancies, which obtain credit around us, deserve at least a hearing. For me they weigh just more than nothing, but they do weigh. Vulgar and unfounded opinions are besides, as regards weight, other than nothing in nature. And one who will not yield so far may perhaps, whilst avoiding the error of superstition, fall into that of opinionativeness.

Opinions then that are opposed to mine do not offend or estrange me; they only arouse and exercise my mind.

We dislike correction; we should meet it half-way and welcome it, especially if it comes in the form of conversation and not of a school-lesson. At every contradiction we do not consider whether it be just, but by what means, fair or foul, we may get rid of it. Instead of extending our arms, we extend our claws to it.

1 Pyrrhonians, i.e. sceptics.

I could endure hard knocks from my friends: 'You are a fool; you are dreaming!' Among gentlemen I like bold expressions of opinion, and to have them speak as they think. We must fortify and harden our ears against that delicate and ceremonious sound of words. I love a strong and manly fellowship and familiarity, a friendship that delights in the rudeness and vigour of its intercourse, as love does in bites and scratches that draw blood.

It is not vigorous and generous enough if it is not quarrelsome; if it is all civility and art; if it fears a shock and walks in constraint. *For there can be no discussion without reprehension* (CICERO).

When a man opposes me he arouses my attention, not my anger; I meet him half-way if he contradicts and corrects me. The cause of truth ought to be the cause common to both of us. What will he reply? The passion of anger has already knocked his judgement on the head. Confusion has usurped the place of reason.

It would be a boon if our disputes were decided by way of wager, and if there were a substantial mark of our losses, that we might keep them in mind; and if my serving-man could say to me, 'Your ignorance and wilfulness on twenty occasions last year cost you a hundred crowns.'

I hail and welcome the truth, in whatever hand I find it; I cheerfully surrender and tender my vanquished sword to her, as soon as I see her approach in the distance.

And, as long as it does not come with too overbearing and schoolmasterly a mien, I encourage criticism of my writings; and I have often altered them more from civility than because they were improved by it; preferring, by readily giving way, to gratify and foster their freedom to admonish me; yea, even at my own expense.

And yet it is difficult to draw the men of my time into it; they have not the courage to correct because they have not the courage to suffer correction, and always speak with dissimulation in presence of one another. I take so much pleasure in being known and criticized that it is almost a matter of indifference to me which of the two forms it takes. My imagination so often contradicts and condemns itself that it is all one to me if another do it, chiefly in view of the fact that I allow his criticism only as much authority as I please. But I shall fall out with him who holds his head too high, as does one man I know, who thinks his advice is thrown away if it is not taken seriously, and takes it as an insult if you do not immediately follow it.

That Socrates always welcomed with a smile the contradictions offered to his arguments was due, we might say, to his strength; and that, the advantage being certain to fall to his side, he accepted them as occasions for fresh triumphs. But we may, on the other hand, observe that there is nothing that makes us so delicately sensitive to contradiction as the feeling we have of our adversary's superiority, and his contempt of us; and that, in reason, it is the part of the weaker rather to accept with a good grace the opposition which corrects and sets him right.

In fact I seek the society of those who drub me rather than of those who fear me. It is a flat and harmful satisfaction to have to do with people who admire and give way to you. Antisthenes recommended his children 'never to regard with gratitude or favour the man who praised them'. I feel much prouder of the victory I gain over myself when, in the very heat of the combat, I make myself give way to the force of my adversary's argument, than I feel gratified by the victory I gain over him through his own weakness.

In short, I accept and admit any kind of blow that is delivered according to the rules of the game, however weak it may be; but I am much too intolerant of those that are given irregularly. I care little about the matter, and all opinions are the same to me; and I am pretty indifferent as to who wins. I can argue peaceably for a whole day, if the debate is carried on according to the rules.

It is not so much force and subtlety that I expect, as order; the order that we may see any day in the altercations of shepherds and shop-boys, never with us. If they go wrong, it is in want of civility; and so it is with us. But their turbulence and impatience never put them off their theme; their argument keeps its course. If they speak out of their turn without waiting for the other to finish, they at least understand one another.

To my mind a man answers only too well if he answers to the purpose. But when the discussion becomes confused and disorderly, I leave the subject to take care of itself, and, losing my temper and my head, I cling to the form; I fall into a testy, spiteful, and overbearing style of debate, for which I have afterwards to blush.

It is impossible to deal honestly with a fool; not only my judgement but also my conscience is vitiated at the hands of so impetuous a master.

Our wranglings ought to be forbidden and punishable like other verbal crimes. How much vice they always stir and pile up, when ruled and governed by anger! We quarrel, first with the reasons, and then with the men. We learn to debate only that we may contradict; and when everyone contradicts and is contradicted, it follows that the fruit of debate is to suppress and nullify the truth. So Plato, in his *Republic*, forbids debates among fools and ill-bred people.

What is the good of starting in quest of truth with one who has no pace and no walking-power to speak of?

We do no wrong to the subject when we leave it in order to find a better method of treating it; I do not mean a scholastic method, a method according to the rules, but a natural method, carried out with a sound understanding.

What will be the end of it all? One will go East, the other West; they drop the main point and lose sight of it among a crowd of incidental questions. After an hour's storming they forget what they are after; one shoots low, the other high, the other wide. One catches at a word and a simile. Another forgets his opponent's point, so intent is he on steering his own course; he can only think of following up his own reasons instead of yours. Another, finding he is weak in the back, is afraid and declines all argument; at the very outset he mixes up and confuses the issues. Or, in the thick of the debate, he stops dead, holds his tongue and sulks, in spiteful ignorance, affecting a proud contempt, or a silly modesty in giving up the struggle.

Provided that he gets in his blow, one man does not care how much he lays himself open. Another counts his words and weighs them as if they were so many reasons. Another only takes advantage of his voice and lung-power. Here we have one who sums up against himself, and another who deafens you with futile preambles and digressions. This one arms himself with downright insults, and seeks a Dutch quarrel to rid himself of the society and conversation of a wit who presses too hard upon him. This last can see nothing in reason, but keeps you enclosed within the barriers of his logical clauses and the formulas of his art.

Now who will not begin to distrust the sciences and doubt if he can derive any substantial gain from them for the needs of life, when he considers the use we put them to? *Learning which cures nothing* (SENECA). Who has ever gained any intelligence from Logic? Where are her fine promises? *She teaches neither to live any better, nor to reason any more pertinently* (CICERO). Do you hear any worse jumble in the cackle of herring-wives than in the public debates of the professors of Logic? I would rather my son learned to speak in the taverns than in the talking schools.

Take a Master of Arts,[2] converse with him; why does he not make us sensible of excelling in those arts, and captivate the ladies and ignoramuses like ourselves with admiration for the solidity of his reasons and the beautiful arrangement of his matter? Why can he not use his powers of persuasion and guide us at his pleasure? Why is a man with all his advantages in learning, and in conducting a debate, unable to fence without getting furiously angry and insulting his opponent? Let him put away his hood and gown and his Latin, and cease to beat his quite raw and undigested Aristotle about our ears, and you will take him for one of us, or worse.

When they become entangled and involved in the words with which they drive us into a corner, they remind me of a juggler; their sleight of hand imposes

2 i.e. a professor of the Humanities and Philosophy.

upon and vanquishes our senses, but it does not by any means shake our belief. Leave out their legerdemain, and what they do is but commonplace and mean. They may be more learned than we, but they are none the less fools.

I love and honour learning as much as those who possess it; and, if rightly used, it is the noblest and most powerful human acquisition. But in those (and there is an endless number of their kind) who make it the ground of their worth and excellence, who appeal from their understanding to their memory, *covering under the shelter of others* (SENECA), who are powerless without their book, I hate it, if I may venture to say so, a little more than I do stupidity.

In my country, and in my time, learning often enough mends the purse, but rarely the soul. If it lights upon a mind that is dull and heavy, like a crude and undigested mass it makes it duller and heavier, and chokes it up; if upon an acute mind, it usually purifies, clarifies, and subtilizes it, even to exhaustion. It is a thing of almost indifferent quality; a very useful accessory in a naturally gifted mind, pernicious and harmful to another. Or rather it is a thing of very precious use, which is not to be purchased at a low price; in some hands it is a sceptre, in others a fool's bauble.

But to proceed. What greater triumph can you expect than to teach your enemy that he is not your match? When you gain the advantage by the substance of your argument, it is the truth that wins; when you gain the advantage by your method of conducting it, it is you who win.

I am of opinion that, in Plato and Xenophon, Socrates debates more for the sake of the debaters than for the sake of the debate, and more to teach Euthydemus and Protagoras to know their own irrelevance than the irrelevance of their art. He lays hold of the first matter that comes to hand, as one who has a more useful purpose than to clear it up, namely, to clear up the minds he undertakes to direct and exercise.

The excitement of the chase is properly our quarry. We are not to be pardoned if we carry it on badly or foolishly; to fail to seize the prey is a different matter. For we are born to search after the truth; to possess it belongs to a greater power. It is not, as Democritus said, hidden in the depths of chasms, but rather raised to an infinite height in divine knowledge.

The world is but a school of research. The question is not who shall hit the ring, but who shall run the best course. He can be as great a fool who speaks true, as he who speaks false; for we are concerned with the manner, not the matter, of speaking. It is my nature to regard the form as much as the substance, the advocate as much as the cause, as Alcibiades ordained that we should.

And every day I spend time in dipping into authors without any care about their learning; in searching their style, not their matter. Just as I eagerly seek the society of any man renowned for his intellectual qualities; not that he may teach me, but that I may know him and knowing him, imitate him, if he is worthy of it.

Any man may speak truthfully; but to speak methodically, with wisdom and talent, is given to few. So the errors that proceed from ignorance do not offend me; it is the foppery of it. I have broken off several transactions which might have profited me, because of the impertinent protestations of those with whom I was transacting.

I do not once in a year excite myself over the faults of those over whom I have authority; but when they stupidly and obstinately persist in their brutish and asinine assertions, excuses and defences, we are every day ready to fly at each other's throats. They neither understand what is said to them nor why, and reply accordingly; it is enough to drive one to despair.

My head only hurts when it comes into rough contact with another. And I can sooner put up with the vices of my men than their want of thought, their unreasonableness and stupidity. Let them do less, provided they are capable of doing. You live in hopes of warming up their willingness. But we cannot hope to get any good out of a log.

But what if I take things otherwise than they are? It may be so; and therefore I condemn my intolerance and hold, firstly, that it is equally a blemish in one who is right and in one who is wrong. For it is always a sign of an arbitrary and sour nature to be unable to suffer any way of thinking differing from our own; and besides, there can be no worse, no more obstinate and more eccentric fatuity than to be annoyed and exasperated by the fatuities of the world. For it irritates us chiefly with ourselves. And that philosopher[3] of olden times would never have lacked an occasion for shedding tears as long as he had himself to look at.

Miso, one of the Seven Sages, who was of a Timonian and Democritian[4] humour, being asked

3 Heraclitus, called the 'weeping philosopher'.

4 The humour of Timon of Athens, the misanthrope, and Democritus, the laughing philosopher.

why he was laughing to himself, replied, 'Because I am laughing to myself.'

How frequently I make remarks and replies every day that appear foolish to myself; therefore how much more commonly and frequently they must appear so to others! If I bite my lips over it, what must they do.

In short, we must live among the living, and let the river flow under the bridge, without caring, or at least without being upset by it.

True, but why can we meet a man with a crooked and deformed body without being moved, when we cannot bear to meet with an illogical mind without getting angry? The hardness of the judge is here more to blame than the fault.

Let us ever keep that saying of Plato on our lips: 'If I find a thing unsound, is it not because I am myself unsound? Am I not myself at fault? May not my observations reflect upon myself?' A wise and divine refrain, which scourges the most common and universal error of mankind! Not only the blame we cast at one another, but also our reasons and arguments and matters in dispute may usually be turned against us; we wound ourselves with our own weapons. Of which antiquity has left me pregnant examples enough. This was cleverly said, and much to the purpose, by him who first thought of it:

Every man's ordure well
To his own sense doth smell.

ERASMUS, *slightly altered*

Our eyes can see nothing behind us. A hundred times a day we laugh at ourselves when we laugh at our neighbours; and we detest in others the faults which are much more glaring in ourselves, and with marvellous impudence and thoughtlessness we express our astonishment at them. Only yesterday I had the opportunity to hear a man, an intelligent and well-mannered person, ridiculing with as much humour as aptness, the fatuity of another who pesters everybody with his pedigrees and his alliances, which are more than half imaginary (for they are most ready to pounce upon this silly subject whose quality is most doubtful and least certain). And this man, if he had retired within himself, would have seen that he was hardly less extravagant and tedious in publishing and extolling his wife's family prerogatives. Oh, the meddlesome presumption with which the wife sees herself armed by the hands of her own husband!

If they understood Latin we might say to them:

As if she were not mad enough already,
You now provoke her to a greater madness.

TERENCE

I do not mean that no man should judge unless he himself be spotless, for then no man could judge; not even if he were free from the same kind of blemish. But I do mean that our judgement, when laying blame on another who is in question, should not save us from self-judgement. It is a charitable office in one who cannot rid himself of a fault to endeavour none the less to rid another of it, in whom it may have taken less deep and stubborn root.

Nor do I think it a proper answer to one who apprises me of a fault, to say that he also has it. What of that? The warning is still true and useful. If our sense of smell were good, our ordure should stink the more in our nostrils because it is ours. And Socrates is of opinion that if a man and his son and a stranger were guilty of some violence and injustice, he should begin by offering himself to be condemned by justice, and implore, for his purgation, the help of the executioner's hand; secondly for his son and in the last place for the stranger. If this precept strikes rather too high a note, he should at least present himself first for punishment to his own conscience.

The senses are our first and proper judges, which perceive things only by external accidents; and it is not to be wondered at if in all the parts of the service of our social life there is so perpetual and universal a mingling of ceremonious and superficial appearances; so much so that therein consists the best and most effective part of our regulations. It is, after all, man with whom we have to do, whose condition is wonderfully corporeal.

Let those who, in these latter years, have tried to establish for us so contemplative and immaterial a practice of religion,[5] not wonder if there are people who think that it would have melted and slipped through their fingers, if it had not held together amongst us as a mark, title, and instrument of division and faction, more than by its own power.

So in conversation the gravity, the gown, and the fortune of the speaker often gain credit for his empty and foolish remarks. It cannot be supposed that a gentleman so formidable and with such a following should not have inside him more than ordinary talents; and that a man so arrogant and supercilious, who has been trusted with so many offices and missions, is not more able than this other who salutes

5 The Protestant Reformers.

him from afar, and whom nobody will employ. Not only the words, but even the grimaces of these people are pondered and weighed, and everyone labours to discover some fine and deep meaning in them. If they condescend to familiar talk, and if you do not approve and bow to everything they say, they will knock you down with the authority of their experience: they have heard this, they have seen that, they have done the other; you are crushed with examples. I should be inclined to say to them that the result of a surgeon's experience is not the history of his patients, and the recollection that he has cured four plague-stricken and three gouty people, unless from that experience he has been able to draw conclusions wherewith to form his judgement, and has given us reason to believe that he has become the wiser in the practice of his profession.

So in an instrumental concert we do not hear a lute, a spinet, and the flute; we hear a general harmony, the effect of the blending of the whole band.

If their travels and their experience in office have improved them, they should make it apparent in the product of their intelligence. It is not enough to sum up their experiences, they should weigh and sort them; they should have digested and distilled them, in order to extract from them the reasons and conclusions they admit of.

There were never so many historians. It is always good and profitable to give ear to them, for they keep us fully provided with good and commendable instruction from the store-house of their memory; they assist us no doubt, for a great part, in the conduct of life. But that is not what we look for at present; we seek to know if those tellers and gatherers are themselves commendable.

I hate any kind of tyranny, whether of words or deeds. I commonly battle against those unreal surroundings that delude our judgement through our senses; and, when I keep a strict watch on those who have risen to any extraordinary eminence, I find that they are for the most part only men, like the rest of us:

> In those high places common sense
> Is rarely to be found.
>
> JUVENAL

Perhaps in our estimation they appear smaller than they are, by reason of their attempting more and being more in evidence than others; they are not equal to the burden they have taken on their shoulders. There must be more strength and power in the porter than in the load. He who has not fully tried his strength leaves you to guess if he has any power left, and if he has been tested to his utmost; he who sinks under his burden, betrays his measure and the weakness of his shoulders. That is why we see so many incapables among the scholarly, outnumbering the capable. They might have made good husbandmen, good tradesmen, good artisans. Their natural powers were cut out to those proportions.

Knowledge is a thing of great weight, and they sink under it. Their mental machine is not powerful nor manageable enough to spread out and distribute that noble and powerful matter, to use it and derive help from it. It can only dwell in a strong nature, and strong natures are very rare. And the weak, says Socrates, by their handling mar the dignity of philosophy. It appears not only useless but harmful when it is badly encased. See how they prejudice and undo themselves!

As when an ape, the counterfeit of man,
By grinning schoolboy dressed in silken coat,
Leaving his backside bare, is ushered in
To amuse the dining guests! CLAUDIAN

So too it is not enough for our rulers and administrators, who hold the world in their hands, to have no more than an ordinary intelligence, no more ability than we. They are very much below if they are not very much above us. As they promise more, so they owe more.

And therefore their silence not only gives them an air of solemnity and gravity, but it is often profitable and economical. For Megabysus, visiting Apelles in his studio, stood a great while without speaking a word. Then he began to deliver his opinion of the painter's work, and received this rude snub, 'As long as you held your tongue, I thought you somebody out of the common, because of your chains and your fine clothes; but now that I have heard you speak, there is not a boy in my workshop who does not despise you.' His gorgeous attire, his elevated rank, were no excuse for being ignorant with a common ignorance, and for speaking impertinently of painting. He should have kept his external and presumptive abilities under a mask of silence.

For how many foolish souls, in my time, has not a frigid and taciturn demeanour served as a mark of wisdom and capability!

Dignities, offices, are necessarily conferred more by fortune than according to merit; and we are often wrong when we blame the King for it. Rather is it a marvel that they are so successful, when they have so little skill in it:

> A Prince's virtue is his folk to know.
>
> MARTIAL

For nature has not given them eyes to take in so many people, to discern our pre-eminence and penetrate our bosoms, where lies the knowledge of our intentions and our greatest worth. They must sift us by conjecture and experiment, by family, wealth, learning, the voice of the people: very feeble testimonies. If any man could discover a means of judging and choosing men correctly and rationally, he would, by that act alone, establish a perfect form of government.

'Yes, but he has conducted this great business with success.' That is something, but it is not enough: for this is a maxim which is rightly accepted: 'That we must not judge the plan by the issue.'

The Carthaginians punished the badly-laid plans of their generals, although they were set right by a happy issue; and the Roman people often refused a triumph for a great and very advantageous victory, because the conduct of the commander did not correspond with his good fortune.

We may commonly observe, in the actions of this world, that Fortune, to apprise us of her power in all things, and because she takes a pleasure in confounding our presumption, being unable to make a blockhead wise, makes him successful, to spite the virtuous; and she is fond of stepping in and favouring those actions in which she has done most of the weaving. Hence we may see every day that the simplest of us may successfully carry through an important affair, either public or private. And, as Siramnez the Persian replied to someone who wondered that his affairs should turn out so badly, seeing that he planned them so wisely: 'That he was sole master of his plans, but that of the success of his affairs Fortune was mistress;' these may answer the same, but with a contrary bias.

Most part of the things of this world work themselves out of their own accord:

> For the Fates will find a way. VIRGIL

The issue often justifies a very foolish conduct. Our intervention is little more than a routine, and most commonly we consult custom and example rather than reason. Being once astonished at the greatness of some affair, and having learned from those who carried it through their motives and their proceedings, I found that their schemes were no more than commonplace. And the most commonplace and timeworn are perhaps also the surest and most adapted to the purpose, in practice if not in appearance.

What if the shallowest reasons are the most suitable; the loosest, most commonplace and threadbare the best adapted for affairs? For the King's Council to maintain its authority, outsiders should not be allowed to join it, or to see further than the nearest barrier. It must command respect on trust and in the lump, if it would keep up its reputation.

In my deliberations I outline the matter a little, and consider it cursorily in its first aspect; the main and chief part of the business I usually entrust to heaven:

> All else unto the gods I leave. HORACE

Good and bad fortune are, in my opinion, two sovereign powers. It is folly to imagine that human wisdom can play the part of Fortune. And vain is his undertaking who has the presumption to embrace both causes and consequences, and to lead the progress of his affair by the hand; especially vain in military deliberations.

There was never more caution and circumspection in military matters than is observed at times in this country. Can it be that they are afraid of losing themselves on the way, and reserve themselves for the catastrophe of that drama? I go further, and say that our wisdom itself and our deliberation follow, for the most part, whither chance leads them.

My will and my reason are stirred now by one breath, now by another; and many of these movements take place without my guidance. My reason is impelled and stirred by accidental causes varying from day to day:

> The phases of their minds are changed;
> their breasts
> Conceive emotions now far otherwise
> Than when the storm-wind drove
> the scudding clouds. VIRGIL

If you will observe who are the most influential people in the cities, and who are most successful in business, you will usually find that they are the least talented. It has fallen to the lot of women, of children and madmen, to rule great states equally well with the most able princes; and the gross-witted, according to Thucydides, are usually more successful than the clever. We attribute to their wisdom the results of their good fortune.

He makes his way who uses Fortune right,
And all the world calls, 'What a clever man!'

PLAUTUS

Wherefore I confidently say that in every way results are a poor testimony of our worth and ability.

Now I was about to say that we have but to look at a man who has been raised to dignity. Although we knew him three days before as a man of very little account, there steals imperceptibly into our minds a picture of greatness and excellence, and we are persuaded that, having grown in pomp and reputation, he has grown in merit. We estimate him, not according to his worth, but after the manner of counters, according to the prerogative of his rank. Let his luck turn, let him fall again and mingle with the crowd, everyone will ask with wonder what it was that lifted him to such a height.

'Is this the man, they will say; did he know no more about it when he was there? Are princes so easily satisfied? We were in good hands, forsooth!'

That is a thing I have often seen in my time. Yea, and the mask of greatness they put on in stage-plays affects and deludes us to a certain degree.

What I myself reverence in kings is the crowd of their reverers. All obeisance and submission is due to them except that of the understanding; my reason is not trained to bow and bend, it is only my knees.

Melanthius, being asked what he thought of Dionysius' tragedy, said, 'I did not see it, it was so obscured by words.' So most of those who judge a great man's speeches might say, 'I did not understand his meaning, his discourse was so obscured by solemnity, grandeur and majesty.'

Antisthenes one day advised the Athenians to order their asses to be used for field-labour, as well as their horses; whereupon somebody replied that that animal was not born for such service. 'That does not matter, he replied; your order will be sufficient, for the most ignorant and incapable man you appoint to a command in your wars, immediately and invariably becomes most worthy of it, just because you appoint him.'

Which comes very near the custom in so many nations of canonizing the King they have elected from among themselves; not satisfied with honouring, they must also worship him. The Mexicans, as soon as the ceremony of crowning their King is over, dare no more look him in the face; nay, as if his royalty had raised him to the gods, with the oaths they make him take to maintain their religion, their laws, and their liberties, to be valiant, just, and mild, he also swears to make the sun run its course with its accustomed light, to make the clouds drop their water at the proper seasons, to make the rivers flow in their channels, and cause the earth to bring forth all things necessary for his people.

I am opposed to this common way of treating them, and I am inclined rather to doubt a man's ability when I see it attended by exalted fortune and the popular favour. We must be on our guard and think how much it means, when a man is able to speak at his own time, to choose his points, to interrupt the course of a discussion or to change it, with a magisterial authority, to defend himself against opposition of others by a motion of the head, by a smile or by silence, in the presence of an assembly trembling with reverence and respect.

A man of prodigious fortune, putting in his word in a certain trifling discussion that was running its even course at his table, began with these very words, 'He can only be a liar or an ignoramus who says otherwise than, etc.' Follow up this philosophical point with a dagger in your hand!

Here is another observation which I find very useful: That in discussions and conversations, not all the sayings which we approve of should be immediately accepted. Most men are rich in borrowed excellence. It may very well happen that a man will make a good point, give a good answer, cite a good maxim and put it forth, without perceiving the force of it.

(That a man does not possess all that he borrows may perhaps be verified in my case.)

We must not always grant it, whatever truth or beauty it may contain. Either we must oppose it seriously, or retire under colour of not understanding it, to feel on all sides how it came into the head of the man who gave utterance to it. We may happen to run upon the point of his sword and assist his stroke, although we were out of his reach.

Sometimes, when forced to it and hard pressed in the combat, I have employed a riposte that told beyond my intention and expectation. I only gave it by measure, and it was received by weight. Just as, when disputing with a strong man, I delight in meeting his conclusions half-way, relieving him of the trouble of explaining himself, and anticipating his idea whilst still unformed and nascent (the order and precision of his understanding warning and threatening me from afar); in the case of those others I do quite the contrary: I am obliged to understand and presume nothing but what they say. If they give their opinion in general terms, 'This is good, that is not good,' and they happen to hit the mark, see if it is not Fortune that hits it for them. Let them circumscribe and limit their judgements a little: why it is so, how it is so.

Those sweeping judgements which are so common are meaningless. They are like men who salute a whole crowd of people in the mass. Those who really know them salute and take notice of them individually and by name. But it is a hazardous experiment. For I have observed, more often than every day, that a man with a poor intellectual foundation, trying to show off his cleverness when reading a book, by remarking upon some fine passage, will fix his admiration with so poor a choice, that instead of showing up the excellence of the author, he only betrays his own ignorance.

After hearing a whole page of Virgil, it is safe to exclaim, 'That is fine!' In that way the artful save their faces. But when you attempt to follow him line by line, and, with positive and discriminating judgement, to point out where a good author surpasses himself, where he rises to sublime heights, weighing his words, phrases, ideas, one after the other, away with you! *We must consider not only what each one says, but what he thinks, and why he thinks it* (CICERO).

Every day I hear stupid people saying things that are not stupid.

They say a good thing; let us know how far they understand it; let us see whereby they grasp it. We assist them when they use this fine maxim and that fine argument, which is none of theirs; it is only in their keeping. They will have brought it out at a venture and diffidently; it is we who give it value and credit. You lend them a hand. What is the good? They do not thank you for it, and only become more foolish. Do not back them up, let them go; they will handle this matter like people who are afraid of burning their fingers; they dare not alter its setting and light, nor probe its meaning. Shake it ever so little, and it will escape them; they will give it up to you, be it never so strong and beautiful. They are fine weapons, but they are ill-hafted.

How often I have had this experience!

Now, if you happen to enlighten them and corroborate them, they will catch at it and forthwith rob you of the advantage of your interpretation: 'That is what I was about to say; that was exactly my idea, and if I failed to make myself so clear, it was only for want of words.' Blow your hardest! One must employ even cunning to correct this arrogant stupidity.

Hegesias' dogma, 'That we should neither hate nor condemn, but instruct,' is reasonable in other cases, but in this case it is unjust and inhuman to help and set him right who stands in no need of it, and is the worse for it. I like to leave them sticking in the mud and becoming more entangled than ever, and so deeply, if it is possible, that they will at last come to acknowledge their error.

Stupidity and a confused mind are not to be cured by a word of admonition; and we may fitly say of this kind of correction what Cyrus replied to one who urged him to harangue his army when on the point of entering into battle, 'That men are not suddenly made brave and warlike by a fine harangue, any more than a man immediately becomes a musician after hearing a good song.' It needs a preliminary apprenticeship, a long and continued education.

This attention, this assiduity in correcting and instructing, we owe to our families; but to go preaching to the first passer-by, to be schoolmaster to the ignorance and stupidity of any chance person, is a thing I greatly grudge. I rarely do so even in private conversation with another; and rather give up the whole thing than impart pedantic instruction to such backward people. I am naturally no more adapted to speak than to write for beginners. But when things are said in company or before others, however false and absurd they may appear to me, I never interfere either by word or sign.

Moreover, nothing exasperates me so much in a stupid person as that he is more self-satisfied than any reasonable person can reasonably be. It is a pity that wisdom forbids you to be satisfied with yourself and to trust your own judgement, and always dismisses you discontented and diffident; whilst a bold opinionativeness always fills its possessors with delight and assurance. It is the most empty-headed who look at other men over their shoulders, and always return from the combat full of glee and triumph. And besides, as a rule their arrogant language and cheerful looks make them the victors in the eyes of the audience, who are usually of weak intelligence and incapable of judging and discerning on which side the advantage really lies.

Obstinacy and heat in sticking to one's opinions is the surest proof of stupidity. Is there anything so cocksure, so immovable, so disdainful, so contemplative, so solemn and serious as an ass?

May we not include under the heading of conversation and intercourse the quick and smart repartees that mirth and intimacy introduce among friends, pleasantly and wittily chaffing and poking fun at each other? A sport for which my natural gaiety makes me fit enough. And if it is not so strained and serious as the other exercise I have spoken of, it is no less subtle and intellectual, and, as Lycurgus thought, no less profitable.

For my part I contribute to it more licence than wit, and have therein more luck than originality. But in patience I am perfect, and can bear a retaliation that is not only rude but impertinent, without being moved. And when attacked, if I have not a brisk retort ready to hand, I do not waste time in following up that point with feeble and tiresome persistence, bordering on obstinacy; I let it pass, cheerfully letting my ears drop and deferring my revenge to some better opportunity. There is no merchant who always gains.

Most people change countenance and raise their voices when their strength begins to fail; and with unreasonable anger, instead of getting their revenge, only betray their weakness and their impatience at the same time. In this mirthful mood we sometimes pluck some secret string of each other's imperfections, which, in a more sober mood, we cannot touch without offence. And we profitably give one another a hint of our defects.

There are other kinds of rough play, which are unwise and cruel, after the French manner, for which I have a deadly hatred; for I have a tender and sensitive skin. I have seen in my time two Princes of our royal blood brought to their graves as a consequence of them.[6] It is an ugly thing to fight in play.

For the rest, when I wish to size up a man, I ask him how far he is satisfied with himself, how much he is

6 King Henri II and Henri de Bourbon-Montpensier, both of whom died of wounds received in the last two tournaments that were held in France, one at Paris in 1559, the other at Orleans in 1560.

pleased with his conversation and his work. I will have none of those fine excuses: 'I only did it in play;

This work unfinished from the anvil comes; OVID

I was not an hour over it; I have not looked at it since.' Well then, I reply, put this piece aside; give me one that does you full justice, by which you would like to be measured. And then, what do you consider best in your work; is it this passage, or this? Is it the charm, or the matter, or the idea, or the judgement, or the learning?

For I observe generally that men are as wide of the mark in judging their own work as in judging that of others, not only by reason of the affection that creeps in, but for want of capacity to know and discriminate it. The work, by its own power and fortune, may second the workman, and outstrip him, beyond his own inventiveness and knowledge.

For my part, I do not judge of the value of another's work less clearly than my own; very changeably and hesitatingly I rate the Essays now low, now high.

There are many books that are useful by reason of their subject, for which the author earns no praise; and there are good books, as well as good works, which shame the workman. I may write of the fashions of our dinner-parties and our clothes, and write without enthusiasm; I may publish the edicts of my time, and the letters of Princes, which will pass into the hands of the public; I may make an abridgement of a good book (and every abridgement of a good book is a foolish abridgement), and the book itself may be lost; and the like things. Posterity may derive singular benefit from such compositions; but what honour shall I gain, except through my good fortune? A good number of famous books are in this plight.

When, some years ago, I read Philip de Commines, truly a very good writer, I noticed this for no common remark: 'That we must take good care not to serve our master so well as to make it difficult for him to requite us adequately for our services.' I ought to have commended the idea, not the writer. I came across it, not long ago, in Tacitus: *Benefits are only so far acceptable as they appear capable of being returned; if they pass much beyond that limit, they reap hatred rather than gratitude.* And Seneca says with vigour: *The man who thinks it disgraceful not to pay back, would rather have no man for a creditor.* And Q. Cicero,[7] from a meaner point of view: *The man who thinks he cannot requite you can in no way be your friend.*

The subject, according to its nature, may gain a man a reputation for learning and a good memory; but in order to appreciate those qualities in the book which are most original and most valuable, the power and beauty of the writer's mind, we must know how much of it is original, how much not. And, with respect to what is not original, how much we owe him in consideration of the choice, the disposition, embellishment and style which he has contributed to it. What if he has borrowed the matter and impaired the form, as so often happens? We others who have little acquaintance with books are in this strait that, when we come across some beautiful idea in a new poet, some forcible argument in a preacher, we dare not commend them for it until we have been informed by some man of learning whether that element is their own, or some other's. Till then I always stand on my guard.

7 Quintus Cicero, brother of the great orator.

I have just run through Tacitus' *History* without a break (a thing that seldom happens with me; it is twenty years since I have devoted a whole hour at a time to a book); I did so at the instigation of a gentleman who enjoys great esteem in France, both for his own worth, and for a consistent kind of excellence and goodness which he shares with several brothers.

I know no writer who introduces into the annals of public affairs so many reflections on the manners and dispositions of private persons. And I totally disagree with him when he says that, having made it his special task to trace the lives of the Emperors of his time, so abnormal and so outrageous in every direction, and to tell of the many remarkable deeds which their cruelties in particular called forth in their subjects, he had a more solid and attractive material on which to build his narrative and his reflections, than if he had had to tell of battles and general insurrections. So that often I find him sterile, hurrying over those noble deaths, as if he feared to weary us with their number and length.

This form of history is by far the most useful. Public movements are more dependent on the guidance of Fortune; private ones on our own.

It is rather a summing up than an historical narrative; there are more precepts than stories. It is not a book to read, it is a book to study and learn; it is so full of maxims, that they seem to have been brought in by hook and by crook. It is a nursery of ethical and political dissertations, for the benefit and improvement of those who hold a place in the management of the world.

He always pleads with strong and solid reasons, in pointed and subtle fashion, in accordance with the affected style of that age; they were so fond of inflated language that when they could find no point or subtlety in things they borrowed them of words.

He writes not unlike Seneca; he appears to me more fleshy, Seneca more pointed. His services were better adapted to a sick and disturbed state, as ours is at present; you might often think he were describing us and criticizing us.

They who doubt his sincerity plainly betray themselves as ill-disposed to him on some other account. His opinions are sound, and he leans to the right side in Roman affairs. Yet I blame him a little for having judged Pompey more harshly than is consistent with the opinion of the honest men who lived at the time and had dealings with him; and for placing him entirely on a par with Marius and Sulla, except in so far as he was more close. In aiming at the government of affairs he was not acquitted of ambition and a feeling of revenge; and even his friends feared that victory would have carried him beyond the bounds of reason, but not to so unbridled a degree. There was nothing in his life to suggest a threat of such purposeful cruelty and tyranny. Besides we should not weigh suspicion against evidence; so I do not agree with Tacitus in that matter.

That his narrative is simple and straightforward may perhaps be argued even from this, that it does not always fit in with the conclusions his judgement comes to, which he follows according to the bias he has taken, often beyond the matter he is presenting to us, which he has not deigned to twist in the least degree.

He needs no excuse for having countenanced the religion of his time, in accordance with the laws which commanded him to do so, and of having been ignorant of the true faith. That was his misfortune, not his fault.

I have considered chiefly his judgement, and am not very clear about it in every case. For example, those words in the letter which Tiberius, sick and aged, sent to the Senate: 'What to write, Conscript Fathers; in what terms to express myself, or what to refrain from writing, is a matter of such perplexity, that if I know how to decide, may the just gods and the goddesses of vengeance doom me to die in pangs worse than those under which I linger every day!' I cannot see why he so positively attributes them to a poignant remorse tormenting Tiberius' conscience; at least I did not see it when I was best able to do so.

This too appeared to me a little mean-spirited, that having occasion to mention a certain honourable office that he filled at Rome, he excuses himself by saying that it is not out of ostentation that he mentions it. This seems to me a cheap thing to say, coming from a mind like his; for not to dare to speak roundly of oneself betrays some want of spirit. A man of staunch and lofty judgement, who judges soundly and surely, will unhesitatingly use himself as an example, as if he were some other person, and give as frank testimony of himself as of anything else. He should override those common rules of politeness for the sake of truth and liberty.

I dare not only to speak of myself, but to speak only of myself; when I speak of other things I wander away and escape from my subject. I am not so inordinately in love, so wholly bound and mixed up with myself, that I cannot consider and distinguish myself apart, as I do a neighbour or a tree. Not to see how much we are worth is as great a fault as to tell more of ourselves than we are able to discover. We owe more love to God than to ourselves, and we know him less well; and yet we speak of him to our heart's content.

If the writings of Tacitus in any way reflect his character, he was a great man, upright and courageous, not of a superstitious, but of a philosophic and generous virtue. We may think him venturesome in his testimony, as when he tells of a soldier, who was carrying a load of wood, that his hands were so stiffened by cold, that they stuck to the wood, and there remained fixed and dead, having come away from his arms. In such matters I usually bow to the authority of such great witnesses.

And when he says that Vespasian, by the grace of the god Serapis, cured a blind woman of Alexandria by anointing her eyes with his spittle, and I know not what other miracle, he follows the example and duty of all good historians. They keep a record of important events, and among matters of public interest are to be numbered popular rumours and ideas. It is their part to cite common beliefs, not regulate them. That part concerns divines and philosophers, the directors of consciences.

Very wisely too his fellow-historian, a great man like himself, said: *Indeed I set down more things than I believe; for I neither affirm things I doubt, nor suppress what I have heard* (QUINTUS CURTIUS). And this other: *These are things we need not be at pains either to affirm or refute; we must abide by report* (LIVY). And, writing in an age when the belief in prodigies was beginning to decline, he says he will not on that account forbear to insert in his *Annals* and lend currency to things accepted by so many worthy men, and with so much reverence for antiquity. That is very well said. Let them deliver history as they receive it rather than as they believe it.

I, who am monarch of the matter I treat of, and am accountable for it to no man, yet do not trust myself with regard to everything; I often venture on intellectual flights of fancy which are suspicious to myself, and certain verbal quibbles at which I shake my ears. But I let them run their chance. I observe that some are praised for such things; it is not for me alone to judge. I present myself standing and lying, front and back, right and left, and in all my natural attitudes.

Minds, even if alike in strength, are not always alike in tastes and inclinations.

That is what my memory of Tacitus pictures to me in the gross, and with uncertainty enough. All generalizations are loose and imperfect.

ry of Essential Thinkers Collector's Library of Essential Thinkers
brary of Essential Thinkers Collector's Library of Essential Think
Library of Essential Thinkers Collector's Library of Essential Th
or's Library of Essential Thinkers Collector's Library of Essential
f Essential Thinkers Collector's Library of Essential Thinkers C
ry of Essential Thinkers Collector's Library of Essential Thinkers
brary of Essential Thinkers Collector's Library of Essential Think
Library of Essential Thinkers Collector's Library of Essential Th
or's Library of Essential Thinkers Collector's Library of Essential
f Essential Thinkers Collector's Library of Essential Thinkers C
y of Essential Thinkers Collector's Library of Essential Thinkers
rary of Essential Thinkers Collector's Library of Essential Think
Library of Essential Thinkers Collector's Library of Essential Th
r's Library of Essential Thinkers Collector's Library of Essentia
Essential Thinkers Collector's Library of Essential Thinkers C
y of Essential Thinkers Collector's Library of Essential Thinker
rary of Essential Thinkers Collector's Library of Essential Thin
Library of Essential Thinkers Collector's Library of Essential T
r's Library of Essential Thinkers Collector's Library of Essentia
Essential Thinkers Collector's Library of Essential Thinkers C
y of Essential Thinkers Collector's Library of Essential Thinker
rary of Essential Thinkers Collector's Library of Essential Thin